Chemistry 1

Brian Ratcliff

Helen Eccles

David Johnson

John Nicholson

John Raffan

Series editor: Brian Ratcliff

CAMBRIDGE
UNIVERSITY PRESS

PUBLISHED BY THE PRESS SYNDICATE OF THE UNIVERSITY OF CAMBRIDGE
The Pitt Building, Trumpington Street, Cambridge CB2 1RP, United Kingdom

CAMBRIDGE UNIVERSITY PRESS
The Edinburgh Building, Cambridge CB2 2RU, UK
40 West 20th Street, New York, NY 10011-4211, USA
10 Stamford Road, Oakleigh, VIC 3166, Australia
Ruiz de Alarcón 13, 28014 Madrid, Spain
Dock House, The Waterfront, Cape Town 8001, South Africa

http:// www.cambridge.org

First published 2000

Reprinted 2001

Printed in the United Kingdom at the University Press, Cambridge

Typeface   Swift   *System*   QuarkXPress®

A catalogue record for this book is available from the British Library

ISBN 0 521 78778 5 paperback

Produced by Gecko Ltd, Bicester, Oxon

Front cover photograph: Reaction synthesis, Images Colour Library

Contents

Introduction

Cambridge Advanced Sciences

The *Cambridge Advanced Sciences* series has been developed to meet the demands of all the new AS and A level science examinations. In particular, it has been endorsed by OCR as providing complete coverage of their specifications. The AS material is presented as a single text for each of biology, chemistry and physics. Material for the A2 year comprises six books in each subject: one of core material and one for each option. Some material has been drawn from the existing *Cambridge Modular Sciences* books; however, the majority is entirely new.

During the development of this series, the opportunity has been taken to improve the design, and a complete and thorough new writing and editing process has been applied. Much more material is now presented in colour. Although the existing *Cambridge Modular Sciences* texts do cover some of the new specifications, the *Cambridge Advanced Sciences* books cover every OCR learning objective in detail. They are the key to success in the new AS and A level examinations.

OCR is one of the three unitary awarding bodies offering the full range of academic and vocational qualifications in the UK. For full details of the new specifications, please contact OCR:

OCR
1 Hills Rd
Cambridge CB1 2EU
Tel: 01223 553311

Chemistry 1 – the AS chemistry text

Chemistry 1 is all that is needed to cover the whole of the AS chemistry material. It is divided into three parts which correspond to the modules Foundation chemistry, Chains and rings, and How far, how fast? It is designed to be accessible to students with a double-award science GCSE background. This book combines entirely new text and illustrations with revised and updated material from *Foundation Chemistry*, *Chains and Rings*, *How Far? How Fast?*, and *Trends and Patterns*, formerly available in the *Cambridge Modular Sciences* series.

Part 1, Foundation chemistry, is a combination of new material and sections based on chapters from *Foundation Chemistry* and *Trends and Patterns*. Specifically, chapters 1–3 in *Foundation Chemistry* have been adapted to form chapters 1–3 in this book. Chapter 4, 'Periodic patterns', is a combination of *Foundation Chemistry* chapter 5 and a new section on successive ionisation energies. Chapter 5 introduces the elements and compounds of Group II of the Periodic Table, pulling together sections from *Trends and Patterns* chapter 4, *Foundation Chemistry* chapter 5 and new material dealing with the formation of salts and aspects of chalk and lime chemistry. Chapter 6, on the topic of the Group VII elements and their compounds, uses material previously found in *Trends and Patterns* chapter 6 and includes a new section on identifying halides.

Chapter 7 begins Part 2 and introduces the subject of organic chemistry. Much of this chapter has been revised from chapter 1 of *Chains and Rings*. In addition, there is a section on the naming of organic compounds which is based on material from *Foundation Chemistry* chapter 6. Chapters 8, 9 and 10 introduce the chemistry of hydrocarbons in the form of fuels, alkanes and alkenes respectively. Sections of *Chains and Rings* chapter 2 and *Foundation Chemistry* chapter 6 are used in these three chapters, enhanced by new material, including sections on the separation of hydrocarbons for use as fuels and the chemical properties of alkanes. Chapter 11, 'Alcohols', combines *Chains and Rings* chapter 4 with new text on the physical properties of alcohols and structural identification using infrared spectroscopy. Part 2 concludes with 'Halogenoalkanes', which is adapted from chapter 3 of *Chains and Rings*.

Part 3 begins with chapter 13, 'Enthalpy changes'. It makes use of *Foundation Chemistry* chapter 4 and *How Far? How Fast?* chapter 1. In addition there is a large new section on the construction and use of enthalpy cycles. *How Far? How Fast?* chapters 3 and 4 respectively form the basis of the final two chapters. However, there is a substantial amount of entirely new material in chapter 14, on measuring the rates of reactions, collision theory and the concept and application of catalysis; and in chapter 15, 'Equilibria', on Le Chatelier's principle, the Haber process, and finally acids and their reactions.

Acknowledgements

2, 26, 69, 70*l*, 77, 78, 91, 92, 93*t*, 113, 114, 118, 120*r*, 129, 130, 131, 139, 165*b*, 166*t*, 168, 170, 188, Andrew Lambert; 4, 7, University of Cambridge Cavendish Laboratory, Madingley Road, Cambridge; 5, Manchester University/Science and Society Picture Library, Science Museum, London; 18, NSSDC/NASA; 20*t*, 22, 93*b*, courtesy of Aventis Pasteur MSD; 20*b*, 41(*gold*), 44*l*, Dr B. Booth, GeoScience Features Picture Library; 21, Heine Schneebeli/Science Photo Library; 31*b*, Photo Library International; 31*tl*, cr, A. Fisher/ GeoScience Features Picture Library; 31*tr*, *cl*, 35, 41*tl*, *tr*, 44*r*, 46, 51*tl*, *cr*, GeoScience Features Picture Library; 32*t*, NASA/Science Photo Library; 32*b*, courtesy of ICI; 34*tl*, The Natural History Museum, London; 34*br*, 71, 124, ©Brian Ratcliff; 36, courtesy of Argonne National Laboratory; 41*c*, *b*, Ancient Art & Architecture Collection; 44*tr*, *br*, 109*r*, 147*tr*, 166*br inset*, Tick Ahearn; 45*l*, 47, 51*bl*, 66*b*, 123*bl*, Peter Gould; 45*r*, Britstock-IFA/TPL; 48*t*, courtesy of Dr Jonathan Goodman, Department of Chemistry, Cambridge University, using the program Eadfrith (©J.M.Goodman, Cambridge University, 1994)/photo by Cambridge University Chemistry Department Photographic Unit; 48*b*, Dr Arthur Lesk, Laboratory of Molecular Biology/ Science Photo Library; 51*tc*, Astrid & Hanns–Frieder Michler/Science Photo Library; 51*cb*, Vaughan Fleming/Science Photo Library; 51*br*, Erich Schrempp/Science Photo Library; 51*tr*, *cl*, US Dept of Energy/Science Photo Library; 52, courtesy of the Library & Information Centre of the Royal Society of Chemistry; 53*r*, courtesy of Gordon Woods, Malvern School; 65, 82, 104, 155, Ann Ronan at Image Select; 66*t*, 70*r* Leslie Garland Picture Library; 72, ©Martyn Chillmaid/ www.osf.uk.com; 76, Steve Davey/La Belle Aurore; 90, Barry Mayes/Life File; 101, 102, Shell Photo Service; 103, Paolo Koch/Robert Harding Picture Library; 105*t*, Kieran Murray/Ecoscene, 105*b*, 107*r*, Schaffer/Ecoscene; 106*t*, Martin Bond/Science Photo Library; 106*b*, ©Geoff Miller; 107*l*, US Department of Energy/Science Photo Library; 108*tl*, John Mead/Science Photo Library; 108*tr*, br, Simon Fraser/Science Photo Library; 108*bl*, Wilkinson/Ecoscene; 108*cr*, Helene Rogers/Art Directors & TRIP Photo Library; 109*tl*, reproduced by kind permission of Mercedes-Benz; 109*bl*, FPG Int/Robert Harding Picture Library; 117, Images Colour Library; 120*l*, courtesy of Van den Berg Foods Limited; 123*tr*, E.J. Bent/Ecoscene; 123*br*, James Holmes/Science Photo Library; 128, H. Schmidbauer/Britstock-IFA; 140*b*, 153, 162*b*, 165*t*, 166*b*, Michael Brooke; 140*t*, courtesy of civil Aviation Authority, International Fire Training Centre, UK and Robert Hartness; 141 NASA/Science Photo Library; 146, Astrid & Hanns-Frieder-Michler/Science Photo Library; 147*l*, courtesy of Buxton Lime Industries/photo by SJ Hambleton; 147*br*, Tim Fisher/Life File; 162*a*, Popperfoto; 171, Juliet Coombe/La Belle Aurore; 174, courtesy of Catalytic Systems Division, Johnson Matthey; 176, Budd Titlow/f/stop Pictures; 186, Billingham Ammonia Plant, Terra Nitrogen (UK) Ltd.

Part 1
Foundation Chemistry

CHAPTER 1

Atomic structure

By the end of this chapter you should be able to:

1 recognise and describe *protons*, *neutrons* and *electrons* in terms of their relative charges and relative masses;

2 describe the distribution of *mass* and *charge* within an *atom*;

3 describe the contribution of protons and neutrons to atomic nuclei in terms of *atomic number* and *mass number*;

4 deduce the numbers of protons, neutrons and electrons present in both atoms and *ions* from given atomic and mass numbers;

5 distinguish between *isotopes* on the basis of different numbers of neutrons present;

6 explain the terms *first ionisation energy* and *successive ionisation energies* of an *element* in terms of 1 mole of gaseous atoms or ions;

7 explain that ionisation energies are influenced by *nuclear charge*, *atomic radius* and *electron shielding*;

8 predict the number of electrons in each principal *quantum shell* of an element from its successive ionisation energies;

9 describe the shapes of s and p *orbitals*;

10 describe the numbers and relative energies of the s, p and d orbitals for the principal quantum numbers 1, 2, 3 and also the 4s and 4p orbitals;

11 deduce the *electronic configurations* of atoms up to $Z = 36$ and ions, given the atomic number and charge, limited to s and p *blocks* up to $Z = 36$.

hemistry is a science of change. Over the centuries people have heated rocks, distilled juices and probed solids, liquids and gases with electricity. From all this activity we have gained a great wealth of new materials – metals, medicines, plastics, dyes, ceramics, fertilisers, fuels and many more (*figure 1.1*). But this creation of new materials is only part of the science and technology of chemistry. Chemists also want to *understand* the changes, to find patterns of behaviour and to discover the innermost nature of the materials.

Our 'explanations' of the chemical behaviour of matter come from reasoning and model-building based on the limited evidence available from

● **Figure 1.1** All of these useful products, and many more, contain chemicals that have been created by applying chemistry to natural materials. Chemists must also find answers to problems caused when people misuse chemicals.

experiments. The work of chemists and physicists has shown us the following:

■ All known materials, however complicated and varied they appear, can be broken down into the fundamental substances we call **elements**. These elements cannot be broken down further into simpler substances. So far, about 115 elements are recognised. Most exist in combinations with other elements in **compounds** but some, such as gold, nitrogen, oxygen and sulphur, are also found in an uncombined state. Some elements would not exist on Earth without the artificial use of nuclear reactions. Chemists have given each element a symbol. This symbol is usually the first one or two letters of the name of the element; some are derived from their names in Latin. Some examples are:

Element	Symbol
carbon	C
lithium	Li
iron	Fe (from the Latin *ferrum*)
lead	Pb (from the Latin *plumbum*)

■ Groups of elements show patterns of behaviour related to their atomic masses. A Russian chemist, Dmitri Mendeleev, summarised these patterns by arranging the elements into a 'Periodic Table'. Modern versions of the Periodic Table are widely used in chemistry. (A Periodic Table is shown in the appendix on page 191 and explained, much more fully, in chapter 4.)

■ All matter is composed of extremely small particles (atoms). About 100 years ago, the accepted model for atoms included the assumptions that (i) atoms were tiny particles, which could not be divided further nor destroyed, and (ii) all atoms of the same element were identical. The model had to give way to other models, as science and technology produced new evidence. This evidence could only be interpreted as atoms having other particles inside them – they have an internal structure.

Scientists now believe that there are two basic types of particles – 'quarks' and 'leptons'. These are the building-blocks from which everything is made, from microbes to galaxies. For many explanations or predictions, however, scientists find it helpful to use a model of atomic structure that includes three basic particles in any atom, the

electron, the **proton** and the **neutron**. Protons and neutrons are made from quarks, and the electron is a member of the family of leptons.

Discovering the electron

Effect of electric current in solutions (electrolysis)

When electricity flows in an aqueous solution of silver nitrate, for example, silver metal appears at the negative electrode (cathode). This is an example of **electrolysis** and the best explanation is that:

■ the silver exists in the solution as positively charged particles known as **ions** (Ag^+);

■ one silver ion plus one unit of electricity gives one silver atom.

The name 'electron' was given to this unit of electricity by the Irish scientist George Johnstone Stoney in 1891.

Study of cathode rays

At normal pressures gases are usually very poor conductors of electricity, but at low pressures they conduct quite well. Scientists, such as William Crookes, who first studied the effects of passing electricity through gases at low pressures, saw that the glass of the containing vessel opposite the **cathode** (negative electrode) glowed when the applied potential difference was sufficiently high.

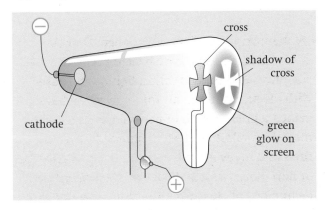

● **Figure 1.2** Cathode rays cause a glow on the screen opposite the cathode, and the 'Maltese Cross' casts a shadow. The shadow will move if a magnet is brought near to the screen. This shows that the cathode rays are deflected in a magnetic field. The term 'cathode ray' is still familiar today, as in 'cathode-ray oscilloscopes'.

A solid object, placed between the cathode and the glow, cast a shadow (*figure 1.2*). They proposed that the glow was caused by rays coming from the cathode and called these **cathode rays**.

For a while there was some argument about whether cathode rays are waves, similar to visible light rays, or particles. The most important evidence is that they are strongly deflected in a magnetic field. This is best explained by assuming that they are streams of electrically charged particles. The direction of the deflection (towards the positive pole) shows that the particles in cathode rays are negatively charged.

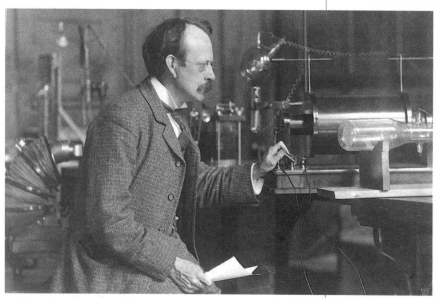

● **Figure 1.3** Joseph (J. J.) Thomson (1856–1940) using his cathode-ray tube.

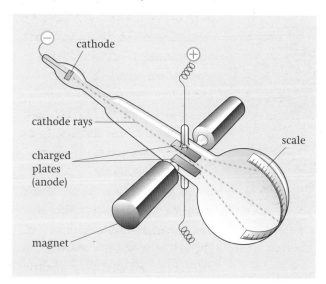

● **Figure 1.4** A drawing of Thomson's apparatus. The electrons move from the hot cathode (negative) through slits in the anode (positive).

J. J. Thomson's *e/m* experiment

The great leap in understanding came in 1897, at the Cavendish Laboratory in Cambridge (*figures 1.3* and *1.4*). J. J. Thomson measured the deflection of a narrow beam of cathode rays in both magnetic and electric fields. His results allowed him to calculate the charge-to-mass ratio (e/m) of the particles. Their charge-to-mass ratio was found to be exactly the same, whatever gas or type of electrodes were used in the experiment. The cathode-ray particles had a tiny mass, only approximately 1/2000 th of the mass of a hydrogen atom. Thomson then decided to call them **electrons** – the name suggested earlier by Stoney for the 'units of electricity'.

Millikan's 'oil-drop' experiment

The electron charge was first measured accurately in 1909 by the American physicist Robert Millikan using his famous 'oil-drop' experiment (*figure 1.5*). He found the charge to be 1.602×10^{-19} C (coulombs). The mass of an electron was calculated to be 9.109×10^{-31} kg, which is 1/1837 th of the mass of a hydrogen atom.

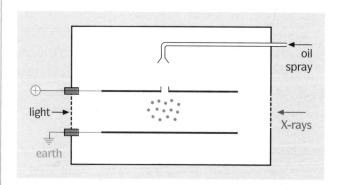

● **Figure 1.5** Robert Millikan's 'oil-drop' experiment. Millikan gave the oil drops negative charge by spraying them into air ionised by X-ray bombardment. He adjusted the charge on the plates so that the upward force of attraction equalled the downward force due to gravity, and a drop could remain stationary. Calculations on the forces allowed him to find the charges on the drops. These were multiples of the charge on an electron.

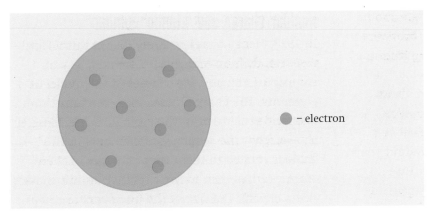

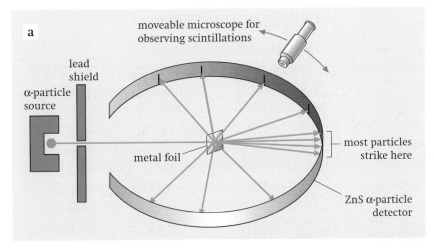

● **Figure 1.6** J. J. Thomson's 'plum-pudding' model of the atom. The electrons (plums) are embedded in a sphere of uniform positive charge.

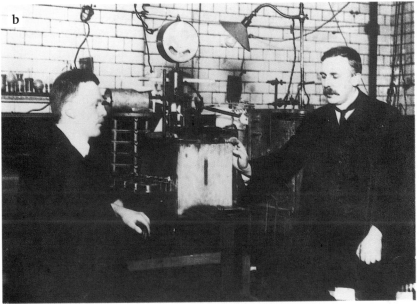

● **Figure 1.7** Geiger and Marsden's experiment, which investigated how α-particles are deflected by thin metal foils.
a A drawing showing the arrangement of the apparatus.
b Ernest Rutherford (right) and Hans Geiger using their apparatus for detecting α-particle deflections. Interpretation of the results led Rutherford to propose the nuclear model for atoms.

Discovering protons and neutrons

New atomic models: 'plum-pudding' or 'nuclear' atom

The discoveries about electrons demanded new models for atoms. If there are negatively charged electrons in all electrically neutral atoms, there must also be a positively charged part. For some time the most favoured atomic model was J. J. Thomson's 'plum-pudding', in which electrons (the plums) were embedded in a 'pudding' of positive charge (*figure 1.6*).

Then, in 1909, came one of the experiments that changed everything. Two members of Ernest Rutherford's research team in Manchester University, Hans Geiger and Ernest Marsden, were investigating how α-particles (α is the Greek letter alpha) from a radioactive source were scattered when fired at very thin sheets of gold and other metals (*figure 1.7*). They detected the α-particles by the small flashes of light (called 'scintillations') that they caused on impact with a fluorescent screen. Since (in atomic terms) α-particles are heavy and energetic, Geiger and Marsden were not surprised that most particles passed through the metal with only slight deflections in their paths. These deflections could be explained, by the 'plum-pudding' model of the atom, as small scattering effects caused while the positive α-particles moved through the diffuse mixture of positive charge and electrons.

However, Geiger and Marsden also noticed some large deflections. A few (about one in 20 000) were so large that scintillations were seen on a screen placed on the same side of the gold sheet as the source of positively charged α-particles. This was unexpected. Rutherford said: 'it was almost as incredible as if you had fired a 15-inch shell at a piece of tissue paper and it came back and hit you!'

The plum-pudding model, with its diffuse positive charge, could not explain the surprising Geiger–Marsden observations. However, Rutherford soon proposed his convincing **nuclear model** of the atom. He suggested that atoms consist largely of empty space and that the mass is concentrated into a very small, positively charged, central core called the **nucleus**. The nucleus is about 10 000 times smaller than the atom itself – similar in scale to a marble placed at the centre of an athletics stadium.

Most α-particles will pass through the empty space in an atom with very little deflection. When an α-particle approaches on a path close to a nucleus, however, the positive charges strongly repel each other and the α-particle is deflected through a large angle (*figure 1.8*).

Nuclear charge and 'atomic' number

In 1913, Henry Moseley, a member of Rutherford's research team in Manchester, found a way of comparing the positive charges of the nuclei of elements. The charge increases by one unit from element to element in the Periodic Table. Moseley showed that the sequence of elements in the Table is related to the nuclear charges of their atoms, rather than to their relative atomic masses (see page 54). The size of the nuclear charge was then called the **atomic number** of the element. Atomic number defined the position of the element in the Periodic Table.

Particles in the nucleus

The proton

After he proposed the nuclear atom, Rutherford reasoned that there must be particles in the nucleus which are responsible for the positive nuclear charge. He and Marsden fired α-particles through hydrogen, nitrogen and other materials. They detected new particles with positive charge and the approximate mass of a hydrogen atom. Rutherford eventually called these particles **protons**. A proton carries a positive charge of 1.602×10^{-19} C, equal in size but opposite in sign to the charge on an electron. It has a mass of 1.673×10^{-27} kg, about 2000 times as heavy as an electron.

Each electrically neutral atom has the same number of electrons outside the nucleus as there are protons within the nucleus.

The neutron

The mass of an atom, which is concentrated in its nucleus, cannot depend only on protons; usually the protons provide around half of the atomic mass. Rutherford proposed that there is a particle in the nucleus with a mass equal to that of a proton but with zero electrical charge. He thought of this particle as a proton and an electron bound together.

Without any charge to make it 'perform' in electrical fields, detection

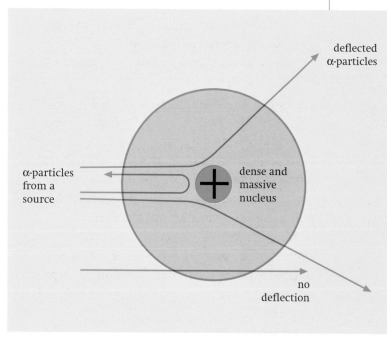

• **Figure 1.8** Ernest Rutherford's interpretation of the Geiger–Marsden observations. The positively charged α-particles are deflected by the tiny, dense, positively charged nucleus. Most of the atom is empty space.

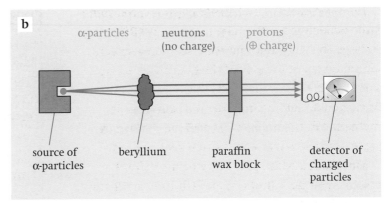

● **Figure 1.9**
a Using this apparatus, James Chadwick discovered the neutron.
b Drawing of the inside of the apparatus. Chadwick bombarded a block of beryllium with α-particles ($^4_2$He). No charged particles were detected on the other side of the block. However, when a block of paraffin wax (a compound containing only carbon and hydrogen) was placed near the beryllium, charged particles were detected and identified as protons (H⁺). Alpha-particles had knocked neutrons out of the beryllium, and in turn these had knocked protons out of the wax.

of this particle was very difficult. It was not until 12 years after Rutherford's suggestion that, in 1932, one of his co-workers, James Chadwick, produced sufficient evidence for the existence of a nuclear particle with a mass similar to that of the proton but with no electrical charge (*figure 1.9*). The particle was named the neutron.

Atomic and mass numbers

Atomic number (Z)

The most important difference between atoms of different elements is in the number of protons in the nucleus of each atom. The number of protons in an atom determines the element to which the atom belongs. The atomic number of an element shows:

■ the number of protons in the nucleus of an atom of that element;
■ the number of electrons in a neutral atom of that element;
■ the position of the element in the Periodic Table.

Mass number (A)

It is useful to have a measure for the total number of particles in the nucleus of an atom. This is called the **mass number**. For any atom:

■ the mass number is the sum of the number of protons and the number of neutrons.

Summary table

Particle name	Relative mass	Relative charge
electron	negligible	−1
proton	1	+1
neutron	1	0

Isotopes

In Rutherford's model of the atom, the nucleus consists of protons and neutrons, each with a mass of one atomic unit. The relative atomic masses of elements should then be whole numbers. It was thus a puzzle why chlorine has a relative atomic mass of 35.5.

The answer is that atoms of the same element are not all identical. In 1913, Frederick Soddy proposed that atoms of the same element could have different atomic masses. He named such atoms **isotopes**. The word means 'equal place', i.e. occupying the same place in the Periodic Table and having the same atomic number.

The discovery of protons and neutrons explained the existence of isotopes of an element. In isotopes of one element, the number of protons must be the same, but the number of neutrons may be different.

Remember:

atomic number (Z) = number of protons
mass number (A) = number of protons
    + number of neutrons

Isotopes are atoms with the same atomic number, but different mass numbers. The symbol for isotopes is shown as

$$_{\text{atomic number}}^{\text{mass number}}X \quad \text{or} \quad _Z^AX$$

For example, hydrogen has three isotopes:

	Protium, $_1^1H$	Deuterium, $_1^2H$	Tritium, $_1^3H$
protons	1	1	1
neutrons	0	1	2

It is also common practice to identify isotopes by name or symbol plus mass number only. For example, uranium, the heaviest naturally occurring element ($Z = 92$), has two particularly important isotopes of mass numbers 235 and 238. They are often shown as uranium-235 and uranium-238, as U-235 and U-238 or as ^{235}U and ^{238}U.

Numbers of protons, neutrons and electrons

It is easy to calculate the composition of a particular atom or ion:

number of protons $= Z$
number of neutrons $= A - Z$
number of electrons in neutral atom
$= Z$
number of electrons in positive ion
$= Z - $ charge on ion
number of electrons in negative ion
$= Z + $ charge on ion

For example, magnesium is element 12; it is in Group II, so it tends to form doubly charged (2+) ions. The ionised isotope magnesium-25 thus has the full symbol $_{12}^{25}Mg^{2+}$, and

number of protons $= 12$
number of neutrons $= 13$
number of electrons $= 10$

SAQ 1.1
a What is the composition (numbers of electrons, protons and neutrons) of neutral atoms of the two main uranium isotopes, U–235 and U–238?
b What is the composition of the ions of potassium-40 (K^+) and chlorine-37 (Cl^-)?
(Use the Periodic Table, page 191, for the atomic numbers.)

Electrons in atoms

Electrons hold the key to almost the whole of chemistry. Protons and neutrons give atoms their mass, but electrons are the outer part of the atom and only electrons are involved in the changes that happen during chemical reactions. If we knew everything about the arrangements of electrons in atoms and molecules, we could predict most of the ways that chemicals behave, purely from mathematics. So far this has proved very difficult, even with the most advanced computers – but it may yet happen.

SAQ 1.2
Suggest why the isotopes of an element have the same chemical properties, though they have different relative atomic masses.

What models are currently accepted about how electrons are arranged around the nucleus? The first simple idea – that they just orbit randomly around the nucleus – was soon rejected. Calculations showed that any moving, electrically charged particles, like electrons, would lose energy and fall into the nucleus.

A model you may have used considers the electrons to be arranged in shells. These 'shells' correspond to different energy levels occupied by the electrons.

Arrangements of electrons: energy levels and 'shells'

There was a great advance in atomic theory when, in 1913, the Danish physicist Niels Bohr proposed his ideas about arrangements of electrons in atoms.

Earlier the German physicist Max Planck had proposed, in his 'Quantum Theory' of 1901, that energy, like matter, is 'atomic'. It can only be transferred in packets of energy he called **quanta**; a single packet of energy is a **quantum**. Bohr applied this idea to the energy of electrons. He suggested that, as electrons could only possess energy in quanta, they would not exist in a stable way, anywhere outside the nucleus, unless they were in fixed or 'quantised' energy levels. If an electron gained or lost energy, it could move to higher or lower energy levels, but not somewhere

	Atomic number	Number of electrons in shell		
		$n = 1$	$n = 2$	$n = 3$
H	1	1		
He	2	2		
Li	3	2	1	
Be	4	2	2	
B	5	2	3	
C	6	2	4	
N	7	2	5	
O	8	2	6	
F	9	2	7	
Ne	10	2	8	
Na	11	2	8	1

● **Table 1.1** Electronic configurations of the first 11 elements in the Periodic Table.

in between. It is a bit like climbing a ladder; you can only stay in a stable state on one of the rungs. You will find that, as you read more widely, there are several names given to these energy levels. The most common name is **shells**.

Shells are numbered 1, 2, 3, 4, etc. These numbers are known as **principal quantum numbers** (symbol n). Such numbers correspond to the numbers of rows (or Periods) in the Periodic Table.

We can now write the simple electronic configurations as shown in *table 1.1*. Remember that the atomic number tells us the number of electrons present in an atom of the element. For a given element, electrons are added to the shells as follows:

■ up to 2 electrons in shell 1;
■ up to 8 electrons in shell 2;
■ up to 18 electrons in shell 3.

Some of the best evidence for the existence of electron shells comes from ionisation energies.

Ionisation energy

When an atom loses an electron it becomes a positive ion. We say that it has been **ionised**. Energy is needed to remove electrons and this is generally called **ionisation energy**. More precisely, the **first ionisation energy** of an element is the amount of energy needed to remove one electron from each atom in a mole of atoms of an element in the gaseous state.

The general symbol for ionisation energy is ΔH_i and for a first ionisation energy it is ΔH_{i1}. The process may be shown by the example of calcium as:

$$Ca(g) \rightarrow Ca^+(g) + e^-; \qquad \Delta H_{i1} = +590\,kJ\,mol^{-1}$$

(If the symbols seem unfamiliar at this stage, see page 148.)

The energy needed to remove a second electron from each ion in a mole of gaseous ions is the **second ionisation energy**. For calcium:

$$Ca^+(g) \rightarrow Ca^{2+}(g) + e^-; \qquad \Delta H_{i2} = +1150\,kJ\,mol^{-1}$$

Note that the second ionisation energy is much larger than the first. The reasons for this are discussed on page 10.

We can continue removing electrons until only the nucleus of an atom is left. The sequence of first, second, third, fourth, etc. ionisation energies (or **successive ionisation energies**) for the first 11 elements in the Periodic Table are shown in *table 1.2*.

We see that the following hold for any one element:

■ The ionisation energies increase. As each electron is removed from an atom, the remaining ion becomes more positively charged. Moving the next electron away from the increased positive charge is more difficult and the next ionisation energy is even larger.
■ There are one or more particularly large rises within the set of ionisation energies of each element (except hydrogen and helium).

Ionisation energies of elements are measured mainly by two techniques:

■ calculating the energy of the radiation causing particular lines in the emission spectrum of the element;
■ using electron bombardment of gaseous elements in discharge tubes.

We now know the ionisation energies of all of the elements.

These data may be interpreted in terms of the atomic numbers of elements and their simple electronic configurations.

Before doing so, we must consider the factors which influence ionisation energies.

		Electrons removed										
		1	2	3	4	5	6	7	8	9	10	11
1	H	1310										
2	He	2370	5250									
3	Li	520	7300	11 800								
4	Be	900	1760	14 850	21 000							
5	B	800	2420	3660	25 000	32 800						
6	C	1090	2350	4620	6220	37 800	47 300					
7	N	1400	2860	4580	7480	9450	53 300	64 400				
8	O	1310	3390	5320	7450	11 000	13 300	71 300	84 100			
9	F	1680	3470	6040	8410	11 000	15 200	17 900	92 000	106 000		
10	Ne	2080	3950	6120	9370	12 200	15 200	–	–	–	131 400	
11	Na	510	4560	6940	9540	13 400	16 600	20 100	25 500	28 900	141 000	158 700

● **Table 1.2** Successive ionisation energies for the first 11 elements in the Periodic Table (to nearest $10 \, kJ \, mol^{-1}$).

Factors influencing ionisation energies

The three strongest influences on ionisation energies of elements are the following:

■ *The size of the positive nuclear charge*
This charge affects all the electrons in an atom. The increase in nuclear charge with atomic number will tend to cause an increase in ionisation energies.

■ *The distance of the electron from the nucleus*
It has been found that, if F is the force of attraction between two objects and d is the distance between them, then

F is proportional to $1/d^2$
(the 'inverse square law')

This **distance effect** means that all forces of attraction decrease rapidly as the distance between the attracted bodies increases. Thus the attractions between a nucleus and electrons decrease as the quantum numbers of the shells increase. The further the shell is from the nucleus, the lower are the ionisation energies for electrons in that shell.

■ *The 'shielding' effect by electrons in filled inner shells*
All electrons are negatively charged and repel each other. Electrons in the filled inner shells repel electrons in the outer shell and reduce the effect of the positive nuclear charge. This is called the **shielding effect**. The greater the shielding effect upon an electron, the lower is the energy required to remove it and thus the lower the ionisation energy.

Consider the example of the successive ionisation energies of lithium. We see a low first ionisation energy, followed by much larger second and third ionisation energies. This confirms that lithium has one electron in its outer shell $n = 2$, which is easier to remove than either of the two electrons in the inner shell $n = 1$. The large increase in ionisation energy indicates where there is a change from shell $n = 2$ to shell $n = 1$.

The pattern is seen even more clearly if we plot a graph of ionisation energies (y axis) against number of electrons removed (x axis). As the ionisation energies are so large, we must use logarithm to base 10 ($\log_{10}$) to make the numbers fit on a reasonable scale. The graph for sodium is shown in *figure 1.10*.

SAQ 1.3

a In *figure 1.10* why are there large increases between the first and second ionisation energies and again between the ninth and tenth ionisation energies?

b How does this graph confirm the suggested simple electronic configuration for sodium of (2,8,1)?

Successive ionisation energies are thus helpful for predicting or confirming the simple electronic configurations of elements. In particular, they

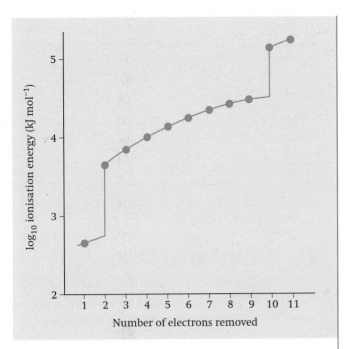

● **Figure 1.10** Graph of logarithm (log$_{10}$) of ionisation energy of sodium against the number of electrons removed.

confirm the number of electrons in the outer shell. This leads also to confirmation of the position of the element in the Periodic Table. Elements with one electron in their outer shell are in Group I, elements with two electrons in their outer shell are in Group II, and so on.

SAQ 1.4

The first four ionisation energies of an element are, in kJ mol^{-1}: 590, 1150, 4940 and 6480. Suggest the Group in the Periodic Table to which this element belongs.

Need for a more complex model

Electronic configurations are not quite so simple as the pattern shown in *table 1.1*. You will see in chapter 4 (page 60) that the first ionisation energies of the elements 3 (lithium) to 10 (neon) do not increase evenly. This, and other, variations show the need for a more complex model of electron configurations than the Bohr model.

The newer models depend upon an understanding of the mathematics of **quantum mechanics** and, in particular, the **Schrödinger equation** and **Heisenberg's uncertainty principle**. Explanations of these will not be attempted in this book, but an

outline of some implications for the chemist's view of atoms is given.

It is now thought that the following hold:
■ The energy levels (shells) of principal quantum numbers n = 1, 2, 3, 4, etc. do not have precise energy values. Instead, they each consist of a set of subshells, which contain **orbitals** with different energy values.
■ The subshells are of different types labelled **s**, **p**, **d** and **f**. An s subshell contains one orbital; a p subshell contains three orbitals; a d subshell contains five orbitals; and an f subshell contains seven orbitals.
■ An electron orbital represents a region of space around the nucleus of an atom, within which there is a high chance of finding that particular electron.
■ Each orbital has its own approximate, three-dimensional shape. It is not possible to draw the shape of orbitals precisely. They do not have exact boundaries but are fuzzy, like clouds; indeed, they are often called 'charge-clouds'.

Approximate representations of orbitals are shown in *figure 1.11*. Some regions, where there is a greater chance of finding an electron, are shown as more dense than others. To make drawing easier, however, we usually show orbitals as if they

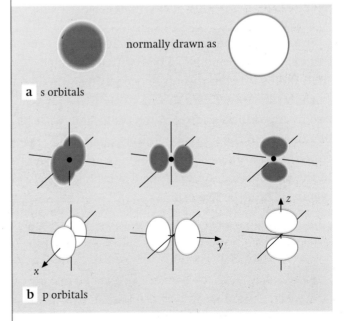

● **Figure 1.11** Representations of orbitals (the position of the nucleus is shown by the black dot):
a s orbitals with spherical symmetry;
b p orbitals, p$_x$, p$_y$ and p$_z$, with 'lobes' along x, y and z axes.

have a boundary; this encloses over 90% of the space where you can find the electron. Note that there is only one type of s orbital but three different p orbitals (p_x, p_y, p_z). There are five different d orbitals and seven f orbitals.

Orbitals: Pauli exclusion principle and spin-pairing

The shell $n = 1$ consists of a single s orbital called 1s; $n = 2$ consists of s and p orbitals in subshells called 2s and 2p; $n = 3$ consists of s, p and d orbitals in subshells called 3s, 3p and 3d.

There is an important principle concerning orbitals that affects all electronic configurations. This is the theory that any individual orbital can hold *one* or *two* electrons but *not more*. The principle was proposed by the Austro-Swiss physicist Wolfgang Pauli in 1921 and is called the **Pauli exclusion principle**.

You may wonder how an orbital can hold two electrons with negative charges that repel each other strongly. It is explained by the idea of **spin-pairing**. Along with charge, we say that electrons have a property called **spin**. We can visualise spin as an electron rotating at a fixed rate. Two electrons can exist as a pair in an orbital through each having opposite spin (*figure 1.12*); this reduces the effect of repulsion (see also later in this chapter). Clockwise spin is shown as ↑, anticlockwise spin as ↓.

From all the known evidence, including the Pauli exclusion principle, scientists have decided that: shell $n = 1$ contains up to two electrons in an s orbital; shell $n = 2$ contains up to eight electrons, two in an s orbital and six in the p subshell, with two in each of the p_x, p_y, p_z orbitals; shell $n = 3$ contains up to 18 electrons, two in an s orbital, six in the p subshell and ten in the d subshell, with two in each of the five orbitals.

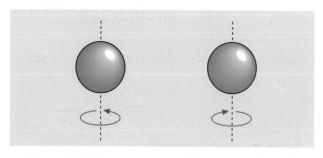

● **Figure 1.12** Representation of opposite spins of electrons.

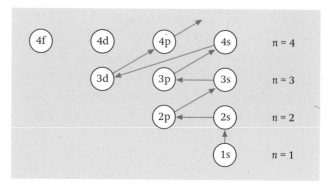

● **Figure 1.13** Diagram to show the order in which orbitals are filled up to shell $n = 4$.

Order of filling shells and orbitals

In each successive element of the Periodic Table, the order of filling the shells and orbitals is the order of their relative energy. The electronic configuration of each atom is the one that gives as low an energy state as possible to the atom as a whole. This means that the lowest-energy orbitals are filled first. The order of filling is:

first 1s, then 2s, 2p, 3s, 3p, 4s, 3d, 4p, ...

As you see, the order (shown diagrammatically in *figure 1.13*) is not quite what we might have predicted! An expected order is followed up to the 3p subshell, but then there is a variation, as the 4s is filled before the 3d. This variation and other variations further along in the order are caused by the increasingly complex influences of nuclear attractions and electron repulsions upon individual electrons.

Electronic configurations

Representing electronic configurations

The most common way of representing the electronic configurations of atoms is shown below. For example, hydrogen has one electron in an s orbital in the shell with principal quantum number $n = 1$. We show this as

Helium has two electrons, both in the 1s orbital, and is shown as $1s^2$.

The electronic configurations for the first 18 elements (H to Ar) are shown in *table 1.3*.

For the set of elements 19 (potassium) to 36 (krypton), it is more convenient to represent part of the configuration as a 'noble-gas core'. In this case the core is the configuration of argon. For convenience we sometimes represent $1s^2 2s^2 2p^6 3s^2 3p^6$ as [Ar] rather than write it out each time. Some examples are shown in *table 1.4*.

The following points should be noted:

■ When the 4s orbital is filled, the next electron goes into a 3d orbital (see scandium). This begins a pattern of filling up the 3d subshell, which finishes at zinc. The elements that add electrons to the d subshells are called the **d-block elements**; a subset of these is called **transition elements**.

■ There are variations in the pattern of filling the d subshell at elements 24 (chromium) and 29 (copper). These elements have only one electron in their 4s orbital. Chromium has five d electrons, rather than the expected four; copper has ten d electrons rather than nine. This is the outcome of the complex interactions of attractions and repulsions in their atoms.

■ From element 31 (gallium) to 36 (krypton) the electrons add to the 4p subshell. This is similar to the pattern of filling the 3p subshell from elements 13 (aluminium) to 18 (argon) in Period 3.

1	H	$1s^1$
2	He	$1s^2$
3	Li	$1s^2 2s^1$
4	Be	$1s^2 2s^2$
5	B	$1s^2 2s^2 2p^1$
6	C	$1s^2 2s^2 2p^2$
7	N	$1s^2 2s^2 2p^3$
8	O	$1s^2 2s^2 2p^4$
9	F	$1s^2 2s^2 2p^5$
10	Ne	$1s^2 2s^2 2p^6$
11	Na	$1s^2 2s^2 2p^6 3s^1$
12	Mg	$1s^2 2s^2 2p^6 3s^2$
13	Al	$1s^2 2s^2 2p^6 3s^2 3p^1$
14	Si	$1s^2 2s^2 2p^6 3s^2 3p^2$
15	P	$1s^2 2s^2 2p^6 3s^2 3p^3$
16	S	$1s^2 2s^2 2p^6 3s^2 3p^4$
17	Cl	$1s^2 2s^2 2p^6 3s^2 3p^5$
18	Ar	$1s^2 2s^2 2p^6 3s^2 3p^6$

● **Table 1.3** Electronic configurations for the first 18 elements in the Periodic Table.

19	Potassium (K)	$[Ar] 4s^1$
20	Calcium (Ca)	$[Ar] 4s^2$
21	Scandium (Sc)	$[Ar] 3d^1 \ 4s^2$
24	Chromium (Cr)	$[Ar] 3d^5 \ 4s^1$
25	Manganese (Mn)	$[Ar] 3d^5 \ 4s^2$
29	Copper (Cu)	$[Ar] 3d^{10} \ 4s^1$
30	Zinc (Zn)	$[Ar] 3d^{10} \ 4s^2$
31	Gallium (Ga)	$[Ar] 3d^{10} \ 4s^2 \ 4p^1$
35	Bromine (Br)	$[Ar] 3d^{10} \ 4s^2 \ 4p^5$
36	Krypton (Kr)	$[Ar] 3d^{10} \ 4s^2 \ 4p^6$

● **Table 1.4** Electronic configurations for some of the elements 19 to 36, where [Ar] is the electronic configuration of argon, $1s^2 2s^2 3s^2 3p^6$.

Filling of orbitals

Whenever possible, electrons will occupy orbitals singly. This is due to the repulsion of electron charges. Electrons remain unpaired until the available orbitals *of equal energy* have one electron each. When there are more electrons than the orbitals can hold as singles, they pair up by spin-pairing. This means that, if there are three electrons available for a p subshell, one each will go to the p_x, p_y and p_z orbitals, rather than two in p_x, one in p_y and none in p_z. When there are four electrons available, two will spin-pair in one orbital, leaving single electrons in the other orbitals. Similarly, five electrons in a d subshell will remain unpaired in the five orbitals (see *figure 1.14*).

As an example, we can show how orbitals are occupied in atoms of carbon, nitrogen and oxygen as:

carbon (six electrons)　　　$1s^2 \ 2s^2 \ 2p_x^1 \ 2p_y^1 \ 2p_z^0$
nitrogen (seven electrons)
　　　　　　　　　　$1s^2 \ 2s^2 \ 2p_x^1 \ 2p_y^1 \ 2p_z^1$
oxygen (eight electrons)　$1s^2 \ 2s^2 \ 2p_x^2 \ 2p_y^1 \ 2p_z^1$

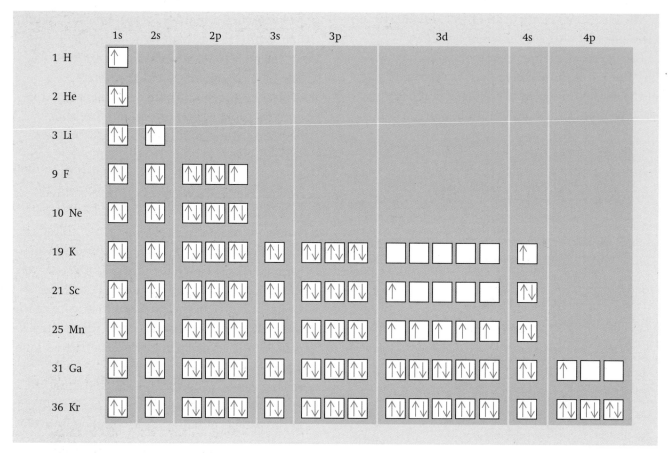

● **Figure 1.14** Electronic configurations of some elements in box form.

(Normally electronic configurations are shown in less detail – as in *table 1.4*.)

Electronic configurations of ions

The number of electrons in an ion is found from the atomic number of the element and the charge of the ion. Some examples are shown in *table 1.5*.

Note that both the sodium ion Na^+ and the fluoride ion F^- have the same electronic configuration as the noble gas neon. This has implications for the formation of, and bonding in, the compound sodium fluoride (see chapter 3, page 31 for a discussion of ionic bonding).

Electronic configurations in boxes

Another useful way of representing electronic configurations is in box form. We can show the electrons as arrows with their clockwise or anti-clockwise spin as ↑ or ↓.

Figure 1.14 shows the electronic configurations of some of the first 36 elements represented in this way.

	Sodium atom	Sodium ion	Fluorine atom	Fluoride ion
Symbol	Na	Na^+	F	F^-
Atomic number	11	11	9	9
Electrons	11	10	9	10
Configuration	$1s^2\ 2s^2\ 2p^6\ 3s^1$	$1s^2\ 2s^2\ 2p^6$	$1s^2\ 2s^2\ 2p^5$	$1s^2\ 2s^2\ 2p^6$

● **Table 1.5**

SAQ 1.5
Draw box-form electronic configurations for: boron, oxygen, argon, nickel and bromine.

SUMMARY

◆ Any atom has an internal structure with almost all of the mass in the nucleus, which has a diameter about 10^{-4} that of the diameter of the atom.

◆ The nucleus contains protons (+ charge) and neutrons (0 charge). Electrons (– charge) exist outside the nucleus.

◆ All atoms of the same element have the same atomic number (Z); that is, they have equal numbers of protons in their nuclei.

◆ The mass number (A) of an atom is the total number of protons and neutrons. Thus the number of neutrons = $A - Z$.

◆ The isotopes of an element are atoms with the same atomic number but different mass numbers. If neutral, they have the same number of protons and electrons but different numbers of neutrons.

◆ Electrons can exist only at certain energy levels and gain or lose 'quanta' of energy when they move between the levels.

◆ The main energy levels or 'shells' are given principal quantum numbers $n = 1, 2, 3, 4,$ etc. Shell $n = 1$ is the closest to the nucleus.

◆ The shells consist of subshells known as s, p, d or f and each subshell consists of orbitals. Subshells s, p, d and f have one, three, five and seven orbitals respectively. Orbitals s, p, d, and f have different, distinctive shapes; we have looked at the shapes of s and p orbitals.

◆ Each orbital holds a maximum of two electrons, so that full subshells of s, p, d and f orbitals contain two, six, ten and fourteen electrons respectively. The two electrons in any single orbital are spin-paired.

◆ Electrons remain unpaired among orbitals of equal energy until numbers require them to spin-pair.

◆ The first ionisation energy of an element is the energy required to remove one electron from each atom in a mole of atoms of the element in the gaseous state.

◆ Successive ionisation energies are the energies required to remove first, second, third, fourth, etc. electrons from a mole of gaseous ions of an element.

◆ Large changes in the values of successive ionisation energies of an element indicate that the electrons are being removed from different shells. This gives evidence for the electronic configuration of atoms of the element and helps to confirm the position of the element in the Periodic Table.

Questions

1 What are the electronic configurations of the following atoms or ions: Li^+, K^+, Ca^{2+}, N^{3-}, O^{2-}, S^{2-}, Cl and Cl^-?

2 Chemists use a model of an atom that consists of sub-atomic particles (protons, neutrons and electrons).

a State the relative mass and relative charge of each of these three particles.

b The particles in each of the following pairs differ **only** in the number of protons **or** neutrons **or** electrons. Explain what the difference is within each pair.

(i) ^6Li and ^7Li

(ii) ^{32}S and $^{32}S^{2-}$

(iii) $^{39}K^+$ and $^{40}Ca^{2+}$

3 Hydrogen fluoride in water produces hydrofluoric acid. This acid is extremely corrosive and, because it reacts with glass, is often stored in nickel containers. This is possible because the hydrofluoric acid reacts with the nickel to form a protective coating of nickel(II) fluoride.

a What is the electronic configuration of a nickel atom?

b Predict the electronic configuration of a nickel(II) ion.

4 In 1911, a 40 kg meteorite fell in Egypt. Isotopic and chemical analysis of oxygen extracted from this meteorite showed a different relative atomic mass to that of oxygen normally found on Earth. This value matched measurements made of the Martian atmosphere by the Viking landing in 1976, proving that the meteorite had originated from Mars.

a (i) Explain what you understand by the word **isotopes**.

(ii) Oxygen has three main isotopes, ^{16}O, ^{17}O and ^{18}O. State the number of protons, neutrons and electrons in ^{16}O and ^{17}O.

(iii) Explain what you understand by the term **relative atomic mass**.

(iv) Suggest why the relative atomic mass of Martian oxygen is different from that of oxygen obtained from Earth.

b The first ionisation energy of oxygen is $1310\,kJ\,mol^{-1}$.

(i) Explain what is meant by the first ionisation energy of an element.

(ii) Write an equation, including state symbols, to represent the first ionisation energy of oxygen.

(iii) Suggest why there is very little difference between the first ionisation energies of ^{16}O, ^{17}O and ^{18}O.

5 Values of the successive ionisation energies of nitrogen are shown below:

Ionisation energy	1st	2nd	3rd	4th	5th	6th	7th
$(kJ\,mol^{-1})$	1400	2860	4590	7480	9450	53 300	64 400

a Explain why the successive ionisation energies increase.

b Explain why there is a particularly large difference between the 5th and 6th ionisation energies of nitrogen.

CHAPTER 2

Atoms, molecules and stoichiometry

By the end of this chapter you should be able to:

1 define the terms *relative atomic mass*, *relative isotopic mass*, *relative molecular mass* and *relative formula mass*, based on the ^{12}C scale;

2 describe the basic principles of the mass spectrometer;

3 outline the use of *mass spectrometry* in the determination of *relative isotopic mass*, *isotopic abundance* and *relative atomic mass*, and as a method for identifying elements;

4 interpret mass spectra in terms of isotopic abundances;

5 calculate the relative atomic mass of an element given the relative abundances of its isotopes, or its mass spectrum;

6 define the *mole* in terms of *Avogadro's constant* and *molar mass* as the mass of 1 mole of a substance;

7 define the terms *empirical formula* and *molecular formula*;

8 calculate empirical and molecular formulae, using composition by mass;

9 construct *balanced* chemical equations (full and ionic);

10 perform calculations involving reacting masses, volumes of gases and volumes and concentrations of solutions in simple acid–base *titrations*, and use those calculations to deduce *stoichiometric* relationships.

Counting atoms and molecules

If you have ever had to sort and count coins, you will know that it is a very time-consuming business! Banks do not need to count sorted coins, as they can quickly check the amount by weighing. For example, as a 2p coin has twice the mass of a 1p coin, a bag containing £2.00 could contain one hundred 2p coins or two hundred 1p coins. Chemists are also able to count atoms and molecules by weighing them. This is possible because atoms of different elements also have different masses.

We rely on tables of relative atomic masses for this purpose. The **relative atomic mass**, A_r, of an element is the mass of the element relative to the mass of carbon-12; one atom of this isotope (see chapter 1, page 7) is given a relative isotopic mass of exactly 12. The relative atomic masses, A_r, of the other elements are then found by comparing the average mass of their atoms with that of the carbon-12 isotope. Notice that we use the average mass of their atoms. This is because we take into account the abundance of their naturally occurring isotopes. Thus the precise relative atomic mass of hydrogen is 1.0079, whilst that of chlorine is 35.49. (Accepted relative atomic masses are shown on the Periodic Table on page 191.)

We use the term **relative isotopic mass** for the mass of an isotope of an element relative to carbon-12. For example, the relative isotopic mass of carbon-13 is 13.003. If the natural abundance of each isotope is known, together with their relative isotopic masses, we can calculate the relative atomic mass of the element as follows.

Chlorine, for example, occurs naturally as chlorine-35 and chlorine-37 with percentage natural abundances 75.5% and 24.5% respectively. So

$$\text{relative atomic mass} = \frac{(75.5 \times 35 + 24.5 \times 37)}{100}$$
$$= 35.5$$

SAQ 2.1

Naturally occurring neon is 90.9% neon–20, 0.3% neon–21 and 8.8% neon–22. Use these figures to calculate the relative atomic mass of naturally occurring neon.

The masses of different molecules are compared in a similar fashion. The **relative molecular mass**, M_r, of a compound is the mass of a molecule of the compound relative to the mass of an atom of carbon-12, which is given a mass of exactly 12.

To find the relative molecular mass of a molecule, we add up the relative atomic masses of all the atoms present in the molecule. For example, the relative molecular mass of methane, CH_4, is $12 + (4 \times 1) = 16$.

Where compounds contain ions, we use the term **relative formula mass**. Relative molecular mass refers to compounds containing molecules.

SAQ 2.2

Use the Periodic Table in the appendix (page 191) to calculate the relative formula mass of the following:

a magnesium chloride, $MgCl_2$;
b copper sulphate, $CuSO_4$;
c sodium carbonate, $Na_2CO_3 \cdot 10H_2O$ (10H_2O means ten water molecules).

In the next section we shall see how we determine relative isotopic masses and isotopic abundances.

Determination of A_r from mass spectra

You may have wondered how tables of relative atomic masses have been obtained. An instrument called a **mass spectrometer** is used for this purpose; such instruments are too expensive to be found in most schools or colleges. Academic or industrial chemical laboratories may have one or two, depending on their needs and resources. Mass spectrometers have even been sent into space (*figure 2.1*).

In order to obtain the mass and the percentage abundance for the isotopes of an element, a method for separating atoms of different masses is required. The principles for this separation are relatively simple and are as follows:

■ Atoms are first converted into singly charged, positive ions. A vaporised sample of an element is bombarded with high-energy electrons. An ion forms when a high-energy electron collides with an atom of the element. Providing the electron has sufficient energy, the collision will

The Viking space probe
When the two *Viking* space probes were launched by NASA in 1975, they carried mass spectrometers. The purpose of these spectrometers was to look for traces of organic compounds on the surface of Mars. Scientists had put forward the hypothesis that living organisms would have left behind traces of organic compounds. However, the soil sampled on Mars showed no trace of organic compounds.

● **Figure 2.1** The surface of Mars, seen from the *Viking I* space probe.

remove an electron from the atom, forming a positive ion.

- A beam of these positive ions is accelerated by using a positively charged electrode to repel it.
- The beam of positive ions passes through a magnetic field where ions are deflected according to their masses.
- As the magnetic field deflects lighter ions more than heavier ions, separation occurs.
- A suitable detector measures the relative abundance of each isotope present. The charge on each ion produces a tiny electric current at the detector. The more ions there are of the same mass, the higher the current.

A simplified diagram of a mass spectrometer is shown in *figure 2.2*. In practice, mass spectrometers are very sophisticated pieces of equipment involving mechanical, electrical, electronic and computer engineering. A very low pressure is needed inside a mass spectrometer to avoid loss of ions by collision with air molecules. The results are displayed on a computer monitor as a chart of abundance against mass (see, for example, *figure 2.3*, the mass spectrum of zirconium).

Notice that the abundance is on the vertical axis. The horizontal axis displays the mass-to-charge ratio (m/e). Remember, the mass spectrometer sorts and detects positive ions. The ions almost always carry a single positive charge. Hence you often see this axis simply labelled mass because, numerically, mass/charge = mass.

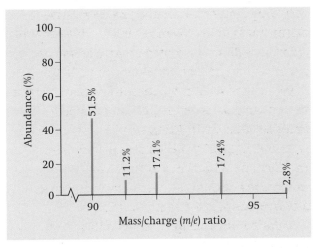

● **Figure 2.3** The mass spectrum of zirconium, Zr.

SAQ 2.3

a List the isotopes present in zirconium.

b Use the percentage abundance of each isotope to calculate the relative atomic mass of zirconium.

Some modern mass spectrometers can be set up to determine isotopic masses to four or five decimal places. *Figure 2.4* shows a photograph of such a spectrometer.

Counting chemical substances in bulk

The mole and Avogadro's constant

When chemists write a formula for a compound, it tells us how many atoms of each element are present in the compound. For example, the formula of water is H_2O, and this tells us that two atoms of hydrogen are combined with one atom of oxygen. As the A_r of hydrogen is 1 and the A_r of oxygen is 16, the M_r is 2 + 16 = 18 and the hydrogen and oxygen are combined in a mass ratio of 2:16. Although atoms are too small to be weighed individually, any mass of water will have hydrogen and oxygen in this ratio.

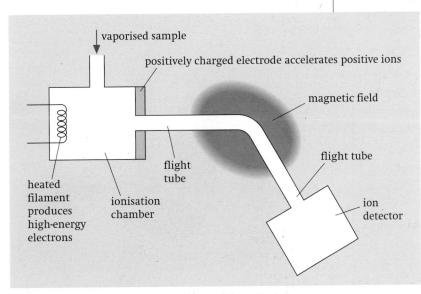

● **Figure 2.2** Simplified diagram of a mass spectrometer.

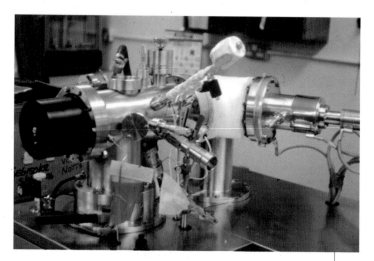

● **Figure 2.4** A high-resolution mass spectrometer, which may be used to determine accurately isotopic masses of elements.

For example, consider 18 g of water (2 + 16 = 18). This will actually contain 2 g of hydrogen and 16 g of oxygen. We can use any unit of mass as long as we keep to the same mass ratio. In 18 tonnes of water there will be 2 tonnes of hydrogen and 16 tonnes of oxygen. The actual number of atoms present will be very large indeed!

When we take the relative molecular mass or relative atomic mass of a substance in grams, we say that we have one mole of the substance. The mole is the chemist's unit of amount. A **mole** of substance is the mass of substance that has the same number of particles as there are atoms in exactly 12 g of carbon-12. The particles may be atoms, molecules, ions or even electrons.

The number of atoms or molecules in one mole is a constant known as Avogadro's constant. Avogadro's constant, L, is approximately $6 \times 10^{23} \, \text{mol}^{-1}$.

Units used by chemists:

Mass is measured in g (kg in SI units).
Volume is measured in cm^3 or dm^3
　($1 \, \text{dm}^3 = 1000 \, \text{cm}^3 = 1 \, \text{litre}$).
Amount of substance is measured in moles
　(abbreviation is mol).

You need to remember that *amount* has a specific meaning, as do *mass* and *volume*. Each has its own unit. SI is an abbreviation for the Système International d'Unités. In this internationally recognised system, kilogram, metre and mole are three of the seven base units from which all supplementary units are derived.

We often refer to the mass of one mole of a substance as the molar mass, M. The units of molar mass are g mol^{-1}.

In *figure 2.5* a mole of some elements may be compared.

Moles are particularly helpful when we need to measure out reactants or calculate the mass of product from a reaction. Such information is very important when manufacturing chemicals. For example, if the manufacture of a drug requires a particularly expensive reagent, it is important to mix it with the correct amounts of the other reagents to ensure that it all reacts and none is wasted. You will need to be able to write formulae in order to calculate amounts in moles. (See page 23 for some help with writing formulae.)

To find the amount of substance present in a given mass, we must divide that mass by the molar mass, M, of the substance. For example, for NaCl, $M = 23 + 35.5 = 58.5 \, \text{g mol}^{-1}$; so in 585 g of sodium chloride (NaCl) there are 585/58.5 mol of NaCl, i.e. 10 mol NaCl.

SAQ 2.4

What amount of substance is there in:
a 35.5 g of chlorine **atoms**?
b 71 g of chlorine **molecules**, Cl_2?

● **Figure 2.5** From left to right, one mole of each of copper, bromine, carbon, mercury and lead.

SAQ 2.5

Use Avogadro's constant to calculate the total number of atoms of chlorine in:

a 35.5 g of chlorine atoms.

b 71 g of chlorine molecules.

To find the mass of a given amount of substance, we multiply the number of moles of the substance by the molar mass.

SAQ 2.6

Calculate the mass of the following:

a 0.1 mol of carbon dioxide.

b 10 mol of calcium carbonate, $CaCO_3$.

Calculations involving reacting masses

If we are given the mass of a reactant, we can find out the mass of products formed in a chemical reaction. To do this, a balanced equation is used. (See page 24 for revision on balancing equations.)

Consider the formation of water from hydrogen and oxygen:

	$2H_2$	$+ O_2$	$\rightarrow 2H_2O$
this reads	2 molecules hydrogen	+ 1 molecule oxygen	→ 2 molecules water
or	2 moles hydrogen	+ 1 mole oxygen	→ 2 moles water
masses (g)	$2 \times 2 = 4$	+ 32	→ $2 \times (2 + 16) = 36$

If we mix 4 g of hydrogen with 32 g of oxygen we should produce 36 g of water on exploding the mixture. Notice that the number of moles of water does *not* equal the sum of the number of moles of hydrogen and oxygen, because they have chemically reacted to produce molecules with a different molecular mass.

Suppose we wish to calculate the mass of iron that can be obtained from a given mass of iron oxide, Fe_2O_3. When iron ore is reduced by carbon monoxide in a blast furnace (*figure 2.6*), the equation for the reaction is:

$$Fe_2O_3 + 3CO \rightarrow 2Fe + 3CO_2$$

The molar mass of Fe_2O_3 is $(2 \times 56) + (3 \times 16) = 160\,\text{g mol}^{-1}$. One mole of Fe_2O_3 produces two moles of iron.

Hence 160 g of Fe_2O_3 will produce $2 \times 56 = 112$ g iron; or

1000 g of Fe_2O_3 will produce

$$112 \times \frac{1000\,\text{g}}{160} = 700\,\text{g iron.}$$

SAQ 2.7

Hydrogen burns in chlorine to produce hydrogen chloride:

$$H_2 + Cl_2 \rightarrow 2HCl$$

a Calculate the ratio of the masses of reactants.

b What mass (in g) of hydrogen is needed to produce 36.5 g of hydrogen chloride?

SAQ 2.8

Calculate the mass of iron produced from 1000 tonnes of Fe_2O_3. How many tonnes of Fe_2O_3 would be needed to produce 1 tonne of iron? If the iron ore contains 12% of Fe_2O_3, how many tonnes of ore are needed to produce 1 tonne of iron? (Note: 1 tonne = 1000 kg)

● **Figure 2.6** Workers taking the slag from the top of the molten iron in an open-hearth blast furnace.

Calculation of empirical and molecular formulae

The **empirical formula** of a compound shows the simplest whole-number ratio of the elements present. For many simple compounds it is the same as the molecular formula. The **molecular formula** shows the total number of atoms of each element present in a molecule of the compound. Some examples are shown below:

Compound	Empirical formula	Molecular formula
water	H_2O	H_2O
methane	CH_4	CH_4
butane	C_2H_5	C_4H_{10}
benzene	CH	C_6H_6

SAQ 2.9
Write down the empirical formulae of the following:
a hexane, C_6H_{14}; **b** hydrogen peroxide, H_2O_2.

The molecular formula is far more useful. It enables us to write balanced chemical equations and to calculate masses of compounds involved in a reaction. It is not possible to calculate the molecular formula from the percentage composition by mass of a compound. This information alone does not tell us how atoms are arranged in a molecule. However, the empirical formula can be found in this way. To find this, experimental methods that determine the mass of each element present in a compound are needed.

For example, if magnesium is burned in oxygen, magnesium oxide is formed. Suppose that a piece of magnesium of known mass is burned completely and the magnesium oxide produced is weighed. The weighings enable us to calculate the empirical formula of magnesium oxide.

In such an experiment, 0.240 g of magnesium ribbon produced 0.400 g of magnesium oxide:

	Mg	O
Mass (g)	0.240	0.400 − 0.240
		= 0.160
Amount (mol)	$= \dfrac{\text{mass}}{M}$	$= \dfrac{\text{mass}}{M}$
	$= \dfrac{0.240}{24}$	$= \dfrac{0.160}{16}$
	= 0.0100	= 0.0100

Divide by the smallest amount to give whole numbers:

Atoms (mol)	1	1

Magnesium and oxygen atoms are present in the ratio 1 : 1. Hence the empirical formula of magnesium oxide is MgO. Notice that we convert the mass of each element to the amount in moles, as we need the ratio of the number of atoms of each element present.

SAQ 2.10
An oxide of copper has the following composition by mass: Cu, 0.635 g; O, 0.080 g. Calculate the empirical formula of the oxide.

Combustion analysis

The composition by mass of organic compounds can be found by combustion analysis. This involves the complete combustion in oxygen of a sample of known mass. In combustion analysis, all the carbon is converted to carbon dioxide and all the hydrogen to water. The carbon dioxide and water produced are carefully collected by absorption and weighed. The apparatus is shown in *figure 2.7*. Calculation then gives the mass of carbon and hydrogen present. If oxygen is also present, its mass is found by subtraction (see example below). Other elements require further analytical determinations.

Let us consider an example. Suppose that 0.500 g of an organic compound X (containing only carbon, hydrogen and oxygen) produces

● **Figure 2.7** Modern microanalytical equipment used for routine determination of percentage of carbon and hydrogen in a compound.

0.733 g of carbon dioxide and 0.300 g of water on complete combustion. The mass spectrum of the compound shows it has a molecular mass of 60. How can we determine the molecular formula of the compound?

Remember that the A_r of H = 1, C = 12, O = 16. The calculation goes as follows. As 12 g of carbon are present in 1 mol (= 44 g) CO_2,

$$\text{mass of carbon in } 0.733 \text{ g of } CO_2 = \frac{12}{44} \times 0.733 \text{ g}$$
$$= 0.200 \text{ g}$$
$$= \text{mass of carbon in X}$$

As 2 g of hydrogen are present in 1 mol (= 18 g) H_2O,

$$\text{mass of hydrogen in } 0.300 \text{ g of } H_2O = \frac{2}{18} \times 0.300 \text{ g}$$
$$= 0.033 \text{ g}$$
$$= \text{mass of hydrogen in X}$$

Hence

$$\text{mass of oxygen in X} = 0.500 - 0.199 - 0.033$$
$$= 0.268 \text{ g}$$

	C	H	O
Mass (g)	0.200	0.033	0.268
Amount (mol)	0.200/12	0.033/1	0.268/16
	= 0.0167	= 0.033	= 0.0168

Divide by the smallest amount to give whole numbers:

Atoms (mol)	1	2	1

Hence the empirical formula is CH_2O. This has $M_r = 12 + 2 + 16 = 30$. As M_r of X is 60, the molecular formula of the compound is $C_2H_4O_2$.

SAQ 2.11

On complete combustion of 0.400 g of a hydrocarbon, 1.257 g of carbon dioxide and 0.514 g of water were produced.
a Calculate the empirical formula of the hydrocarbon.
b If the relative molecular mass of the hydrocarbon is 84, what is its molecular formula?

Writing chemical formulae

By this point in your study of chemistry you will already know the formulae of some simple compounds. For advanced chemistry you will need to learn the formulae of a wide range of compounds. These formulae are determined by the electronic configurations of the elements involved and the ways in which they combine with other elements to form compounds. The chemical bonding of elements in compounds is studied in chapter 3. It will help if you learn some generalisations about the names and formulae of compounds.

In the formula of an ionic compound, the total number of positive charges in the compound must exactly equal the total number of negative charges. For magnesium oxide, magnesium (in Group II) forms Mg^{2+} ions. Oxygen (in Group VI) forms O^{2-} ions. Magnesium oxide is thus MgO (+2 − 2 = 0). Aluminium forms 3+ ions. Two Al^{3+} ions and three O^{2-} ions are needed in aluminium oxide ($2 \times (+3) + 3 \times (-2) = 0$). The formula is Al_2O_3. Note how the number of ions of each element in the formula is written as a small number following and below the element symbol.

Some compounds do not contain ions. These compounds contain covalent bonds. The formulae of simple covalent compounds may be deduced from the numbers of electrons required to complete the outer electron shell of each atom present. For example, in methane, carbon requires four more electrons to complete its second shell. Hydrogen requires one. This means that one carbon will combine with four hydrogen atoms to form CH_4 (methane). In chapter 3, you will see that each hydrogen forms one bond to carbon whilst the carbon forms four bonds to the four hydrogen atoms.

Table 2.1 summarises the charges on some of the common ions that you need to learn. The position of the elements in the Periodic Table is helpful. In many instances, the Group in which an element lies indicates the charge on an ion of the element. Note that metals form positive ions, whilst non-metals form negative ions.

Metals do not usually change their names in compounds. However, non-metals change their name by becoming -ides. For example, chlorine becomes chloride in sodium chloride. Sodium has not changed its name, although its properties are now dramatically different! Many non-metals (and some metals) combine with other non-metals such as oxygen to form negative ions. These negative

Charge	Examples
1+	H^+ and Group I, the alkali metal ions, e.g. Li^+, Na^+, K^+
2+	Group II, the alkaline earth metal ions, e.g. Mg^{2+}, Ca^{2+}
3+	Al^{3+}
1–	Group VII, the halogens, e.g. F^-, Cl^-, Br^-, I^-
	Nitrate, NO_3^-
2–.	Group VI, O^{2-} and S^{2-}
	Carbonate, CO_3^{2-}
	Sulphate, SO_4^{2-} and sulphite, SO_3^{2-}
3–	Phosphate, PO_4^{3-}

● **Table 2.1** Charges on some common ions.

ions start with the name of the element and end in -ate (or sometimes -ite), e.g. sulphate (sulphite). Some of these ions are also included in *table 2.1*.

SAQ 2.12

Write the molecular formula for each of the following compounds:
a magnesium bromide　d sodium sulphate
b hydrogen iodide　e potassium nitrate
c calcium sulphide　f nitrogen dioxide

SAQ 2.13

Name each of the following compounds:
a K_2CO_3　c $LiNO_3$　e SiO_2
b Al_2S_3　d $Ca_3(PO_4)_2$

Balancing chemical equations

Atoms are neither created nor destroyed in a chemical reaction. When we write a chemical equation we must, therefore, ensure we have the same number of atoms of each element on each side of the chemical equation. We do this by *balancing* the equation, as follows:
■ Write down the formulae of all the reactants and all the products. It may help you to write these in words first.
■ Now inspect the equation and count the atoms of each element on each side. As the elements present cannot be created or lost in the chemical reaction, we must balance the number of each element.

■ Decide what numbers must be placed in front of each formula to ensure that the same number of each atom is present on each side of the equation.

It is most important that the formulae of the reactants and products are not altered; only the total number of each may be changed.

We shall now do an example. When iron(III) oxide is reduced to metallic iron by carbon monoxide, the carbon monoxide is oxidised to carbon dioxide. (The III in iron(III) oxide indicates that the iron has an oxidation state of +3. See page 67 for more on oxidation states.)

Iron(III) oxide + carbon monoxide
　→ iron + carbon dioxide

The formulae are:

$$Fe_2O_3 + CO \rightarrow Fe + CO_2$$

On inspection we note that there are two iron atoms in the oxide on the left-hand side but only one on the right-hand side. We thus write

$$Fe_2O_3 + CO \rightarrow 2Fe + CO_2$$

Next we count the oxygen atoms: three in the oxide plus one in carbon monoxide, on the left-hand side. As there are only two on the right-hand side in carbon dioxide, we must double the number of CO_2 molecules in order to balance the number of oxygen atoms.

$$Fe_2O_3 + CO \rightarrow 2Fe + 2CO_2$$

On checking we see we have solved one problem but created a new one. There are now two carbon atoms on the right but only one on the left. Doubling the number of CO molecules balances the carbon atoms but unbalances the oxygen atoms again!

If we examine the equation again, we see that in the reaction between Fe_2O_3 and CO, each CO molecule requires only one oxygen atom to form CO_2. Thus three CO molecules combine with the three oxygen atoms lost from Fe_2O_3. Three CO_2 molecules will be formed:

$$Fe_2O_3 + 3CO \rightarrow 2Fe + 3CO_2$$

The equation is now balanced.

We often need to specify the physical states of chemicals in an equation. This can be important when, for example, calculating enthalpy changes (see chapter 13). The symbols used are: (s) for solid; (l) for liquid; (g) for gas. A solution in water is described as aqueous, so (aq) is used. Addition of the physical states to the equation for the reaction of iron(III) oxide with carbon monoxide produces:

$$Fe_2O_3(s) + 3CO(g) \rightarrow 2Fe(s) + 3CO_2(g)$$

SAQ 2.14

Balance the equations for the following reactions.

a The thermite reaction (used for chemical welding of lengths of rail):
$$Al + Fe_2O_3 \rightarrow Al_2O_3 + Fe$$

b Petrol contains octane, C_8H_{18}. Complete combustion in oxygen produces only carbon dioxide and water.

c Lead nitrate, $Pb(NO_3)_2$, decomposes on heating to produce PbO, NO_2 and O_2.

Balancing ionic equations

In some situations, chemists prefer to use ionic equations. Such equations are simpler than the corresponding full equation (which show the full formulae of all compounds present). For example, when a granule of zinc is placed in aqueous copper sulphate, copper metal is displaced, forming a red-brown deposit on the zinc. In the reaction, zinc dissolves to form zinc sulphate. The full equation for the reaction is:

$$Zn(s) + CuSO_4(aq) \rightarrow ZnSO_4(aq) + Cu(s)$$

During this reaction copper ions, Cu^{2+}, are converted to copper atoms, Cu, and zinc atoms, Zn, are converted to zinc ions, Zn^{2+}. The sulphate ion has remained unchanged. It is known as a spectator ion: it stays on the sidelines. The ionic equation does not show the ions that remain unchanged. It therefore provides a shorter equation which focusses our attention on the change taking place:

$$Zn(s) + Cu^{2+}(aq) \rightarrow Zn^{2+}(aq) + Cu(s)$$

In an ionic equation we must balance the overall charge on the ions on each side of the equation.

Notice that the charge on each side of this ionic equation is 2+. Ensure that the charges are balanced *before* balancing the number of atoms of each element.

The reaction of $Cu^{2+}(aq)$ with Zn(s) involves transfer of electrons. It is known as a **redox** reaction. You will learn more about such reactions in chapter 5 (see page 68). Ionic equations are frequently used for redox reactions. Chemists also prefer to use ionic equations for **precipitation** reactions. For example, when sodium hydroxide is added dropwise to copper sulphate a pale blue precipitate of copper(II) hydroxide, $Cu(OH)_2(s)$, is formed. The full equation is:

$$CuSO_4(aq) + 2NaOH(aq)$$
$$\rightarrow Cu(OH)_2(s) + Na_2SO_4(aq)$$

The ionic equation is:

$$Cu^{2+}(aq) + 2OH^-(aq) \rightarrow Cu(OH)_2(s)$$

Both sodium ions, $Na^+(aq)$, and sulphate ions, $SO_4^{2-}(aq)$, are spectator ions, meaning that they are unchanged, and can be omitted.

SAQ 2.15

Try balancing the following ionic equations:

a $Cl_2(aq) + Br^-(aq) \rightarrow Cl^-(aq) + Br_2(aq)$

b $Fe^{3+}(aq) + OH^-(aq) \rightarrow Fe(OH)_3(s)$

Calculations involving concentrations and gas volumes

Concentrations of solutions

When one mole of a compound is dissolved in a solvent to make one cubic decimetre (1 dm^3) of solution, the concentration is 1 $mol\,dm^{-3}$. Usually the solvent is water and an aqueous solution is formed.

Traditionally, concentrations in $mol\,dm^{-3}$ have been expressed as **molarities**. For example, 2 $mol\,dm^{-3}$ aqueous sodium hydroxide is 2M aqueous sodium hydroxide, where M is the molarity of the solution. Although this is still a convenient method for labelling bottles, etc., it is better to use the units of $mol\,dm^{-3}$ in your calculations. Although you may have used mol/dm^3 or $mol/litre$

in the past, advanced chemistry requires you to use $mol\,dm^{-3}$.

An experimental technique in which it is essentail to know the concentration of solutions is a titration. A **titration** (*figure 2.8*) is a way of measuring quantities of reactants, and can be very useful in determining an unknown concentration or following the progress of a reaction. In titrations there are five things you need to know:

- the balanced equation for the reaction showing the moles of the two reactants;
- the volume of the solution of the first reagent;
- the concentration of the solution of the first reagent;
- the volume of the solution of the second reagent;
- the concentration of the solution of the second reagent.

● **Figure 2.8** A titration enables the reacting volumes of two solutions to be accurately determined. One solution is measured with a graduated pipette into a conical flask, the other is added slowly from a burette. The point where complete reaction just occurs is usually shown using an indicator, which changes colour at this point (called the end-point).

If we know four of these, we can calculate the fifth. Remember that concentrations may be in $mol\,dm^{-3}$ or $g\,dm^{-3}$.

Many titration calculations start by finding the amount of a reagent (in moles) from a given concentration and volume. For example, what amount of sodium hydroxide is present in $24.0\,cm^3$ of an aqueous $0.010\,mol\,dm^{-3}$ solution?

Convert the volume to dm^3:

$$1\,dm^3 = 10 \times 10 \times 10\,cm^3 = 1000\,cm^3$$

$$24.0\,cm^3 = \frac{24.0}{1000}\,dm^3$$

$$\text{amount of NaOH in } 24.0\,cm^3 = \frac{24.0}{1000} \times 0.010\,mol$$
$$= 2.40 \times 10^{-4}\,mol$$

To check your calculations:

- Notice how the units multiply and cancel: $dm^3 \times mol\,dm^{-3} = mol$. Use this as a check.
- Ensure the units of the answer are those you would expect (e.g. mol for quantity or $mol\,dm^{-3}$ for concentration).
- Think about the size of your answer (e.g. $24\,cm^3$ is much less than $1\,dm^3$, so we expect the quantity of sodium hydroxide in $24\,cm^3$ of $0.01\,mol\,dm^{-3}$ solution to be much less than $0.01\,mol$).

We also often need to find the concentration of a solution from the amount in a given volume. For example, what is the concentration of an aqueous solution containing $2 \times 10^{-4}\,mol$ of sulphuric acid in $10\,cm^3$?

As before, convert the volume to dm^3:

$$10\,cm^3 = \frac{10}{1000}\,dm^3 = 1 \times 10^{-2}\,dm^3$$

$$\text{concentration of sulphuric acid} = \frac{2 \times 10^{-4}}{1 \times 10^{-2}}\,mol\,dm^{-3}$$
$$= 2 \times 10^{-2}\,mol\,dm^{-3}$$

Again check by looking at the units:

$$\frac{mol}{dm^3} = mol\,dm^{-3}.$$

SAQ 2.16

a Calculate the amount in moles of nitric acid in $25.0\,cm^3$ of a $0.1\,mol\,dm^{-3}$ aqueous solution.

b Calculate the concentration in $mol\,dm^{-3}$ of a solution comprising $0.125\,mol$ of nitric acid with water added, up to a volume of $50\,cm^3$.

Changing concentrations expressed in $mol\,dm^{-3}$ to $g\,dm^{-3}$ and vice versa is straightforward. We multiply by the molar mass M to convert $mol\,dm^{-3}$ to $g\,dm^{-3}$. To convert $g\,dm^{-3}$ to $mol\,dm^{-3}$ we divide by M. Notice how the units cancel correctly.

SAQ 2.17

a What is the concentration in $g\,dm^{-3}$ of $0.50\,mol\,dm^{-3}$ aqueous ethanoic acid (CH_3CO_2H)?

b What is the concentration in $mol\,dm^{-3}$ of an aqueous solution containing $4.00\,g\,dm^{-3}$ of sodium hydroxide?

A worked example follows of how such calculations are combined with a balanced chemical equation to interpret the result of a titration. Try to identify the 'five things to know' in this calculation. In the titration $20.0\,cm^3$ of $0.200\,mol\,dm^{-3}$ aqueous sodium hydroxide exactly neutralises a $25.0\,cm^3$ sample of sulphuric acid. What is the concentration of the sulphuric acid in **a** $mol\,dm^{-3}$, **b** $g\,dm^{-3}$?

The working goes as follows:

$$20.0\,cm^3 = \frac{20}{1000}\,dm^3 = 2.00 \times 10^{-2}\,dm^3$$

amount of sodium hydroxide
$$= 2 \times 10^{-2} \times 0.200\,mol$$
$$= 4.00 \times 10^{-3}\,mol$$

The balanced equation for the reaction is:

$$2NaOH(aq) + H_2SO_4(aq) \rightarrow Na_2SO_4(aq) + 2H_2O(l)$$

Exact neutralisation requires 2 mol of NaOH to 1 mol of H_2SO_4. So

amount of H_2SO_4 neutralised in the titration
$$= \tfrac{1}{2} \times \text{amount of NaOH}$$
$$= \tfrac{1}{2} \times 4 \times 10^{-3}\,mol$$
$$= 2 \times 10^{-3}\,mol$$

Volume of $H_2SO_4 = 25.0\,cm^3 = 25.0/1000\,dm^3$
$$= 2.5 \times 10^{-2}\,dm^3.$$

a Concentration of H_2SO_4
$$= \frac{2 \times 10^{-3}}{2.5 \times 10^{-2}}\,mol\,dm^{-3}$$
$$= 0.080\,mol\,dm^{-3}$$

b As $M(H_2SO_4) = 2 + 32 + 4 \times 16 = 98\,g$
concentration of $H_2SO_4 = 98 \times 0.080\,g\,dm^{-3}$
$$= 7.84\,g\,dm^{-3}$$

SAQ 2.18

$20.0\,cm^3$ of $0.100\,mol\,dm^{-3}$ potassium hydroxide exactly neutralises a $25.0\,cm^3$ sample of hydrochloric acid. What is the concentration of the hydrochloric acid in **a** $mol\,dm^{-3}$, **b** $g\,dm^{-3}$?

It is possible to use a titration result to arrive at the reacting mole ratio, called the **stoichiometric ratio**, and the balanced equation for a reaction.

The example that follows illustrates how this is done. A $25.0\,cm^3$ sample of $0.0400\,mol\,dm^{-3}$ aqueous metal hydroxide is titrated against $0.100\,mol\,dm^{-3}$ hydrochloric acid. $20.0\,cm^3$ of the acid were required for exact neutralisation of the alkali.

The working is as follows:

amount of metal hydroxide $= \dfrac{25.0}{1000} \times 0.0400\,mol$
$$= 1.00 \times 10^{-3}\,mol$$

amount of hydrochloric acid $= \dfrac{20.0}{1000} \times 0.100\,mol$
$$= 2.00 \times 10^{-3}\,mol$$

Hence the reacting (i.e. stoichiometric) mole ratio of metal hydroxide : hydrochloric acid is

$$1.00 \times 10^{-3} : 2.00 \times 10^{-3}$$
or $\qquad 1:2$

i.e. exactly one mole of the metal hydroxide neutralises exactly two moles of hydrochloric acid. One mole of HCl will neutralise one mole of hydroxide ions, so the metal hydroxide must contain two hydroxide ions in its formula. The balanced equation for the reaction is

$$M(OH)_2(aq) + 2HCl(aq) \rightarrow MCl_2(aq) + 2H_2O(l)$$

where M is the metal.

SAQ 2.19

Determine the stoichiometric ratio, and hence the balanced equation, for the reaction of an insoluble iron hydroxide with dilute nitric acid, HNO_3. $4.00 \times 10^{-4}\,mol$ of the iron hydroxide is exactly neutralised by $24.0\,cm^3$ of $0.05\,mol\,dm^{-3}$ nitric acid.

Gas volumes

In 1811, Avogadro discovered that equal volumes of all gases contain the same number of molecules. (Note that the volumes must be measured under the same conditions of temperature and pressure.) This provides an easy way of calculating the amount of gas present in a given volume. At room temperature and pressure, one mole of any gas occupies approximately $24.0\,dm^3$. For example, $24.0\,dm^3$ of carbon dioxide (CO_2) and $24.0\,dm^3$ of nitrogen (N_2) both contain one mole of molecules.

SAQ 2.20

a Calculate the amount of helium present in a balloon with a volume of $2.4\,dm^3$. Assume that the pressure inside the balloon is the same as atmospheric pressure and that the balloon is at room temperature.

b Calculate the volume occupied by a mixture of 0.5 mol of propane and 1.5 mol of butane gases at room temperature and pressure.

We can use reacting volumes of gases to determine the **stoichiometry** of a reaction. The experiments must be carried out under the same conditions of temperature and pressure. We can then assume that equal volumes of gases contain the same number of moles. For example, measurements show that $20\,cm^3$ of hydrogen react with exactly $10\,cm^3$ of oxygen to form water. The ratio of reacting volumes of hydrogen : oxygen is 20 : 10 or 2 : 1. Hence the reacting mole ratio for hydrogen : oxygen (the stoichiometry of the reaction) is also 2 : 1, and so the balanced equation is:

$$2H_2(g) + O_2(g) \rightarrow 2H_2O(l)$$

The following example shows how we can find the formula of a hydrocarbon using measurements of reacting volumes.

$10\,cm^3$ of a gaseous hydrocarbon X burned completely in exactly $50\,cm^3$ of oxygen to produce water and $30\,cm^3$ of carbon dioxide. All measurements were made at room temperature and pressure. We need to determine:

■ the formula of the hydrocarbon;
■ the balanced equation for the reaction.

We can present the calculations as follows:

hydrocarbon X(g) + O₂(g) → CO₂(g) + H₂O(l)			
Gas volumes (cm^3)	10	50	30
Gas volume ratio	1	5	3
Gas mole ratio	1	5	3

This tells us that 3 mol of carbon dioxide are obtained from 1 mol of the hydrocarbon, so each hydrocarbon molecule must contain 3 carbon atoms.

The 3 mol of carbon dioxide use up 3 out of the original 5 mol of oxygen.

Hence 2 mol of oxygen molecules, $O_2(g)$, are left to combine with hydrogen atoms from the hydrocarbon, to form 4 mol of water. So there must be $4 \times 2 = 8$ hydrogen atoms present in the hydrocarbon. Therefore:

■ The formula of the hydrocarbon is C_3H_8.
■ The balanced equation for the reaction is:
  $$C_3H_8(g) + 5O_2(g) \rightarrow 3CO_2(g) + 4H_2O(l)$$

SAQ 2.21

$20\,cm^3$ of a gaseous hydrocarbon Y burned completely in exactly $60\,cm^3$ of oxygen to produce water and $40\,cm^3$ of carbon dioxide. All measurements were made at room temperature and pressure.

a What is the formula of the hydrocarbon?
b Write a balanced equation for the reaction.

SUMMARY

◆ Definitions of atomic, isotopic and molecular masses are relative to carbon-12, which has a mass of exactly 12.

◆ One mole of a substance is the amount of substance that has the same number (called Avogadro's constant) of particles as there are atoms in exactly 12 g of carbon-12.

◆ A mass spectrometer enables ionised atoms to be accelerated into a beam of gaseous ions which are deflected in a magnetic field according to their mass.

◆ Mass spectra of elements enable isotopic abundances and relative atomic masses to be found.

◆ Empirical formulae show the simplest whole-number ratio of atoms in a compound whilst molecular formulae show the total number of atoms for each element present. Empirical formulae may be determined from the composition by mass of a compound. The molecular formula may then be found if the molecular mass is known.

◆ Molar masses enable calculations to be made using moles and balanced chemical equations involving reacting masses, volumes and concentrations of solutions and volumes of gases.

◆ Balanced chemical equations (which show the stoichiometry of a reaction) may also be derived by measuring reacting masses, volumes and concentrations of solutions or volumes of gases.

Questions

1 Copper–nickel alloys are used to make some coins. The composition of coins may be checked by using mass spectrometry. The mass spectrum of the copper content of a coin is shown below:

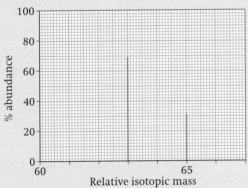

a State, for each of these isotopes of copper,
   (i) the number of protons and neutrons in the nucleus;
   (ii) the percentage abundance.
b Define the term **relative atomic mass**.
c Calculate the relative atomic mass of the copper in the coin.
d Pure nickel was not discovered until 1751 and it was named from the German word 'kupfernickel' meaning 'devil's copper'. A compound of nickel, A, was analysed and shown to have the following percentage composition by mass: Ni, 37.9%; S, 20.7%; O, 41.4%. Calculate the empirical formula of A.

2 Azides are compounds of metals with nitrogen, used mainly as detonators in explosives. However, sodium azide, NaN_3, decomposes non-explosively on heating to release nitrogen gas. This provides a convenient method of obtaining pure nitrogen in the laboratory:
$2NaN_3(s) \rightarrow 2Na(l) + 3N_2(g)$
a A student prepared 1.80 dm^3 of pure nitrogen in the laboratory by this method. This gas volume was measured at room temperature and pressure (r.t.p.).
   (i) How many moles of nitrogen, N_2, did the student prepare? [Assume that 1 mole of gas molecules occupies 24.0 dm^3 at r.t.p.]
   (ii) What mass of sodium azide did the student heat?
b After cooling, the student obtained 1.15 g of solid sodium. She then carefully reacted this sodium with water to form 25.0 cm^3 of aqueous sodium hydroxide:
$2Na(s) + 2H_2O(l) \rightarrow 2NaOH(aq) + H_2(g)$
Calculate the concentration, in mol dm^{-3}, of the aqueous sodium hydroxide.

CHAPTER 3

Chemical bonding and structure

By the end of this chapter you should be able to:

1 describe *ionic bonding* as the electrostatic attraction between two oppositely charged ions, including the use of *dot-and-cross* diagrams;

2 describe, in simple terms, the lattice structure of sodium chloride;

3 describe a covalent bond as a pair of electrons shared between two atoms;

4 describe, including the use of dot-and-cross diagrams, *covalent bonding* and *dative* covalent (co-ordinate) bonding;

5 appreciate that, between the extremes of ionic and covalent bonding, there is a gradual transition from one extreme to the other;

6 describe *electronegativity* as the ability of an atom to attract the bonding electrons in a covalent bond;

7 explain that bond polarity may arise when the atoms joined by a covalent bond have different electronegativities, and that *polarisation* may occur between cations of high charge density and anions of low charge density;

8 explain and predict the shapes of, and bond angles in, *molecules* and ions by using the qualitative model of *electron-pair repulsion* up to 4 electron pairs;

9 describe *metallic bonding*, present in a giant *metallic lattice* structure, as the attraction of a lattice of positive ions to a sea of *mobile electrons*;

10 describe *intermolecular forces* (van der Waals' forces), based on instantaneous and permanent *dipoles*;

11 describe, in simple terms, the *giant molecular structures* of graphite and diamond;

12 describe *hydrogen bonding* between molecules containing −OH and −NH groups, typified by water and ammonia;

13 describe and explain the anomalous properties of water resulting from hydrogen bonding;

14 describe, interpret and/or predict physical properties in terms of the types, motion and arrangement of particles (atoms, molecules and ions) and the forces between them, and the different types of bonding;

15 deduce the type of bonding present in a substance, given suitable information.

Ionic bonding

Many familiar substances are ionic compounds. An example is common salt (sodium chloride). Sodium chloride and many other ionic compounds are present in sea-water. Crystals of salt are readily obtained by the partial evaporation of sea-water in a salt pan (*figure 3.1*).

We need to understand the bonding in compounds in order to explain their structure and physical properties. Ionic compounds:

■ are crystalline solids with high melting points;
■ conduct electricity, with decomposition at the electrodes, in aqueous solution or when they are molten;
■ are hard and brittle with crystals that cleave easily;
■ are often soluble in water.

Ionic bonding results from the **electrostatic attraction** between the **oppositely charged ions**. In sodium chloride, the ions are arranged in a crystal lattice, which determines the shape of the crystals grown from sea-water. Most other minerals are also found as well-formed crystals. The shapes of these crystals arise from the way in which the ions are packed together in the lattice. Some crystals are shown in *figure 3.2*.

Use is often made of the very high melting points of ionic compounds, e.g. aluminium oxide (melting point 2345 K, where K refers to the kelvin scale for temperature, 0 °C = 273 K). A fibrous form

● **Figure 3.2** A selection of minerals.

of aluminium oxide is used in tiles on the Space Shuttle for protection from the high temperatures experienced on re-entry into the atmosphere (*figure 3.3*) and in the lining of the portable gas forges of a modern 'high-tech' farrier.

Another important characteristic of ionic compounds is their ability to conduct electricity, with decomposition, when in aqueous solution or when they are molten. This process is called **electrolysis**. Electrolysis is used to produce chlorine from brine (concentrated aqueous

● **Figure 3.1** A salt mountain with a salt pan in the foreground, Sardinia.

● **Figure 3.3** The space shuttle *Columbia*, seen during the fitting of the thermal insulation tiles.

sodium chloride) (*figure 3.4*) and aluminium from molten aluminium oxide.

Ions are free to move through the aqueous solution or molten compound and are attracted to the oppositely charged electrode. Positive ions (cations) are attracted to the negative electrode (cathode), and negative ions (anions) to the positive electrode (anode). At the electrode, the ions discharge; e.g. chloride ions to chlorine or aluminium ions to aluminium metal. On being discharged, an ion will either gain or lose electrons. Electrons will be gained by **cations** (positively charged ions) and lost by **anions** (negatively charged ions). The number of electrons gained or lost will depend on the magnitude of the charge on the ion. A chloride ion will lose one electron; an aluminium ion will gain three electrons. These changes may be represented as follows:

at the positive electrode (anode): $Cl^- \rightarrow \frac{1}{2}Cl_2 + e^-$

at the negative electrode (cathode):
$$Al^{3+} + 3e^- \rightarrow Al$$

● **Figure 3.4** Industrial electrolysis: chlorine cell.

SAQ 3.1

Write similar equations, including electrons, for the discharge of copper and bromide ions during the electrolysis of copper bromide, $CuBr_2$, using carbon electrodes. Indicate the electrode at which each reaction will occur.

Formation of ions from elements

Positive ions are formed when electrons are removed from atoms. This happens most easily with metallic elements. Atoms of non-metallic elements tend to gain electrons to form negative ions. Hence when metals combine with non-metals, electrons are transferred from the metal atoms to the non-metal atoms. Usually a metal atom will lose all of its outer-shell electrons and a non-metal atom will accept electrons to fill its outer shell. The net result of electron transfer from a metal atom to a non-metal atom is to produce filled outer shells similar to the noble-gas electronic configurations for both elements. The ionic bonding results from the electrostatic attraction between the oppositely charged ions.

Dot-and-cross diagrams are used to show the electronic configurations of elements and ions. The electrons of one element in the compound are shown by dots, those of the second element by crosses. *Table 3.1* shows some examples.

Usually when we draw a dot-and-cross diagram, the filled inner electron shells are omitted. A circle is drawn round the outer-shell electrons. In the case of a sodium ion Na^+, this shell no longer contains any electrons. The nucleus of the element is shown by the symbol for the element. The dot-and-cross diagram for an ion is placed in square brackets with the charge outside the brackets. Electrons are placed in pairs for clarity.

Often only the outer shell dot-and-cross diagram for the compound is needed. For sodium chloride this is:

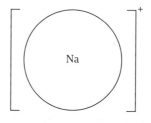
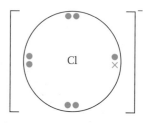

Atom	Electronic configuration	Dot-and-cross diagram	Ion	Electronic configuration	Dot-and-cross diagram
Na	2,8,1	(diagram: Na)	Na$^+$	2,8	(diagram: Na)$^+$
Cl	2,8,7	(diagram: Cl)	Cl$^-$	2,8,8	(diagram: Cl)$^-$

● **Table 3.1** Examples of dot-and-cross diagrams.

SAQ 3.2

Draw dot-and-cross diagrams for the following: **a** KF, **b** Na$_2$O, **c** MgO and **d** CaCl$_2$.

The typical properties of ionic compounds may be explained by the presence of ions, which are arranged in a giant ionic lattice. In the ionic lattice, positive and negative ions alternate in a three-dimensional arrangement. The way in which the ions are arranged depends on their relative sizes. Sodium chloride has a cubic ionic lattice, which is shown in *figure 3.5*.

Magnesium oxide has the same cubic structure with magnesium ions in place of sodium ions and oxide ions in place of chloride ions. In the lattice, the attraction between oppositely charged ions binds them together. These attractions greatly outweigh repulsions between similarly charged ions, as each ion is surrounded by six oppositely charged ions. Hence the melting points of ionic compounds are very high. The melting point usually increases as the charges on the ions increase. Sodium chloride with its singly charged ions has a melting point of 1074 K, and magnesium oxide with its doubly charged ions has a melting point of 3125 K.

Ionic compounds are hard and brittle. The cleavage of gemstones and other ionic crystals occurs between planes of ions in the ionic lattice. If an ionic crystal is tapped sharply in the direction of one of the crystal planes with a sharp-edged knife, it will split cleanly. As a plane of ions is displaced by the force of the knife, ions of similar charge come together and the repulsions between them cause the crystal to split apart. The natural shape of ionic crystals is the same as the arrangement of the ions in the lattice. This is because the crystal grows as ions are placed in the lattice and this basic shape continues to the edge of the crystal. Hence sodium chloride

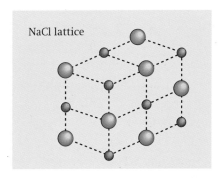

NaCl lattice

● **Figure 3.5** The sodium chloride (NaCl) lattice.

crystals are cubic. The smallest repeating unit in the lattice is known as the **unit cell**.

Gemstones and other semi-precious stones, such as emeralds, sapphires and rubies (*figure 3.6*), are ionic compounds valued for their colour and hardness. Gemstones are crystalline and are cut so that they sparkle in the light. They are cut by exploiting the cleavage planes between layers of ions in the crystal structure.

Ionic compounds may dissolve in water. As a general rule all metal nitrates and most metal chlorides are soluble, as are

● **Figure 3.6** Sapphires in the form of both rough crystals and cut gemstones.

almost all of the salts of the Group I metals. Ionic compounds that carry higher charges on the ions tend to be less soluble or insoluble. For example, whilst Group I hydroxides are soluble, Group II and III hydroxides are sparingly soluble or insoluble in water (a **sparingly soluble** compound has only a very low solubility, e.g. calcium hydroxide as lime water). When ionic compounds dissolve, energy must be provided to overcome the strong attractive forces between the ions in the lattice. This energy is provided by the similarly strong attractive forces that occur in the hydrated ions. In a hydrated ion water molecules are attracted to an anion or cation by strong electrostatic forces. In the case of a cation, the oxygen atoms of the water molecules are attracted by the positive charge on the ion. Negative ions are attracted to the hydrogen end of the water molecule. This is possible as water molecules are polar (see page 45). *Figure 3.7* shows a hydrated sodium ion (grey) and a hydrated chloride ion (green). The water molecules are shown with oxygen = red and hydrogen = white.

In chapter 13, you will learn how to calculate the energy change when an ionic compound dissolves.

Electrolysis of ionic compounds can only occur when the ions are free to move. In the lattice the ions are in fixed positions, and ionic solids will thus not conduct electricity. On melting, or dissolving in water, the ions are no longer in fixed positions so they are free to move towards electrodes (*figure 3.8*).

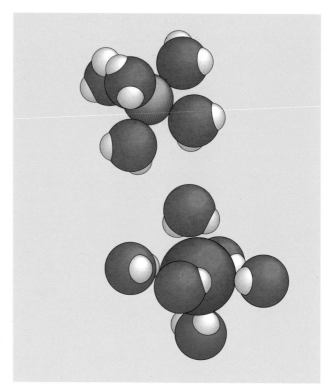

● **Figure 3.7** Hydrated sodium ions (grey) and chloride ions (green).

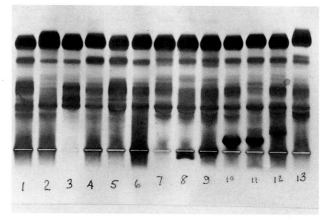

● **Figure 3.8** In this diagnostic test for leukaemia, negatively charged polypeptide ions (proteins) move towards a positive electrode (towards the top of the page).

Covalent bonding

Many familiar compounds are liquids or gases or solids with low melting points, e.g. water, ammonia, methane, ethanol, sucrose and poly(ethene). Such compounds have very different properties to ionic compounds. They all contain molecules in which groups of atoms are held together by covalent bonds. They are non-conductors of electricity and may be insoluble in water. They may dissolve in organic solvents such as ethanol or cyclohexane.

Some crystalline covalent compounds are very hard, have high melting points and are more difficult to cleave than ionic compounds. Such compounds also contain covalent bonds, which extend throughout the crystal in a giant lattice structure, e.g. quartz crystals (*figure 3.9*).

In covalent compounds, electrons are shared in pairs. The negative charge of the electron-pair will attract the positively charged nuclei of the elements, and this holds the atoms together in a molecule. The electron-pair must lie between the nuclei for the attraction to outweigh the repulsion between the nuclei. Under such circumstances two atoms will be bound together by a covalent bond. In a molecule, atoms will share electrons, and, as a general rule, the number shared gives each atom filled outer shells similar to the electronic configuration of a noble gas. Covalent bonds are usually formed between pairs of non-metallic elements.

In a molecule the bonding electrons are now in molecular orbitals rather than atomic orbitals. The molecular orbitals may be considered to arise from the overlap of atomic orbitals. Molecular orbitals are given labels using Greek letters: σ, π, δ, etc. (pronounced sigma, pi, delta, respectively). These parallel the labels for atomic orbitals: s, p, d, etc. A single covalent bond consists of a σ orbital and is often called a σ bond. The σ bond in a hydrogen molecule is shown in *figure 3.10*. The π orbitals are found as π bonds. A double covalent bond consists of a σ bond and a π bond. You will find more on σ and π bonds on page 118.

Dot-and-cross diagrams for some examples of covalent compounds are shown in *figure 3.11*. Diagrams of molecules often show the covalent bonds as lines. A double line is used for a double bond. Such diagrams are called displayed formulae. Examples are shown with the dot-and-cross diagrams in *figure 3.11*. Remember that each covalent bond is a *shared* pair of electrons. Ionic compounds are held together by electrostatic attraction between oppositely charged *ions*.

SAQ 3.3

a Draw dot-and-cross diagrams together with displayed formulae for each of the following:
(i) H_2, (ii) HCl, (iii) O_2, (iv) PCl_3, (v) BF_3 and (vi) SF_6.

b How many electrons are present in the outer shell of boron in BF_3 and of sulphur in SF_6?

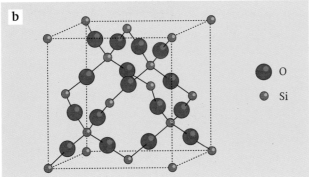

● **Figure 3.9**
a Quartz crystals.
b Model of the arrangement of atoms in a quartz lattice.

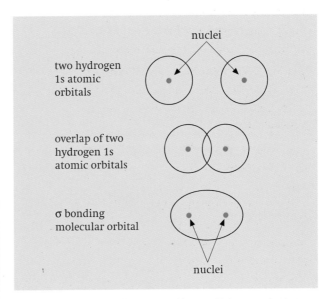

● **Figure 3.10** A σ bond in hydrogen, showing the overlap of 1s orbitals.

For example, SF_6 is now being used as an electrical insulator in large electrical transformers. It has largely replaced polychlorinated biphenyls (PCBs), which were found to cause environmental damage. BF_3 is an example of a molecule in which an atom does not achieve a noble-gas configuration in its outer shell. The sulphur atom in SF_6 has more electrons in its outermost shell than the next noble gas, argon. When chemists realised that it was possible for atoms to expand their outer shells in this way, it was suggested that noble gases, hitherto thought to be unreactive, might form compounds in the same way (*figure 3.12*).

Lone-pairs

Atoms in molecules frequently have pairs of electrons in their outer shells that are not involved in covalent bonds. These

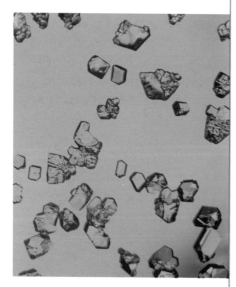

● **Figure 3.12** In compounds of noble gases, the outer electron shell expands beyond eight electrons. Xenon tetrafluoride (XeF_4) contains 12 outer-shell electrons. The photograph shows crystals of XeF_4.

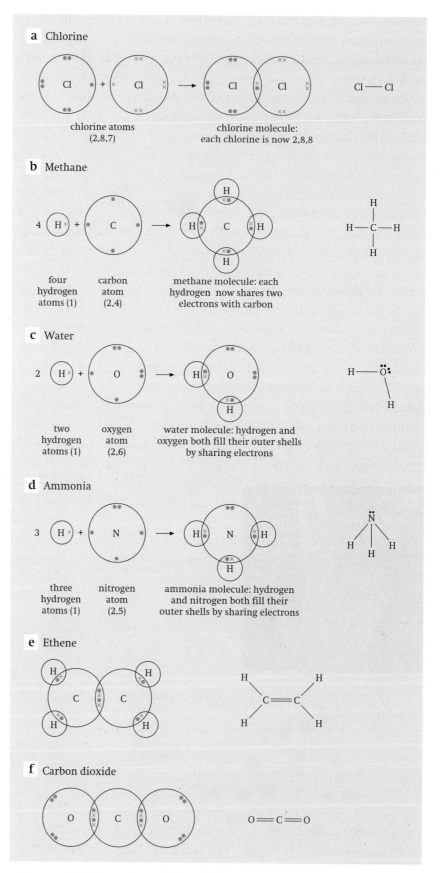

● **Figure 3.11** Dot-and-cross diagrams for some covalent compounds: **a** chlorine (Cl_2), **b** methane (CH_4), **c** water (H_2O), **d** ammonia (NH_3), **e** ethene (C_2H_4) and **f** carbon dioxide (CO_2), also showing the displayed formulae.

non-bonding electron-pairs are called **lone-pairs**. In ammonia, nitrogen has one lone-pair, and in water, oxygen has two lone-pairs. Sometimes these lone-pairs are used to form a covalent bond to an atom that can accommodate two further electrons in its outer shell. An example is when ammonia and the hydrogen ion combine to form the ammonium ion, NH_4^+ (shown below):

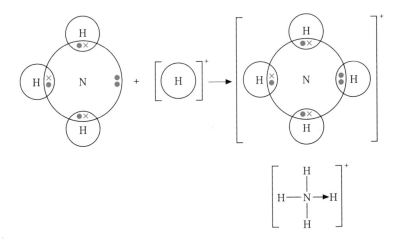

The covalent bond from the nitrogen atom to the H^+ ion is formed by sharing the nitrogen lone-pair. As both electrons come from the nitrogen atom, this is called a **dative covalent bond**. The word 'dative' derives from the Latin for 'give'. Dative covalent bonds are represented by arrows in displayed formulae of molecules. Dative covalent bonds are also called **coordinate bonds** in metal complexes.

SAQ 3.4

a Water molecules will hydrate the aqueous hydrogen ion to form the oxonium ion, H_3O^+. Draw a dot-and-cross diagram and the displayed formula of the oxonium ion.

b BF_3 forms a white solid when it reacts with gaseous ammonia. A bond forms between boron and nitrogen. The formula of the solid is F_3BNH_3. Draw a dot-and-cross diagram and the displayed formula of this product.

c Draw a dot-and-cross diagram and the displayed formula for carbon monoxide.

Bonds of intermediate character

There are compounds that might be expected to be ionic which have properties more typical of covalent compounds. For example, some salts **sublime** (i.e. change from a solid to a gas without melting) at quite low temperatures, e.g. aluminium chloride ($AlCl_3$).

Similarly there are covalent compounds that dissolve readily in water to produce ionic solutions, e.g. hydrogen chloride gas or ammonia.

Compounds that are purely ionic or covalent are best regarded as extremes. Between the two extremes a gradual transition from one to the other takes place. We shall start by examining an ionic compound.

Polarisation of ions

Ionic compounds that show some properties more characteristic of covalent compounds contain anions that have become **polarised**. This means that the cation distorts the electron charge-cloud on the anion. Polarisation brings more electron charge between the ionic nuclei, and thus produces a significant degree of covalent bonding between the ions.

Anions with a greater charge or a larger radius are more easily polarised than those with a smaller charge or smaller radius. Cations with a smaller radius or a greater charge will have a greater charge density. Such cations will exert a greater degree of polarisation on an anion than will cations with a larger radius or lower charge.

Figure 3.13 shows the increasing polarisation of an anion by a cation. The effect of this polarisation is to place some of the electron charge-cloud from the larger ion between the two ions. If the process is continued, a covalent bond is created between the two nuclei. When this occurs, the molecule still has some separation of positive and negative charge. The molecule has an electric dipole; it is described as a **polar molecule**.

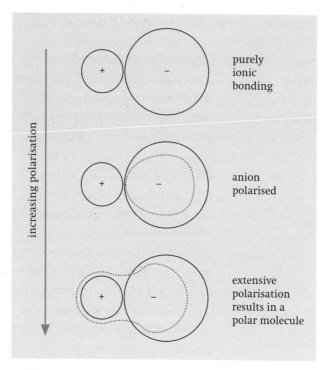

increasing polarisation

purely
ionic
bonding

anion
polarised

extensive
polarisation
results in a
polar molecule

● **Figure 3.13** Polarisation of an anion by a cation.

Polar molecules

Covalent bonds in molecules are polar if there is a difference in electronegativity between the elements. **Electronegativity** is the ability of a bonded atom to attract electron charge.

The electronegativity of the elements increases from Group I to Group VII across the Periodic Table. Electronegativity also increases up a Group of elements as the proton number decreases. Several attempts have been made to put numerical values on electronegativity. For our purposes, it is sufficient to recognise that electronegativities increase **a** moving from left to right across a Period in the Periodic Table and **b** vertically up Groups. The electronegativity of hydrogen is lower than that of most non-metallic elements. In the few cases where it is not lower, it is of a very similar magnitude to that of the non-metal.

increasing electronegativity

$\longrightarrow$

Cl < N < O < F

These electronegativity differences between atoms introduce a degree of polarity in covalent bonds between different atoms. A bigger difference in electronegativity will cause a greater degree of bond polarity. This accounts for the polarity of

many simple diatomic molecules such as hydrogen chloride, HCl.

The situation is more complicated in polyatomic molecules, where the shape of the molecule must be taken into account. A symmetrical distribution of polar covalent bonds produces a non-polar molecule. The dipoles of the bonds exert equal and opposite effects on each other. An example is tetrachloromethane, CCl_4. This tetrahedral molecule has four polar C–Cl bonds. The four dipoles point towards the corners of the tetrahedral molecule, cancelling each other out. In the closely related trichloromethane, $CHCl_3$, the three C–Cl dipoles point in a similar direction. Their combined effect is not cancelled out by the C–H bond. (The C–H bond has a weak dipole, pointing towards the carbon atom.) Hence trichloromethane is a very polar molecule.

polar   polar   non-polar

Predict the polarity of the following molecules: **a** O_2, **b** HF, **c** CH_3Br and **d** SCl_2 (non-linear molecule).

Bond polarity can be a helpful indication of the reactivity of a molecule. This is clearly illustrated by a comparison of nitrogen and carbon monoxide. Both molecules contain triple bonds, which require a similar amount of energy to break them. (The CO bond actually requires more energy than the N_2 bond!) However, carbon monoxide is a very reactive molecule, whereas nitrogen is very unreactive. Non-polar nitrogen will only undergo reactions at high temperatures or in the presence of a catalyst. Carbon monoxide, which is a polar molecule, may be burned in air and it combines more strongly with the iron in haemoglobin than does oxygen. Many chemical reactions are started by a reagent attacking one of the electrically charged ends of a polar bond. Non-polar molecules are consequently much less reactive towards ionic or polar reagents. Other important polar molecules include water and ammonia.

As a knowledge of molecular shape is needed to predict the polarity of a polyatomic molecule, the next section shows how you can predict the shapes of simple molecules.

Shapes of simple molecules

Molecules vary in shape, as shown by the six examples in *figure 3.14*.

Electron-pair repulsion theory

As electrons are negatively charged, they exert a repulsion on each other. In chapter 1 (page 12), you saw that electrons may pair up with opposite spins in orbitals. This is also true in molecules. An electron-pair in the bonding (outermost) shell of the central atom in a simple molecule will exert a repulsion on the other electron-pairs. Each pair will repel each of the other pairs. The effect of these repulsions will cause the electron-pairs to move as far apart as possible within the confines of the bonds between the atoms in the molecule.

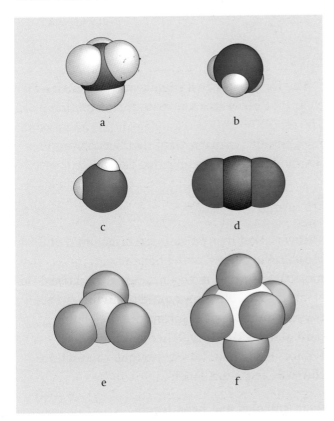

- **Figure 3.14** Shapes of molecules. These space-filling models show the molecular shapes of **a** methane (CH_4), **b** ammonia (NH_3), **c** water (H_2O), **d** carbon dioxide (CO_2), **e** boron trifluoride (BF_3) and **f** sulphur hexafluoride (SF_6).

This will determine the three-dimensional shape of the molecule.

The concept of electron-pair repulsion is a powerful theory, as it successfully predicts shapes, which are confirmed by modern experimental techniques.

In order to predict the shape of a molecule, the number of pairs of outer-shell electrons on the central atom is needed. It is best to start with a dot-and-cross diagram and then to count the electron-pairs, as shown in the following examples.

- *Methane*
  As there are four bonding pairs of electrons, these repel each other towards the corners of a regular tetrahedron. The molecule thus has a tetrahedral shape. A tetrahedron has four faces.

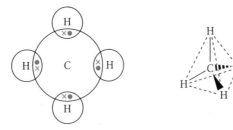

- *Ammonia*
  This has three bonding pairs and one lone-pair on the central atom, nitrogen. The four electron-pairs repel each other and occupy the corners of a tetrahedron as in methane. However, the nitrogen and three hydrogen atoms form a triangular pyramidal molecule.

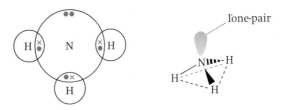

- *Water*
  There are two bonding pairs and two lone-pairs. Again, these repel each other towards the corners of a tetrahedron, leaving the oxygen and two hydrogen atoms as a non-linear (or bent) molecule.

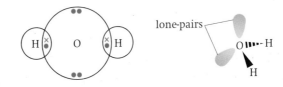

■ *Carbon dioxide*

This has two carbon–oxygen double bonds. Multiple bonds are best considered in the same way as single electron-pairs. If the two double bond pairs repel each other as far as possible, the molecule is predicted to be linear (i.e. the OCO angle is 180°):

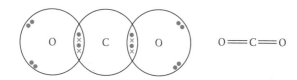

■ *Boron trifluoride*

This is an interesting molecule, as it only has six electrons in the bonding shell on boron, distributed between three bonding pairs. The three bonding pairs repel each other equally, forming a trigonal planar molecule with bond angles of 120°. Boron trifluoride is very reactive and will accept a non-bonding (lone) pair of electrons. For example, with ammonia $H_3N{\rightarrow}BF_3$ is formed (note the dative covalent bond indicated by the arrow).

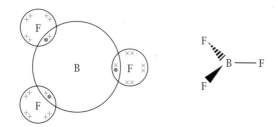

■ *Sulphur hexafluoride*

There are six bonding pairs and no lone-pairs. Repulsion between six electron-pairs produces the structure shown. All angles are 90°. The shape produced is an octahedron (i.e. eight faces).

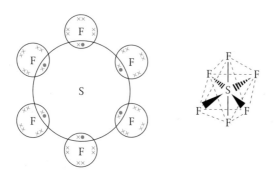

SAQ 3.6

a Draw dot-and-cross diagrams for (i) PCl_3, (ii) NH_4^+, (iii) H_2S and (iv) SCl_2.

b Consider the bonding and lone pairs you have drawn in **a**. Predict the shape of each molecule and illustrate each shape with a diagram.

Lone-pairs, bonding pairs and bond angles

Lone-pairs of electrons are attracted by only one nucleus, unlike bonding pairs, which are shared between two nuclei. As a result, lone-pairs occupy a molecular orbital that is pulled closer to the nucleus than bonding pairs. The electron charge-cloud in a lone-pair has a greater width than a bonding pair. The diagram below shows the repulsions between lone-pairs (pink) and bonding pairs (white) in a water molecule.

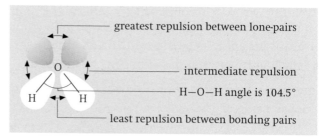

greatest repulsion between lone-pairs

intermediate repulsion

H—O—H angle is 104.5°

least repulsion between bonding pairs

The repulsion between lone-pairs is thus greater than that between a lone-pair and a bonding pair. The repulsion between a lone-pair (LP) and a bonding pair (BP) is greater than that between two bonding pairs. To summarise:

> LP–LP repulsion > LP–BP repulsion > BP–BP repulsion

This variation in repulsion produces small but measurable effects on the bond angles in molecules. In methane, all the HCH angles are the same at 109.5°. In ammonia, the slightly greater repulsion of the lone-pair pushes the bonding pairs slightly closer together and the angle reduces to 107°. In water, two lone-pairs reduce the HOH angle to 104.5°.

Bond enthalpy and bond length

In general, double bonds are shorter than single bonds. In addition, the energy required to break a double bond is greater than that needed to break a single bond. The **bond enthalpy** is the energy

Bond	Bond enthalpy (kJ mol⁻¹)	Bond length (nm)
C–C	347	0.154
C=C	612	0.134
C–O	358	0.143
C=O	805	0.116

● **Table 3.2** Some bond enthalpies and bond lengths. See page 148 for an explanation of enthalpy.

required to break one mole of the given bond in the gaseous molecule (see also chapter 13, page 151). *Table 3.2* shows some examples of bond enthalpies and bond lengths.

Metallic bonding

Metals have very different properties to both ionic and covalent compounds. In appearance they are usually shiny (*figure 3.15*). They are good conductors of both heat and electricity (the latter in the solid state and without decomposition, unlike ionic compounds). They are easily worked and may be drawn into wires or hammered into a different shape, i.e. they are ductile and malleable. They often possess high tensile strengths and they are usually hard. *Table 3.3* provides information on some of the properties of aluminium, iron and copper, with the non-metal sulphur for comparison.

It is this range of properties that has led humans to use them to make tools, weapons and jewellery. Two major periods in our history are named after the metals in use at the time (*figure 3.16*). The change from bronze (an alloy of tin and copper) to iron reflected the discovery of methods for extracting different metals.

A simplified model of metallic bonding is adequate for our purposes. In a metallic lattice, the atoms lose their outer-shell electrons to become positive ions. The outer-shell electrons occupy new energy levels, which extend throughout the metal lattice. The bonding is often described as a 'sea' of mobile electrons surrounding a lattice of positive ions. This is shown in *figure 3.17*. The lattice is held together by the strong attractive forces between the mobile electrons and the positive ions.

● **Figure 3.15** Metals. Clockwise from top left: sodium, gold and zinc.

a

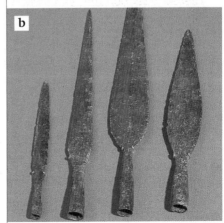

b

● **Figure 3.16 a** Bronze age statue and **b** Iron age spears.

	Density (g cm⁻³)	Tensile strength (10¹⁰ Pa)	Thermal conductivity (W m⁻¹ K⁻¹)	Electrical conductivity (10⁸ S m⁻¹)
Aluminium	2.70	7.0	238	0.38
Iron	7.86	21.1	82	0.10
Copper	8.92	13.0	400	0.59
Sulphur	2.07		0.029	1×10^{-23}

● **Table 3.3** Properties of three metals and sulphur.

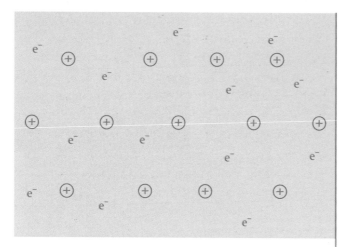

● **Figure 3.17** Metallic bonding. There are strong attractive forces between positively charged ions and a 'sea' of mobile electrons.

The properties of metals can be explained in terms of this model of the bonding. Electrical conduction can take place in any direction, as electrons are free to move throughout the lattice. Conduction of heat occurs by vibration of the positive ions as well as via the mobile electrons.

Metals are both ductile and malleable because the bonding in the metallic lattice is not broken when they are physically deformed. As a metal is hammered or drawn into a wire, the metal ions slide over each other to new lattice positions. The mobile electrons continue to hold the lattice together. Some metals will even flow under their own weight. Lead has a problem in this respect. It is often used on roofs where, over the years, it suffers from 'creep'. This is not only from thieves but also because the metal slowly flows under the influence of gravity.

The transition elements (see chapter 4, page 55) are metals that possess both hardness and high tensile strength. Hardness and high tensile strength are also due to the strong attractive forces between the metal ions and the mobile electrons in the lattice.

SAQ 3.7

Use *table 3.3* to answer the following questions and give full explanations in terms of metallic bonding. (Assume steel and stainless steel have similar properties to iron.)

a Why do some stainless steel saucepans have a copper base?

b Aluminium with a steel core is used for overhead power cables in preference to copper. Why is aluminium preferred? What is the function of the steel core?

c Apart from overhead power cables, copper is chosen for almost all other electrical uses. Suggest reasons for the choice of copper.

Intermolecular forces

Before we discuss the attractive forces that exist between molecules, it may be helpful to review the **kinetic theory of matter**. Matter exists in solid, liquid and gaseous states. In the solid state, the particles are packed together in a regularly ordered way. This order breaks down when a substance melts. In the liquid state, there may be small groups of particles with some degree of order, but, overall in the liquid, particles are free to move past each other. In order to do this, many of the forces that bind the particles together must be overcome on melting. In the gaseous state, the particles are widely separated. They are free to move independently, and all the forces that bind the particles together in the solid or liquid have been overcome on vaporisation. In the gaseous state, the particles move randomly in any direction. As they do so, they exert a pressure (vapour pressure) on the walls of their container.

A multitude of biochemical compounds are involved in the enormous number of chemical reactions found in living organisms. They are also ultimately responsible for a seemingly infinite number of variations within a given species. All biochemical compounds rely significantly on weak attractive forces that exist between their molecules to produce this variety. These intermolecular forces (often called van der Waals' forces) are much weaker than ionic, covalent or metallic bonding forces.

The properties of all small molecules are dependent on intermolecular forces. It is the properties of these small molecules that provide evidence for the existence of intermolecular forces and help us to understand the nature of these forces. If a gas is able to condense to a liquid, which can then be frozen to a solid, there must be an attraction between the molecules of the gas. When a solid melts or a liquid boils, energy is needed to overcome this attraction. For example, water in a kettle will continue to boil only whilst the electricity is switched on. The temperature of the water is constant whilst the water is boiling, and the heating effect of energy from the electricity is separating the water molecules from each other to produce water vapour.

There are three types of intermolecular forces: instantaneous dipole-induced dipole forces, dipole–dipole forces and hydrogen bonds.

Instantaneous dipole-induced dipole forces

Even noble-gas atoms must exert an attraction on each other. *Figure 3.18* shows the enthalpy change of vaporisation of the noble gases plotted against the number of electrons present. (**Enthalpy change of vaporisation** is the energy required to convert the liquid to a gas.) The trend in the enthalpy change of vaporisation shows an increase from helium to xenon as the number of electrons increases. Alkanes (chapter 9) show a similar trend; their enthalpies of vaporisation also increase with increasing numbers of atoms in the molecules (and hence with increasing numbers of electrons). Both the noble gases and the alkanes have attractive forces between atoms and molecules, which are now known to depend on the number of electrons and protons present.

The forces arise because electrons in atoms or molecules are moving at very high speeds in orbitals. At any instant in time it is possible for more electrons to lie to one side of the atom or molecule than the other. When this happens, an instantaneous electric dipole occurs. The momentary imbalance of electrons provides the negative end of a dipole, with the atomic nucleus providing the positive end of the dipole. This instantaneous dipole produces an induced dipole in a neighbouring atom or molecule, which is hence attracted (*figure 3.19*).

This is rather like the effect of a magnet (magnetic dipole) on a pin. The pin becomes temporarily magnetised and is attracted to the magnet. Intermolecular forces of this type are called **instantaneous dipole-induced dipole forces** (also called **van der Waals' forces**). The strength of the force increases with the number of electrons and protons present.

Instantaneous dipole-induced dipole forces are the weakest type of attractive force found between atoms or molecules. They are responsible for the slippery nature of graphite (*figure 3.20a*) in contrast to the great hardness of diamond (*figure 3.20b*), and for the volatility of bromine and iodine (*figure 3.21*).

A polymer is a molecule built up from a large number of small molecules (called monomers). Low-density poly(ethene), LDPE, and high-density poly(ethene), HDPE, have differing properties because of the way the polymer molecules are packed (*figure 3.22*). The HDPE molecules can pack much more closely as they are not branched. LDPE molecules are branched at intervals, which prevents them packing as closely. As a result, the

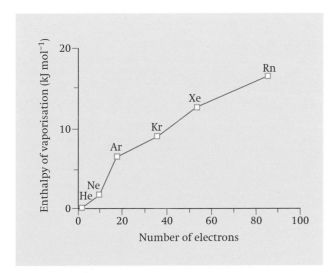

● **Figure 3.18** Enthalpy change of vaporisation of the noble gases plotted against the number of electrons present.

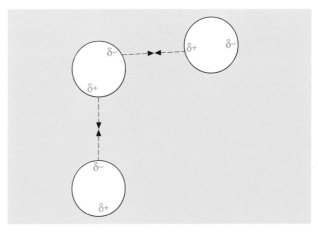

● **Figure 3.19** Induced dipole attractions.

● **Figure 3.20**

a The structure of graphite. In the planar sheets of carbon atoms, all the bonding electrons are involved in covalent bonds. The sheets are held together by much weaker instantaneous dipole-induced dipole forces. These forces are easily overcome, allowing the sheets to slide over each other (rather like a pack of cards). Graphite is often used as a lubricant.

b The structure of diamond. In contrast to graphite, each carbon atom forms four covalent bonds to four other carbon atoms. The resulting network of covalent bonds requires considerable energy to separate the atoms. The strength of the bonding in diamond is responsible for its great hardness.

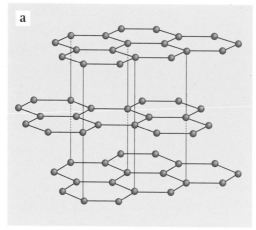

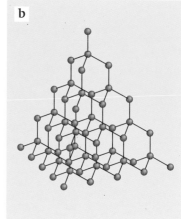

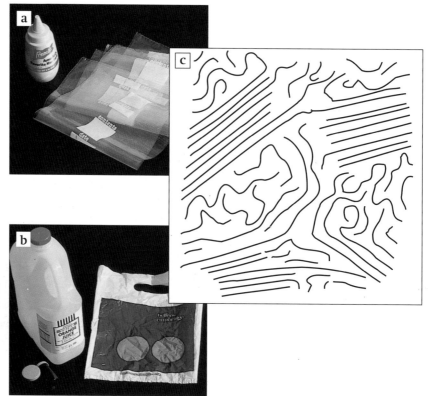

● **Figure 3.21** Bromine **a** and iodine **b** exist as covalent molecules. They are both volatile, as only very weak instantaneous dipole-induced dipole forces need to be overcome to achieve vaporisation.

● **Figure 3.22** Low-density and high-density poly(ethene).

a LDPE is made under high pressure with a trace of oxygen as catalyst. The product consists primarily of a tangled mass of polymer chains with some regions where the chains have some alignment.

b HDPE is made using catalysts developed by the Swiss chemist Ziegler and the Italian chemist Natta. (They received a Nobel Prize for their discoveries.) In HDPE, the polymer chains are arranged in a much more regular fashion. This increases the density of the material and makes it more opaque to light. As the molecules are closer together in HDPE, the instantaneous dipole-induced dipole forces between the non-polar poly(ethene) molecules are greater and the tensile strength of the material is higher.

c Diagram of crystalline and non-crystalline regions in poly(ethene). LDPE has fewer of the crystalline regions than HDPE. In the crystalline regions, polymer chains (shown as lines in the diagram) lie parallel to each other.

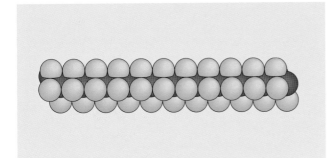

● **Figure 3.23** Model of PTFE. Note how the fluorine atoms (yellow-green) surround the carbon atoms to produce a non-polar polymer.

instantaneous dipole-induced dipole forces are not as strong.

Teflon is poly(tetrafluoroethene), PTFE. A model of part of a PTFE molecule is shown in *figure 3.23*. The instantaneous dipole-induced dipole forces between oil or grease and PTFE are much weaker than those present in the oil or grease itself. This gives rise to the polymer's non-stick properties.

Permanent dipole–dipole forces

A nylon rod may be given a charge of static electricity by rubbing it with a dry sheet of thin poly(ethene). If this is brought near a fine jet of water, the stream of water is attracted by the charge on the nylon rod. You can try this for yourself. Use a nylon comb and as fine a trickle of water from a tap as possible (see *figure 3.24*).

The water molecules are attracted to the charged nylon rod or comb because they have a permanent electric dipole. A force of this type is called a **dipole–dipole force**. The dipole of water

arises because of the bent shape of the molecule and the greater electron charge around the oxygen atom. As we saw earlier in the case of the hydrogen chloride molecule, a molecule is often polar if its atoms have different electronegativities. The diagram shows the lone-pairs and electric dipole of a water molecule (note that the arrow head shows the negative end of the dipole).

SAQ 3.8

The nylon rod carries a positive charge. Which end of the water molecule is attracted to the rod? Why are no water molecules repelled by the rod? A poly(ethene) rod may be given a negative charge when rubbed with a nylon cloth. Will the charge on the poly(ethene) rod attract or repel a thin stream of water?

Many fabrics are made using poly(ester) fibres because of that polymer's strength. Production of poly(ester) fibres together with a section of a poly(ester) molecule are shown in *figure 3.25*.

● **Figure 3.24** Deflection of water by an electrically charged nylon comb.

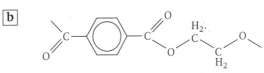

● **Figure 3.25**
a A photograph showing the production of poly(ester) fibre and
b a section of the poly(ester) chain. The strength of poly(ester) fibre is due to the strong dipole–dipole forces between ester groups of adjacent molecules.

SAQ 3.9

Copy the section of the poly(ester) chain shown in *figure 3.25* and mark on your copy the polar groups, showing the δ+ and δ− charges. Draw a second section of poly(ester) chain alongside your first section and mark in the dipole–dipole forces with dotted lines.

Water is peculiar

Figure 3.26 shows the enthalpy changes of vaporisation of water and other hydrides of Group VI elements.

SAQ 3.10

Explain the underlying increase in the enthalpy change of vaporisation with increasing atomic number. Estimate a value for water based on this trend. What is the cause of the much higher value observed for water?

The boiling point of water is also much higher than predicted by the trend in boiling points for other Group VI element hydrides. This trend would suggest that water should be a gas at room temperature and pressure. There are several more ways in which water behaves differently to most other liquids. For example, it has a very high surface tension and a high viscosity. Further, the density of ice is less than the density of water (*figure 3.27*). Most solids are denser than their liquids, as molecules usually pack closer in solids than in liquids.

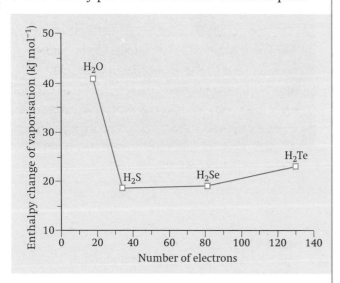

● **Figure 3.26** Enthalpy changes of vaporisation of Group VI hydrides, including water, plotted against number of electrons present.

● **Figure 3.27** Ice floats on water.

> ### Surface tension of water
> You can demonstrate the high surface tension of water for yourself by floating a needle on water. Rinse a bowl several times with water. Fill the bowl with water. Place a small piece of tissue paper on the surface of the water. Now place a needle on the tissue. Leave it undisturbed. The paper will sink, leaving the needle floating. Now carefully add a few drops of washing-up liquid (which lowers the surface tension of water) and observe the effect.

Hydrogen bonds

The peculiar nature of water is explained by the presence of the strongest type of intermolecular force – the hydrogen bond (indicated on diagrams by dotted lines). Water is highly polar owing to the large difference in electronegativity between hydrogen and oxygen. The resulting intermolecular attraction between oxygen and hydrogen atoms on neighbouring water molecules is a very strong dipole–dipole attraction called a **hydrogen bond**. Each water molecule can form two hydrogen bonds to other water molecules. These form in the directions of the lone-pairs. In the liquid state, water molecules collect in groups. On boiling, the hydrogen bonds must be broken. This raises the boiling point significantly as the hydrogen bonds are stronger than the other intermolecular forces. Similarly the enthalpy change of vaporisation is much higher than it would be if no hydrogen bonds were present.

In ice, a three-dimensional hydrogen-bonded lattice is produced. In this lattice, each oxygen is surrounded by a tetrahedron of hydrogen atoms bonded to further oxygen atoms. The structure is shown in *figure 3.28*. The extensive network of hydrogen bonds raises the freezing point

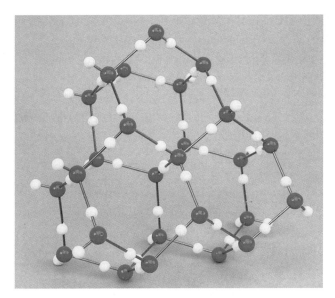

● **Figure 3.28** Model of ice. It is this hydrogen-bonded arrangement of molecules that makes ice less dense than water.

significantly above that predicted by the trend for other Group VI hydrides.

SAQ 3.11

A diamond-type lattice is present in ice. The O⋯H hydrogen bond length is 0.159 nm and the O–H covalent bond length is 0.096 nm. When ice melts, some hydrogen bonds break and the density rises. Use *figure 3.28* and these values to explain why ice has a lower density than water.

The high surface tension of water is explained by the presence of a hydrogen-bonded network of water molecules at the surface. This network is sufficiently strong to enable a needle to be floated on the surface of water.

Within the bulk of water, small groups of molecules are attracted by hydrogen bonds. The hydrogen bonds are constantly breaking and re-forming at room temperature. As the temperature of water is raised towards the boiling point, the number of hydrogen bonds reduces. On boiling, the remaining hydrogen bonds are broken. Water vapour consists of widely separated water molecules.

SAQ 3.12

Why does a needle floating on water sink on the addition of washing-up liquid to the water?

SAQ 3.13

The boiling points for Group V element hydrides are as follows:

Hydride	Boiling point (K)
ammonia, NH_3	240
phosphine, PH_3	185
arsine, AsH_3	218
stibine, SbH_3	256
bismuthine, BiH_3	295

Plot a graph of these boiling points against the relative molecular mass of the hydrides.

a Explain the steadily rising trend in the boiling points from phosphine to bismuthine.

b Explain why the boiling point of ammonia does not follow this trend.

Nylon

This synthetic polymer is an example of a poly(amide). It is similar to poly(ester) with the –O– link replaced by –NH–. The structure of a section of the polymer chain of one type of nylon is shown in *figure 3.29*. The –CO–NH– link is called an amide link. Hence the name poly(amide).

Nylon fibres are produced in the same way as poly(ester) fibres. Their high tensile strength is due to strong hydrogen bonds forming between an –NH– hydrogen atom and a C=O oxygen atom on a neighbouring polymer chain.

SAQ 3.14

a Ammonia is a gas which liquifies easily under pressure due to the formation of hydrogen bonds. Draw a diagram to show hydrogen bond formation between two adjacent molecules.

b Draw two parallel short sections of nylon-6,6 polymer chain and indicate where hydrogen bonds form between them.

● **Figure 3.29** The structure of a section of nylon-6,6. Each building-block (monomer unit) contains six carbon atoms, hence the name nylon-6,6.

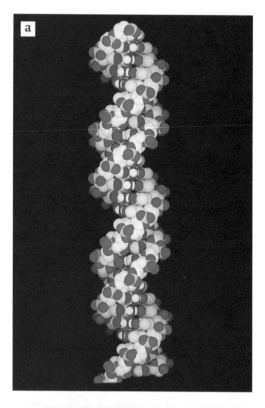

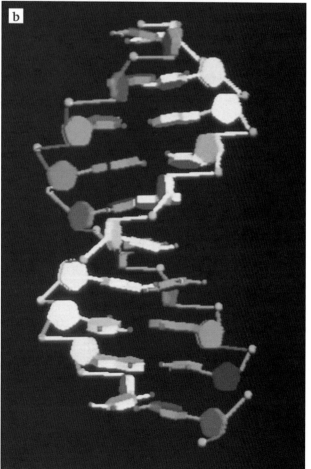

Not all the polymer chains lie close and parallel. When the fibres are stretched, the molecules straighten further but are held by the hydrogen bonds, which return the molecules to their original positions on release. The combination of strength and high elasticity are important properties in a climbing rope. If a climber falls, a nylon rope can stretch by up to half its length to stop the fall without injuring the climber.

Hydrogen bonds play a very important part in the structures and properties of biochemical polymers. For example, protein chains often produce a helical structure, and the ability of DNA molecules to replicate themselves depends primarily on the hydrogen bonds, which hold the two parts of the molecules together in a double helix (*figure 3.30*).

Relative bond strengths

Table 3.4 shows the relative strengths of intermolecular forces and other bonds. Note that all the intermolecular forces are much weaker than the forces of attraction found in typical covalent bonds or in ionic bonding. Instantaneous dipole-induced dipole forces are weaker than dipole–dipole forces. Hydrogen bonds are about twice as strong as the other intermolecular forces.

Table 3.5 provides a summary of the pattern and variety of structures and bonding found among elements and compounds.

	Energy (kJ mol^{-1})
Instantaneous dipole-induced dipole, e.g. in xenon	15
Hydrogen bond, e.g. in water	22
O–H covalent bond in water	464
Ionic bonding, sodium chloride	760

● **Table 3.4** Relative strengths of intermolecular forces and bonds.

● **Figure 3.30** Photographs of models of biochemical polymers: **a** the α-helix formed by a protein molecule and **b** a section of the DNA molecule.

| | Type of structure | | | | | |
| | Giant lattices | | | Macromolecular | Molecular | Atomic |
	Ionic	Covalent	Metallic		Simple	
Where this type of structure is found	compounds formed between metals and non-metals	Group IV elements and some of their compounds	metals	polymers	some elements and some compounds formed between non-metals	noble gases
Some examples	sodium chloride, magnesium oxide	diamond, graphite, silicon(IV) oxide	aluminium, copper	nylon, DNA	hydrogen H_2, chlorine Cl_2, methane, ammonia	helium, neon
Particles present	ions	atoms	positive ions and electrons	long-chain molecules	small molecules	atoms
Attractions that hold particles together	between oppositely charged ions	electrons in covalent bonds attract nuclei	delocalised sea of electrons attracts positive ions	various intermolecular forces between molecules, covalent bonds within molecule	various intermolecular forces between molecules, covalent bonds within molecule	intermolecular forces between atoms: instantaneous dipole-induced dipole only
Common physical state(s) at room temperature and pressure	solid	solid	solid	solid	solids, liquids and gases	gases
Melting and boiling points, enthalpy change of vaporisation	high	very high	moderately high to high	moderate, may decompose	low	very low
Hardness	hard, brittle	very hard	hard, malleable	often soft, flexible	solids usually soft	
Electrical conductivity	conduct when molten or in aqueous solution	usually non-conductors	conduct when solid or molten	usually non-conductors	non-conductors	non-conductors
Solubility in water	many ionic compounds are soluble	insoluble (SiO_2 is very sparingly soluble)	insoluble, some react liberating hydrogen	mostly insoluble, natural polymers more likely to be soluble	usually insoluble unless very polar and capable of forming hydrogen bonds to water	sparingly soluble

● **Table 3.5** Summary of structure and bonding.

SUMMARY

◆ All bonding involves electrostatic attractive forces.

◆ In ionic bonding, the attractive forces are between oppositely charged ions.

◆ In a covalent bond (one electron from each atom) or a dative covalent bond (both electrons from one atom), the forces are between two atomic nuclei and pairs of electrons situated between them.

◆ Ionic and covalent bonds may be seen as extremes. Between the two, there is a gradual transition from one extreme to the other.

◆ In metallic bonding, the forces are between delocalised electrons and positive ions.

◆ Intermolecular attractive forces also involve electrostatic forces.

◆ Intermolecular forces (hydrogen bonds, dipole–dipole and instantaneous dipole-induced dipole forces) are much weaker than ionic, covalent or metallic bonding forces.

◆ Dot-and-cross diagrams enable ionic and covalent bonds to be described. Use of these diagrams with electron-pair repulsion theory enables molecular shapes to be predicted.

◆ In molecules, atomic orbitals combine to produce σ and π molecular orbitals.

◆ Physical properties and structures of elements and compounds may be explained in terms of kinetic theory and bonding (*table 3.5*).

Questions

1 Hydrogen fluoride, HF, is one of the most important fluorine compounds. It can be prepared by reacting calcium fluoride, CaF_2, with sulphuric acid.

  a Showing outer-shell electrons only, draw 'dot-and-cross' diagrams of:
    (i) hydrogen fluoride;
    (ii) calcium fluoride.

  b Predict two differences between the physical properties of HF and CaF_2.

2 a Explain how the model of electron-pair repulsion can be used to explain the shape and bond angles of simple molecules using CH_4, NH_3 and CO_2 as examples.

  b Draw 'dot-and-cross' diagrams for the oxides of sulphur, SO_3 and SO_2, and predict the shape and bond angles of these molecules.

3 At room temperature, iodine, I_2, has a crystal lattice structure.

  a (i) What type of bond holds together the iodine atoms in an iodine molecule?
    (ii) What forces act between the iodine molecules in a crystal lattice of iodine?

  b When iodine is gently heated to 114 °C, it turns directly from a solid into a gas without going through the liquid state. This unusual behaviour is called **sublimation**.

    (i) Explain, in terms of forces, the changes that occur to the structure of iodine as it sublimes.

    (ii) The diamond form of carbon sublimes at a much higher temperature than iodine. Suggest why this higher temperature is required.

CHAPTER 4

Periodic patterns

By the end of this chapter you should be able to:

1 describe the Periodic Table in terms of the arrangement of elements by increasing atomic number, in Periods showing repeating physical and chemical properties, and in Groups having similar physical and chemical properties;

2 classify the elements into s, p and d blocks;

3 describe, for the elements of Period 3, the variation in electronic configurations, atomic radii, electrical conductivities, melting points and boiling points, and explain these variations in terms of the structure and bonding of the elements;

4 interpret successive ionisation energy data of an element in terms of the position of that element within the Periodic Table;

5 describe and explain the variation of the first ionisation energies of elements shown by a general increase across a Period, in terms of increasing nuclear charge;

6 describe and explain the variation of the first ionisation energies of elements shown by a general decrease down a Group, in terms of increasing atomic radius and shielding;

7 interpret data on electronic configurations, atomic radii, electrical conductivities, melting points and boiling points to demonstrate periodicity.

Introduction to periodicity

Patterns of chemical properties and atomic masses

If you were given samples of all the elements (some are shown in *figure 4.1*) and the time to observe their properties, you would probably find many ways of arranging them. You could classify them by their states at a particular temperature (solids, liquids or gases) or as metals and non-metals; you might find patterns in their reactions with oxygen or water or other chemicals. Would you consider trying to link these properties to the relative atomic masses of the elements?

● **Figure 4.1** A few of the 115 known elements.

If you have studied the metallic elements lithium, sodium and potassium, you will know that they have similar reactions with oxygen, water and chlorine, and form similar compounds. The rates of their reactions show that sodium comes between lithium and potassium in reactivity. Now look at their relative atomic masses:

Li	Na	K
6.9	23	39.1

The relative atomic mass of sodium is the mean of the relative atomic masses of lithium and potassium. There is a pattern here which is also shown by other groups of elements in threes – chlorine, bromine and iodine, for example. The 'middle' element has the mean relative atomic mass and other properties inbetween those of the other two. This pattern was first recorded by the German chemist Johann Döbereiner (1780–1849) as his 'Law of Triads' (*figure 4.2*). At the time, however, it was little more than a curiosity, as too few elements were known and values for atomic masses were uncertain.

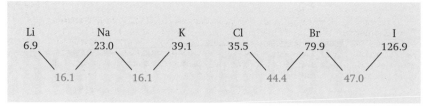

● **Figure 4.2** Two of Döbereiner's 'triads'.

Later in the century, more elements were known and atomic masses could be measured more accurately. A British chemist, John Newlands (1837–98), suggested that, when the elements were arranged in order of increasing atomic mass, 'the eighth element, starting from a given one, is a kind of repetition of the first, like the eighth note in an octave of music'.

Newlands presented his ideas for a 'Law of Octaves' to a meeting of the Chemical Society in 1866 (*figure 4.3*). They were not well received. Unfortunately, his 'octaves' only seemed to apply to the first 16 elements. He had not allowed space in his table for the possibility of new elements to be discovered.

Despite the Chemical Society's sceptical reception of Newlands' ideas, we now know that he had found the important pattern of periodicity. This means that the properties of elements have a regularly recurring or 'periodic' relationship with their relative atomic masses.

Mendeleev's periodic table

The greatest credit for producing chemistry's most famous organisation of elements – 'the Periodic Table' – is always given to Dmitri Mendeleev (1834–1907) from Russia.

Mendeleev arranged the elements, just as Newlands had, in order of increasing relative atomic mass (*figure 4.4*). At the time (late 1860s) over 60 elements were known, and he saw that there was some form of regularly repeating pattern of properties.

CHEMICAL NEWS,}
March 9, 1866. }

Table II.—Elements arranged in Octaves.

No.		No.		No.		No.		No.		No.		No.		No.
H	1	F	8	Cl	15	Co & Ni	22	Br	29	Pd	36	I	42	Pt & Ir	50
Li	2	Na	9	K	16	Cu	23	Rb	30	Ag	37	Cs	44	Os	51
G	3	Mg	10	Ca	17	Zn	24	Sr	31	Cd	38	Ba & V	45	Hg	52
Bo	4	Al	11	Cr	19	Y	25	Ce & La	33	U	40	Ta	46	Tl	53
C	5	Si	12	Ti	18	In	26	Zr	32	Sn	39	W	47	Pb	54
N	6	P	13	Mn	20	As	27	Di & Mo	34	Sb	41	Nb	48	Bi	55
O	7	S	14	Fe	21	Se	28	Ro & Ru	35	Te	43	Au	49	Th	56

● **Figure 4.3**
a John Newlands.
b This is the table Newlands presented to the Chemical Society in 1866 in a paper entitled 'The Law of Octaves, and the Causes of Numerical Relations among the Atomic Weights'. Note that some elements have symbols that we do not use today, e.g. G and Bo. What are these elements?

a
Ueber die Beziehungen der Eigenschaften zu den Atomgewichten der Elemente. Von D. Mendelejeff. — Ordnet man Elemente nach zunehmenden Atomgewichten in verticale Reihen so, dass die Horizontalreihen analoge Elemente enthalten, wieder nach zunehmendem Atomgewicht geordnet, so erhält man folgende Zusammenstellung, aus der sich einige allgemeinere Folgerungen ableiten lassen.

			Ti = 50	Zr = 90	? = 180
			V = 51	Nb = 94	Ta = 182
			Cr = 52	Mo = 96	W = 186
			Mn = 55	Rh = 104,4	Pt = 197,4
			Fe = 56	Ru = 104,4	Ir = 198
		Ni = Co = 59		Pd = 106,6	Os = 199
			Cu = 63,4	Ag = 108	Hg = 200
H = 1		Mg = 24	Zn = 65,2	Cd = 112	
Be = 9,4		Al = 27,4	? = 68	Ur = 116	Au = 197?
B = 11		Si = 28	? = 70	Sn = 118	
C = 12		P = 31	As = 75	Sb = 122	Bi = 210?
N = 14		S = 32	Se = 79,4	Te = 128?	
O = 16		Cl = 35,5	Br = 80	J = 127	
F = 19		K = 39	Rb = 85,4	Cs = 133	Tl = 204
Li = 7	Na = 23	Ca = 40	Sr = 87,6	Ba = 137	Pb = 207
		? = 45	Ce = 92		
		?Er = 56	La = 94		
		?Yt = 60	Di = 95		
		?In = 75,6	Th = 118?		

• Figure 4.4
a Mendeleev's first published periodic table in the *Zeitschrift für Chemie* in 1869. Note that the elements with similar properties (e.g. Li, Na, K) are in horizontal rows in this table.
b This photograph shows a late version of Mendeleev's periodic table on the building where he worked in St Petersburg. Elements with similar properties are now arranged vertically in groups.

Mendeleev made several crucial decisions that ensured the success of his first periodic table. The most important decisions were the following.

■ He left spaces in the table so that similar elements could always appear in the same Group.

■ He said that the spaces would be filled by elements not then known. Furthermore, he predicted what the properties of these elements might be, based on the properties of known elements in the same Group. He made predictions, for example, about the element between silicon and tin in Group IV. This element was only discovered about 15 years later. Mendeleev had called it 'eka-silicon'; it is now known as germanium (*table 4.1*).

SAQ 4.1

From *table 4.1*, how well do you think Mendeleev's predicted properties for eka-silicon compare with the known properties of germanium?

A theory or model is most valuable when it is used to explain and predict. Mendeleev's periodic table was immensely successful. By linking the observed periodicity in the properties of elements with the atomic theory of matter, the table helped to organise and unify the science of chemistry and led to much further research. It has been greatly admired ever since. It was even able to cope with the discovery of a whole new group of elements, now called 'the noble gases' (helium to radon), though these had not been predicted by Mendeleev.

Property	Mendeleev's predictions for 'eka-silicon'	Germanium
Appearance	light-grey solid	dark-grey solid
Atomic mass	72	72.59
Density ($g\,cm^{-3}$)	5.5	5.35
Oxide formula	eka-SiO_2	GeO_2
Oxide density	4.7	4.2
Chloride density	1.9 (liquid)	1.84 (liquid)
Chloride b.p. (°C)	<100	84

• Table 4.1 Comparison of Mendeleev's predictions for eka-silicon with known properties of germanium.

Atomic structure and periodicity

In 1913 the British scientist Henry Moseley was able to show that the real sequence in the Periodic Table is not the order of relative atomic masses. The sequence is the order of atomic numbers – the numbers of protons in the nuclei of atoms of the elements (see chapter 1). This sequence of elements by atomic numbers is close to the sequence by relative atomic masses, but not exactly the same.

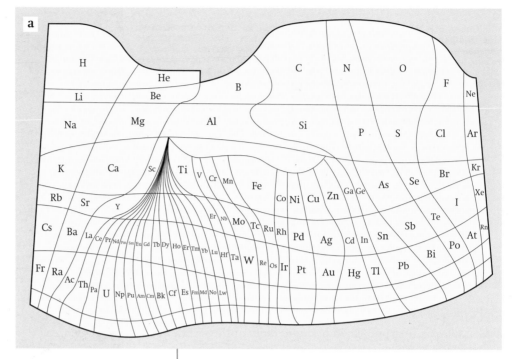

SAQ 4.2

a What is the relationship between atomic numbers and relative atomic masses?

b Why are the relative atomic mass values for tellurium (Te) and iodine (I; J in Mendeleev's table) the 'wrong' way around in the Periodic Table, whereas their atomic numbers fit the Table?

Moseley's work was about the nature of the nucleus and led to the correct sequence of elements. It did not, however, answer questions about the periodic variations in physical and chemical properties. This is because these properties depend much more upon the numbers and distributions of electrons in atoms.

Versions of the Periodic Table

Chemists have enjoyed displaying the Periodic Table in many different ways (for two versions, see *figure 4.5*). You may be able to invent some new versions.

The Periodic Table most often seen is shown in *figure 4.6* (and also in the appendix). Its main features are:

■ the vertical Groups of elements, labelled I, II,

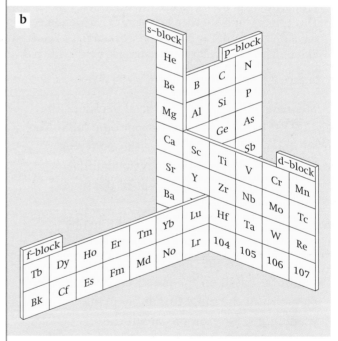

● **Figure 4.5** Two rather unusual versions of the Periodic Table:
a the elements according to relative abundance and
b a three-dimensional, four-vaned model.

III, up to VII; the noble gases are not called Group VIII but Group 0;

■ the horizontal Periods labelled 1, 2, 3, etc.

Blocks of elements in the Periodic Table

Chemists find it helpful to identify 'blocks' of elements by the type of electron orbital most

s-Block / p-Block / d-Block / f-Block

Period	I	II											III	IV	V	VI	VII	0
1							1.0 H Hydrogen 1											4.0 He Helium 2
2	6.9 Li Lithium 3	9.0 Be Beryllium 4											10.8 B Boron 5	12.0 C Carbon 6	14.0 N Nitrogen 7	16.0 O Oxygen 8	19.0 F Fluorine 9	20.2 Ne Neon 10
3	23.0 Na Sodium 11	24.3 Mg Magnesium 12											27.0 Al Aluminium 13	28.1 Si Silicon 14	31.0 P Phosphorus 15	32.1 S Sulphur 16	35.5 Cl Chlorine 17	39.9 Ar Argon 18
4	39.1 K Potassium 19	40.1 Ca Calcium 20	45.0 Sc Scandium 21	47.9 Ti Titanium 22	50.9 V Vanadium 23	52.0 Cr Chromium 24	54.9 Mn Manganese 25	55.8 Fe Iron 26	58.9 Co Cobalt 27	58.7 Ni Nickel 28	63.5 Cu Copper 29	65.4 Zn Zinc 30	69.7 Ga Gallium 31	72.6 Ge Germanium 32	74.9 As Arsenic 33	79.0 Se Selenium 34	79.9 Br Bromine 35	83.8 Kr Krypton 36
5	85.5 Rb Rubidium 37	87.6 Sr Strontium 38	88.9 Y Yttrium 39	91.2 Zr Zirconium 40	92.9 Nb Niobium 41	95.9 Mo Molybdenum 42	– Tc Technetium 43	101 Ru Ruthenium 44	103 Rh Rhodium 45	106 Pd Palladium 46	108 Ag Silver 47	112 Cd Cadmium 48	115 In Indium 49	119 Sn Tin 50	122 Sb Antimony 51	128 Te Tellurium 52	127 I Iodine 53	131 Xe Xenon 54
6	133 Cs Caesium 55	137 Ba Barium 56	La to Lu	178 Hf Hafnium 72	181 Ta Tantalum 73	184 W Tungsten 74	186 Re Rhenium 75	190 Os Osmium 76	192 Ir Iridium 77	195 Pt Platinum 78	197 Au Gold 79	201 Hg Mercury 80	204 Tl Thallium 81	207 Pb Lead 82	209 Bi Bismuth 83	– Po Polonium 84	– At Astatine 85	– Rn Radon 86
7	– Fr Francium 87	– Ra Radium 88	Ac to Lr	– Rf Rutherfordium 104	– Db Dubnium 105	– Sg Seaborgium 106	– Bh Bohrium 107	– Hs Hassium 108	– Mt Meitnerium 109	– Uun Ununnillium 110	– Uuu Unununium 111	– Uub Ununbium 112		– Uuq Ununquadium 114		– Uuh Ununhexium 116		– Uuo Ununoctium 118

Key: a = relative atomic mass, X = symbol, b = proton number (box shows a, X, Name, b).

f-Block

139 La Lanthanum 57	140 Ce Cerium 58	141 Pr Praseodymium 59	144 Nd Neodymium 60	– Pm Promethium 61	150 Sm Samarium 62	152 Eu Europium 63	157 Gd Gadolinium 64	159 Tb Terbium 65	163 Dy Dysprosium 66	165 Ho Holmium 67	167 Er Erbium 68	169 Tm Thulium 69	173 Yb Ytterbium 70	175 Lu Lutetium 71
– Ac Actinium 89	– Th Thorium 90	– Pa Protactinium 91	– U Uranium 92	– Np Neptunium 93	– Pu Plutonium 94	– Am Americium 95	– Cm Curium 96	– Bk Berkelium 97	– Cf Californium 98	– Es Einsteinium 99	– Fm Fermium 100	– Md Mendelevium 101	– No Nobelium 102	– Lr Lawrencium 103

● **Figure 4.6** The Periodic Table of the elements.

affecting the properties. These are shown on the Periodic Table in *figure 4.6*.

- Groups I and II elements are in the **s-block**.
- Groups III to VII and Group 0 (except He) are in the **p-block**.
- The transition elements are included in the **d-block**.
- The lanthanide and actinide elements are included in the **f-block**.

Periodic patterns of physical properties of elements

We shall now look in more detail at the physical properties of elements and their relationships with the electronic configurations of atoms.

Summary of structure and bonding of the first 36 elements

Figure 4.7 shows details of the structures and bonding of elements 1 to 36, hydrogen (H) to krypton (Kr).

H_2(g) mols																	He(g) atoms
Li(s) metal	Be(s) metal											B(s) giant mol	C(s) giant mol	N_2(g) mols	O_2(g) mols	F_2(g) mols	Ne(g) atoms
Na(s) metal	Mg(s) metal											Al(s) metal	Si(s) giant mol	P_4(s) mols	S_8(s) mols	Cl_2(g) mols	Ar(g) atoms
K(s) metal	Ca(s) metal	Sc(s) metal	Ti(s) metal	V(s) metal	Cr(s) metal	Mn(s) metal	Fe(s) metal	Co(s) metal	Ni(s) metal	Cu(s) metal	Zn(s) metal	Ga(s) metal	Ge(s) metal	As(s) giant mol	Se(s) mol	Br_2(l) mols	Kr(g) atoms

● **Figure 4.7** Structures of elements 1 (hydrogen, H) to 36 (krypton, Kr).

Periodic patterns of electronic configurations

Magnesium and calcium are both s-block elements in Group II. Their electronic configurations are:

Mg $1s^2 2s^2 2p^6 3s^2$
Ca $1s^2 2s^2 2p^6 3s^2 3p^6 4s^2$

Notice that they have the same outer-shell configuration, s^2. All the Group II elements have an outer-shell configuration of s^2.

SAQ 4.3

Carbon and silicon are both p-block elements and in Group IV.

a Write down the electronic configurations of carbon and silicon.

b What do you notice about their outer-shell configurations?

c Suggest, giving a reason, the outer-shell configuration for germanium.

In general:

- in the s-block, the outermost electrons are in an s orbital. In the p-block, the outermost electrons are in p orbitals;
- elements in the same Group have the same number of electrons in their outer shell;
- for the elements in Groups I to VII, the number of outer-shell electrons is the same as the Group number. For example, chlorine in Group VII has seven outer-shell electrons: $1s^2 2s^2 2p^6 3s^2 3p^5$, a total of seven electrons in the third shell;
- Group 0 elements, the noble gases, have a full outer shell of eight electrons: $s^2 p^6$. For example, neon has the electronic configuration $1s^2 2s^2 2p^6$.

Periodic patterns of atomic radii

The size of an atom cannot be measured precisely as their electron shells do not define a clear outer limit. However, one measure of the size of an atom is its 'atomic radius'. This can be either the 'covalent radius' or the 'metallic radius' (*figure 4.8*). **Covalent radius** is half the distance between the nuclei of neighbouring atoms in molecules. **Metallic radius** is half the distance between the nuclei of neighbouring atoms in metallic crystals. The covalent radius can be measured for most elements and is usually what is meant when we use the term **atomic radius**.

Atomic radii of elements 1 to 36 are shown in *figure 4.9*. When atomic (covalent) radii are plotted against proton numbers for the first 36 elements, the graph appears as in *figure 4.10*. The noble gases are not included as they do not have covalent radii.

SAQ 4.4

Why do the noble gases not have any measured covalent radii?

Note the relative positions of the elements in any one Group, such as Group I (alkali metals) or

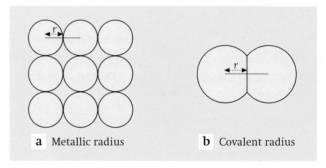

| **a** Metallic radius | **b** Covalent radius |

● **Figure 4.8** Metallic and covalent radii.

H 0.037																	He –
Li 0.123	Be 0.089											B 0.080	C 0.077	N 0.074	O 0.074	F 0.072	Ne –
Na 0.157	Mg 0.136											Al 0.125	Si 0.117	P 0.110	S 0.104	Cl 0.099	Ar –
K 0.203	Ca 0.174	Sc 0.144	Ti 0.132	V 0.122	Cr 0.117	Mn 0.117	Fe 0.116	Co 0.116	Ni 0.115	Cu 0.117	Zn 0.125	Ga 0.125	Ge 0.122	As 0.121	Se 0.117	Br 0.114	Kr –

● **Figure 4.9** The atomic (covalent) radii of elements 1 to 36, measured in nanometres (nm).

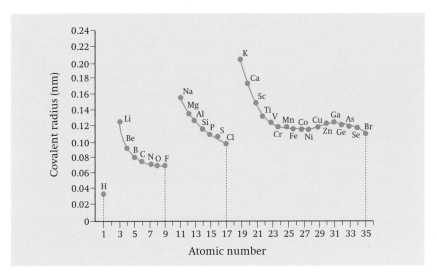

● **Figure 4.10** Plot of atomic (covalent) radii against atomic number of elements. The noble gases (He–Kr) are not included.

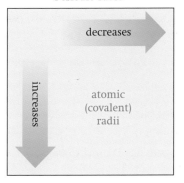

● **Figure 4.11** Trends of atomic (covalent) radii.

Group VII (halogens), and across the Periods 2 and 3. The trends (*figure 4.11*) show that atomic radii:

■ increase down a Group;

■ decrease across a Period;

■ after some decrease, are relatively constant across the transition elements, titanium to copper.

Note that the trends in atomic radii are generally in the opposite direction to the trends in first ionisation energies. As atomic radii become larger, first ionisation energies become smaller. In any one atom, both trends are due to the same combined effects of:

■ the size of the nuclear charge;

■ the distance of the outer electron shell from the nucleus;

■ the shielding effect of filled inner electron shells upon the outer shell.

Down any one Group, the nuclear charges increase, but the distance and shielding effects increase even more, as extra electron shells are added. The overall result is an increase in atomic radii.

Across Periods 2 and 3, the nuclear charges increase from element to element. The distance and shielding effects remain fairly constant, because electrons are added to the same outer shell. As the increasing attraction pulls the electrons closer to the nuclei, the radii of the atoms decrease.

Periodic patterns of boiling points for elements 1 to 36

The variation in boiling points is shown in *figures 4.12* and *4.13*. In any boiling liquid, particles are entering the vapour phase in large numbers. If the forces of attraction between the particles are strong, the boiling point is high; if the forces are weak, the boiling point is low.

Note that the 'peaks' of the graph are occupied by elements from the same Group – carbon and silicon from Group IV. Their extremely high boiling points are due to the strong covalent bonds between atoms of these

H 20																	He 4
Li 1604	Be 2750											B 4200	C 5100	N 77	O 90	F 85	Ne 27
Na 1163	Mg 1390											Al 2720	Si 2950	P 554	S 718	Cl 239	Ar 87
K 1039	Ca 1765	Sc 2750	Ti 3550	V 3650	Cr 2915	Mn 2314	Fe 3160	Co 3150	Ni 3110	Cu 2855	Zn 1181	Ga 2510	Ge 3100	As 886	Se 958	Br 331	Kr 120

● **Figure 4.12** Boiling points of elements 1 to 36, measured in kelvins (K).

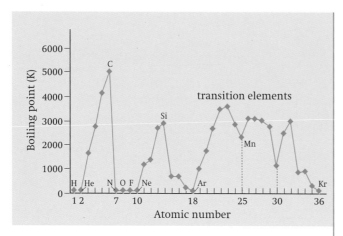

● **Figure 4.13** Plot of boiling points of elements 1 to 36 against atomic numbers.

elements, which exist in the giant molecular lattice structure and persist, to some extent, in the liquid phase. These bonds are broken when the elements boil. Atoms, singly or in groups, separate into the vapour phase.

The 'troughs' are occupied by elements that consist of diatomic molecules (H_2, N_2, O_2, F_2, Cl_2, Br_2) or single atoms (He, Ne, Ar, Kr). The forces of attraction between the particles are very weak, even in the liquid phase, and are readily broken. The diatomic molecules or atoms are easily separated from each other as the temperature rises.

Elements in Groups I, II and III occupy similar positions on the rising parts of the curve. Most of the elements in these Groups are metals, and the rising boiling points show that their metallic bonding persists into the liquid phase. The metallic bonding is stronger on moving from Group I to Group II to Group III, as there are more outer-shell electrons available to be mobile and take part in the bonding.

SAQ 4.5

Why do both phosphorus (P_4) and sulphur (S_8) occupy low positions on the boiling-point curve but are higher than chlorine?

SAQ 4.6

Figure 4.14 shows the melting points of the elements from Period 3. Plot these melting points against the atomic numbers for the elements.

Na	Mg	Al	Si	P (white)	S	Cl	Ar
371	922	933	1683	317	386	172	84

● **Figure 4.14** Melting points of the elements from Period 3, measured in kelvins.

Explain the following in terms of structure and bonding of the elements:
a the increase in the melting points between sodium and aluminium;
b the very high melting point of silicon;
c the low melting points of sulphur to argon.

Periodic patterns of electrical conductivities

Electrical conductivities are measured in units called 'siemens per metre' ($S\,m^{-1}$). Siemens are the reciprocal of the units of electrical resistance (ohms, Ω), $S = \Omega^{-1}$. *Figure 4.15* shows the known values of electrical conductivities, in units of $10^8\,S\,m^{-1}$, for elements up to bromine. Conductivity values give an indication of how easily electrons move through the element. Metallic elements thus have higher electrical conductivities than molecular elements.

H –																	He –
Li 0.108	Be 0.25											B 10^{-12}	C (graphite) 7×10^{-4}	N –	O –	F –	Ne –
Na 0.218	Mg 0.224											Al 0.382	Si 2×10^{-10}	P 10^{-17}	S 10^{-23}	Cl –	Ar –
K 0.143	Ca 0.218	Sc 0.015	Ti 0.024	V 0.04	Cr 0.078	Mn 0.054	Fe 0.010	Co 0.16	Ni 0.145	Cu 0.593	Zn 0.167	Ga 0.058	Ge 2.2×10^{-8}	As 0.029	Se 0.08	Br 10^{-18}	Kr –

● **Figure 4.15** Electrical conductivities of elements 1 to 36, measured in 10^8 siemens per metre ($10^8\,S\,m^{-1}$, or $10^{-8}\,\Omega^{-1}\,m^{-1}$).

SAQ 4.7

a Why do electrical conductivities increase from Group I to Group III elements in Period 3?

b Why are the electrical conductivities of d-block transition elements relatively high, compared with most p-block elements?

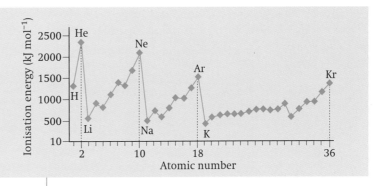

● **Figure 4.17** The first ionisation energies of elements 1 to 36, plotted against atomic number.

Periodic patterns of first ionisation energies

The first ionisation energies of the first 36 elements in the Periodic Table are shown in *figure 4.16*. Their variation with atomic number is displayed in *figure 4.17*. The most significant features of the graph are:

■ The 'peaks' are all occupied by elements of the same Group (Group 0, the noble gases) and the 'troughs' by the Group I elements (the alkali metals).

■ There is a general increase in ionisation energy across a Period, from the Group I elements to the Group 0 elements, but the trend is uneven.

■ The first ionisation energies of the elements 21 (scandium) to 29 (copper) (the d-block elements of Period 4) vary much less than other series of elements.

How are these periodic variations in first ionisation energies to be explained in terms of the model of atomic structure and electronic configurations outlined in chapter 1?

Consider some examples:

fluorine, element 9, has the configuration
$1s^2 \, 2s^2 \, 2p^5$

neon, element 10, has the configuration
$1s^2 \, 2s^2 \, 2p^6$

sodium, element 11, has the configuration
$1s^2 \, 2s^2 \, 2p^6 \, 3s^1$

As you see in *figure 4.17*, the ionisation energy of neon is higher than that of fluorine; sodium's ionisation energy is much lower. The main differences in the atoms of these elements are:

■ the numbers of protons in their nuclei, and hence their positive nuclear charges, are different;

■ the outer occupied orbital in both fluorine and neon is in the 2p subshell but sodium has an electron in the next shell, in its 3s orbital;

■ neon has a completely filled outer shell, fluorine has one electron fewer than a complete shell and sodium has one electron more than a complete shell.

These differences between the atoms may be explained by the factors that influence their first

H 1310																	He 2370
Li 519	Be 900											B 799	C 1090	N 1400	O 1310	F 1680	Ne 2080
Na 494	Mg 736											Al 577	Si 786	P 1060	S 1000	Cl 1260	Ar 1520
K 418	Ca 590	Sc 632	Ti 661	V 648	Cr 653	Mn 716	Fe 762	Co 757	Ni 736	Cu 745	Zn 908	Ga 577	Ge 762	As 966	Se 941	Br 1140	Kr 1350

● **Figure 4.16** The first ionisation energies of elements 1 to 36, measured in kilojoules per mole ($kJ \, mol^{-1}$).

ionisation energies (see chapter 1):

■ An increase in positive nuclear charge will tend to cause an increase in first ionisation energies.

■ The forces of attraction between the positive nuclear charge and the negatively charged electrons decreases as the quantum number of the shells increases. The further the shell is from the nucleus the lower the first ionisation energy is.

■ Filled inner electron shells shield outer electrons. The outer electrons are repelled by the electrons in the filled inner shells so the first ionisation energy falls.

We shall now apply these ideas to the three elements, 9, 10, and 11 – fluorine, neon and sodium.

The outer electrons in both fluorine and neon atoms are in the 2p orbitals. This means that the 'distance' effect and the 'shielding' effect are similar. However, the nuclear charge in a neon atom is larger and attracts the 2p electrons more strongly. This causes the first ionisation energy of neon to be higher than that of fluorine.

The outer electron of sodium is in the 3s orbital, as the 2p orbitals are full. The ionisation energy of sodium is much lower than that of neon, even though a sodium atom has a larger nuclear charge. This shows how the combined effects, of increased distance and of shielding, reduce the effective nuclear charge. The 3s electron in a sodium atom is further from the nucleus than any 2p electrons. It

is also shielded from the attractions of the nuclear charge by two complete inner shells ($n = 1$ and $n = 2$). The electrons in shell $n = 2$ are shielded only by the electrons in one shell ($n = 1$).

First ionisation energies across a Period

From *figure 4.17* you will see that there is a general trend of increasing ionisation energies across a Period. However, the trend is uneven. Look, for example, at elements 3, 4 and 5, lithium ($1s^2\ 2s^1$), beryllium ($1s^2\ 2s^2$) and boron ($1s^2\ 2s^2\ 2p^1$). We might have predicted that boron would have the highest ionisation energy of the three; in fact, it is beryllium. Experimental evidence such as this leads to a further assumption about electronic configurations: it is easier to remove electrons from p orbitals than from s orbitals in the same shell. Our modern theories for electronic structure show that the p orbitals are higher energy levels than the s orbital for a given quantum number. Hence our theories predict that an electron is more easily removed from the p orbital than the s orbital. Thus the 2p electron in boron is easier to remove than one of the 2s electrons. Though the nuclear charge in boron is larger than in beryllium, boron has the lower first ionisation energy.

Now look at the other elements in Period 2:

	Carbon	*Nitrogen*	*Oxygen*
atomic number	6	7	8
electronic config.	$1s^2\ 2s^2\ 2p^2$	$1s^2\ 2s^2\ 2p^3$	$1s^2\ 2s^2\ 2p^4$
box config. for 2p	↑ ↑ ☐	↑ ↑ ↑	↑↓ ↑ ↑

	Fluorine	*Neon*
atomic number	9	10
electronic config.	$1s^2\ 2s^2\ 2p^5$	$1s^2\ 2s^2\ 2p^6$
box config. for 2p	↑↓ ↑↓ ↑	↑↓ ↑↓ ↑↓

In the general trend across the Period, we might expect the ionisation energy of oxygen to be higher than that of nitrogen. In fact, the ionisation energy of nitrogen is the higher of the two. Nitrogen has three electrons in the p orbitals, each of them unpaired; oxygen has four electrons, with two of them paired. The repulsion between the electrons in the pair increases the energy and makes it easier to remove one of them and to ionise an atom of oxygen, even though the nuclear charge is larger than in an atom of nitrogen.

The general trend, of increasing ionisation energies across a Period, is re-established in atoms of fluorine and neon, by the effect of larger nuclear charge.

SAQ 4.8

In terms of their electronic configurations, explain the relative first ionisation energies of:

a sodium, magnesium and aluminium;

b silicon, phosphorus and sulphur.

First ionisation energies in Groups

Elements are placed in Groups in the Periodic Table, as they show many similar physical and chemical properties. Note how elements in Groups occupy similar positions on the plot of first ionisation energy against atomic number (*figure 4.17*). This is evidence that the elements in Groups have similar electronic configurations in their outer orbitals. For example:

Group I (alkali metals, Li–Cs)
all have one (s^1) electron in their outer orbitals
Group II (alkaline-earth metals, Be–Ba)
all have two (s^2) electrons in their outer orbitals
Group VII (halogens, F–At)
all have seven ($s^2 p^5$) electrons in their outer orbitals

The first ionisation energies generally decrease down a vertical Group, with increasing atomic number. This shows the combined result of several factors. With increasing proton number, in any Group:

- the positive nuclear charge increases;
- the atomic radius increases so the distance of the outer electrons from the nucleus also increases with each new shell;
- the shielding effect of the filled inner electron shells increases as the number of inner shells grows.

The distance and shielding effects together reduce the effect of the increasing nuclear charges from element to element down any Group.

SAQ 4.9

Helium has the highest first ionisation energy in the Periodic Table. Suggest which element is likely to have the lowest first ionisation energy and why.

First ionisation energies and reactivity of elements

Ionisation energies give a measure of the energy required to remove electrons from atoms and form positive ions. The lower the first ionisation energy of an element, the more easily the element forms positive ions during reactions:

$$M(g) \longrightarrow M^+(g) + e^-$$

This is the main reason for the metallic nature of the elements on the 'left' of the Periodic Table (Groups I, II and III) and increasingly metallic nature of elements down all Groups.

- In elements with low first ionisation energies, one or more electrons are relatively free to move from atom to atom in the metallic bonding of the structure.
- The characteristic chemical properties of metallic elements include the formation of positive ions. In the reactions of metals with oxygen, chlorine or water, for example, formation of positive ions is one of several stages involving enthalpy changes. The elements with low first ionisation energies usually do react more quickly and vigorously. In any Period, the Group I elements (alkali metals) have the lowest first ionisation energies and are the most reactive metals. They also have lower first ionisation energies going 'down' the Group, with increasing atomic number, and become much more reactive.

The factors that affect the values of ionisation energies thus also influence the reactivities of many elements. We shall examine the effect of ionisation energies on reactivity for Group II metals in the next chapter (see page 69).

Successive ionisation energies and the Periodic Table

Successive ionisation may be interpreted in terms of the position of an element in the Periodic Table. In chapter 1, the pattern of successive ionisation energies for an element was used to:

- provide evidence for the general pattern of electron shells;
- predict the simple electronic configuration of an element;
- confirm the position of an element in the Periodic Table.

For any one element, successive ionisation energies steadily increase as electrons are removed. A large increase occurs between two successive ionisation energies when the next electron is removed from a lower electron shell.

For example, carbon has the following successive ionisation energies:

1090, 2350, 4610, 6220, 37 800, 47 300 kJ mol^{-1}.

The first four values show a steady increase followed by a very large increase at the fifth value. Hence, a total of four electrons are removed from the outer shell of carbon. Carbon has the simple electronic configuration 2,4 which also confirms the position of carbon in Group IV.

SAQ 4.10

a Phosphorus is in Group V. Between which of the first eight ionisation energies will there be a large rise in ionisation energy?

b In which Group of the Periodic Table would you place the element with the following successive ionisation energies?
1680, 3370, 6040, 8410, 11 000, 15 200, 17 900, 92 000, 106 000 kJ mol^{-1}.

SUMMARY

◆ Early periodic patterns (regularly repeating variations) in the properties of elements were based on the elements in order of their relative atomic masses. The modern Periodic Tables are based on the elements in order of their atomic numbers.

◆ A Group in the Periodic Table contains elements with the same outer-shell electronic configuration but very different atomic numbers; the elements and their compounds have many similar chemical properties.

◆ The elements in a Block have their outer-most electrons in the same type of subshell. For example, s-block elements have their outermost electrons in an s subshell.

◆ Periods in the Periodic Table are sequences of elements, differing by one proton and one electron, from Group I to Group 0.

◆ Periodic variations may be observed across Periods in physical properties such as ioni-sation energies, electron configurations, atomic radii, boiling points, melting points and electrical conductivities.

◆ The main influences on ionisation energies and atomic radii are: the size of the positive nuclear charge; the distance of the electron from the nucleus; the shielding effect on outer electrons by electrons in filled inner shells.

◆ Ionisation energies decrease down a Group and tend to increase across a Period; atomic radii increase down a Group (effect of increasing shielding) and decrease across a Period (effect of increasing nuclear charge).

◆ The uneven trend of ionisation energies across a Period is explained by: a change from s to p subshells with a drop in first ionisation energy between Groups II and III; the commencement of electron pairing in a Group VI p orbital resulting from increased energy from electron-pair repulsion and a consequent fall in first ionisation energy between Groups V and VI.

◆ Across a Period (left to right, from Group I to Group VII), the structures of the elements change from giant metallic, through giant molecular to simple molecular. Group 0 elements consist of individual atoms.

◆ Successive ionisation energy data of an element may be interpreted in terms of the position of the element within the Periodic Table.

◆ Data on electronic configurations, atomic radii, electrical conductivity, melting points and boiling points may be inter-preted to demonstrate periodicity.

◆ Chemically, the elements change from reac-tive metals, through less reactive metals and less reactive non-metals to reactive non-metals. Group 0 contains the extremely unreactive noble gases.

Questions

1 Patterns in data have enabled chemists to gain a better understanding of many physical properties of elements. Look at the following figure, which gives the boiling points of the elements in Period 3 of the Periodic Table.

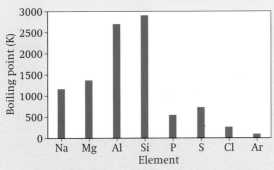

a Explain, in terms of their structures, why:
   (i) the boiling point of phosphorus is different from that of silicon;
   (ii) the boiling point of aluminium is different from that of magnesium.

b Explain why the pattern in the figure is described as being **periodic**.

2 In the Periodic Table there are trends in physical properties of the elements across periods and down groups. Describe and explain:
   a the trend in electrical conductivity for Period 3;
   b the trend in atomic radii down Group II.

3 The Periodic Table is divided into blocks labelled s, p, d and f.
   a Give the full electron configurations of:
      (i) calcium;
      (ii) silicon;
      (iii) selenium;
      (iv) nickel.
   b Give the Periodic Table block in which each of the elements in a may be found.
   c Explain, in terms of electronic configurations, what the elements in the p-block have in common.

CHAPTER 5

The Group II elements and their compounds

By the end of this chapter you should be able to:

1 describe and explain the trends in electronic configurations, atomic radii and ionisation energies of the Group II elements (Mg to Ba);

2 use the rules for assigning oxidation state with elements, compounds and ions;

3 interpret and make predictions from the chemical and physical properties of the Group II elements and their compounds;

4 show awareness of the importance and use of Group II elements and their compounds, with appropriate chemical explanations;

5 describe oxidation and reduction in terms of electron transfer and changes in oxidation state;

6 describe the redox reactions of the elements Mg to Ba with oxygen and water and explain the trend in reactivity in terms of ionisation energies;

7 describe the reactions of Mg, MgO and $MgCO_3$ with hydrochloric acid;

8 describe the thermal decomposition of $CaCO_3$ to form CaO (lime) and the subsequent formation of $Ca(OH)_2$ (slaked lime) with water;

9 describe lime water as an aqueous solution of $Ca(OH)_2$ and state its approximate pH;

10 describe the reaction of lime water with carbon dioxide forming $CaCO_3(s)$, and with excess carbon dioxide, forming $Ca(HCO_3)_2(aq)$, as in hard water.

Introduction

The elements of Group II are often called the **alkaline earth metals**. They are:

beryllium	Be	$[He]2s^2$
magnesium	Mg	$[Ne]3s^2$
calcium	Ca	$[Ar]4s^2$
strontium	Sr	$[Kr]5s^2$
barium	Ba	$[Xe]6s^2$
radium	Ra	$[Rn]7s^2$

Beryllium is markedly different from the other members of the Group, and so we shall not consider it here. We also shall not consider radium (the element discovered and isolated by Marie Curie – *box 5A*), as all its isotopes are radioactive.

The alkaline earth metals from magnesium to barium are white metals, with low melting and boiling points compared to transition metals like iron. They are good conductors of heat and electricity. The white colour is an oxide film – the metals themselves are shiny but react quickly with air, and the oxide film prevents further reaction. These metals burn in air with characteristic flame colours – magnesium white, calcium brick red, strontium red and barium green. Their physical properties are listed in *table 5.1*.

Marie Curie, *née* Marja Skłodowska, was born in Poland in 1867. Her first job was as a governess, which she took to pay for her sister's medical training in France. After her sister qualified Marie also went to Paris to study at the Sorbonne, where she obtained the highest marks in physics. She also met and married Pierre Curie, who was a research scientist.

Marie Curie suspected that in the uranium ore called pitchblende there was another radioactive substance as well as uranium. She treated tonnes of pitchblende and eventually isolated a small quantity of radium chloride – radium was unknown before this. Pierre Curie helped her in this work, which was remarkable in its detective work, as 10 tonnes of pitchblende contain about 1g of radium. The Curies were awarded the Nobel Prize in 1903 (along with Becquerel, who discovered radioactivity in 1896) for this work.

In 1906 Pierre, by then Professor of Physics at the Sorbonne, was killed by a horse-drawn carriage and Marie took over his post. She was the first woman to hold this position. In 1911 she was awarded a second Nobel Prize for her discovery of radium and polonium (which she named after Poland). The Curies' daughter Irene, with her husband Frederic Joliot, was also awarded a Nobel Prize for chemistry in 1935.

● **Figure 5.1** Marie Curie.

The metals of Group II all have two electrons in their outer s subshell, and these are lost when the metal reacts. This means that they always form an ion of oxidation number +2 in their compounds, such as Mg^{2+} and Ca^{2+}. It also means that they are less reactive than Group I metals, because they have to lose two outer-shell electrons, whereas Group I metals lose only one.

SAQ 5.1

a Using *table 5.1*, describe, for magnesium to barium, the trend in: (i) their metallic radii and (ii) their first ionisation energies.

b Explain the trends that you have described in **a**.

c Predict and explain the trend in electronegativity of the Group II elements.

General properties of the Group II elements

The general properties of the Group II elements magnesium to barium are as follows:

- They are all metals.
- They are good conductors of heat and electricity.
- Their compounds are all white or colourless.
- In all their compounds they have an oxidation number +2.
- Their compounds are ionic.
- They are called alkaline earth metals because their oxides and hydroxides are basic.
- They react with acids to give hydrogen.

Compared with the metals of Group I:

- They are harder and denser.

	Mg	Ca	Sr	Ba
Atomic number	12	20	38	56
Metallic radius (nm)	0.160	0.197	0.215	0.224
Ionic radius (nm)	0.072	0.100	0.113	0.136
First ionisation energy (kJ mol⁻¹)	738	590	550	503
Second ionisation energy (kJ mol⁻¹)	1451	1145	1064	965
Third ionisation energy (kJ mol⁻¹)	7733	4912	4210	
Melting point (°C)	649	839	769	725
Boiling point (°C)	1107	1484	1384	1640

● **Table 5.1** Physical properties of Group II elements.

- They have higher melting points.
- They exhibit stronger metallic bonding (because they have two outer-shell electrons instead of one).

Uses

The elements of Group II and their compounds are widely used in commerce and industry.

Magnesium burns with a bright white light, and is used in flares, incendiary bombs and tracer bullets. It was once used in photographic flash bulbs.

Magnesium has such a strong reducing power that it is widely used to protect steel objects such as ships, outboard motors and bridges from corrosion. Its strong reducing power also means that it can be used to extract less electropositive (the ease with which elements lose electrons) metals such as titanium in the Kroll process, which takes place at 1250 K under an argon atmosphere:

$$2Mg(s) + TiCl_4(g) \longrightarrow Ti(s) + 2MgCl_2(l)$$

Magnesium is also found in chlorophyll, the substance in plants which performs photosynthesis.

Magnesium hydroxide is a weak alkali and is used in indigestion remedies and in toothpastes, where it helps to neutralise acids in the mouth which encourage tooth decay. Representing acid as $H^+(aq)$, the following reaction occurs:

$$Mg(OH)_2(s) + 2H^+(aq) \longrightarrow Mg^{2+}(aq) + 2H_2O(l)$$

Magnesium oxide is a refractory material, which means that it is resistant to heat (its melting point is over 3000 K). Its main use is for the lining of furnaces.

Magnesium fluoride is used to coat the surface of camera lenses, to reduce the amount of reflected light. It is responsible for the violet colour on the surface of the lens.

Calcium carbonate is an important compound as it is used in making cement – see *box 5B*.

Lime or *quicklime*, which is *calcium oxide*, was used in cement, mortar (*figure 5.2*) and plaster manufacture. It still has a very important role in purifying iron, as it reacts with impurities in the ore to form a molten slag:

$$\underset{\substack{\text{basic} \\ \text{oxide}}}{CaO(s)} + \underset{\substack{\text{acidic} \\ \text{oxide}}}{SiO_2(s)} \longrightarrow CaSiO_3(l)$$

Box 5B Cement

Calcium carbonate occurs in vast quantities in sedimentary rocks, such as limestone, chalk and dolomite. Marble is also a form of calcium carbonate, in which the marbling effect is caused by the presence of iron oxides. However, the largest use of calcium carbonate is in the manufacture of cement.

Cement is made by heating a finely ground mixture of limestone with clay (aluminosilicate) at 1750 K in a rotary kiln. This process results in clinker, which is reground and mixed with about 3% gypsum (calcium sulphate). This is a complex process, and the final formula of cement can be regarded as

$$2Ca_3SiO_5 + Ca_3Al_2O_6$$

The setting of cement is also a complex process – the cement reacts with water and carbon dioxide from the air.

The annual production of cement worldwide is about 1 billion tonnes.

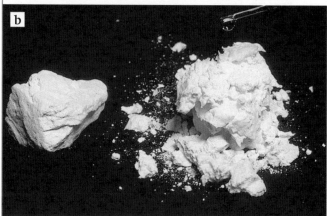

● **Figure 5.2**
a Calcium oxide was used in lime mortar before the introduction of cement mortar.
b Addition of water to dry calcium oxide causes the solid to crumble, in an exothermic reaction producing calcium hydroxide.

Calcium oxide is the origin of the theatrical term 'limelight', because it glows with a bright white light when strongly heated and was originally used in stage lighting.

Solid calcium hydroxide is also used on acidic soil, to reduce the acidity of the soil. This increases crop yields. Representing acid as $H^+(aq)$, the following reaction occurs:

$$Ca(OH)_2(s) + 2H^+(aq) \longrightarrow Ca^{2+}(aq) + 2H_2O(l)$$

Compare this reaction to that of magnesium hydroxide in indigestion remedies, above.

Lime mortar, which is prepared by mixing sand and calcium oxide with water, was widely used in bricklaying until the beginning of the 20th century.

Plaster of Paris, used to set broken bones and for modelling, is an insoluble form of *calcium sulphate*, $2CaSO_4.H_2O$. When it is mixed with water, it hydrates to $CaSO_4.2H_2O$ and sets hard.

The *hydrogencarbonates of calcium and magnesium* are responsible for the hardness of water – the metal ions are originally picked up when rain-water trickles over limestone and other similar rocks.

Barium sulphate is insoluble and, in suspension, is given to patients as a 'barium meal'. The barium ions coat the walls of the stomach and digestive tract and, as they are opaque to X-rays, they make any imperfections visible by X-ray photography. Soluble barium compounds are toxic, but barium sulphate is safe to use because its solubility is so low – for this reason, the presence of a barium sulphate precipitate is also used as a laboratory test for the sulphate ion.

Strontium has few uses. However, the isotope $^{90}_{38}Sr$ has been well studied, as it is produced in many nuclear reactions.

Names of calcium compounds

Several calcium compounds have common names based on the word 'lime', derived from limestone, which is one of the most widespread types of rock:

limestone	calcium carbonate	$CaCO_3$
quicklime	calcium oxide	CaO
slaked lime	solid calcium hydroxide	$Ca(OH)_2(s)$
lime water	a solution of calcium hydroxide (only sparingly soluble)	$Ca(OH)_2(aq)$

Reactions of Group II elements

These elements are powerful reducing agents. Before we study their reactions in detail we shall look at ways of describing oxidation and reduction.

Oxidation states

When you look at the formulae of many compounds you see that there are differences in the ratios of the atoms that combine with each other – MgO and Al_2O_3, for example. Chemists have devised various ways for comparing the 'combining ability' of individual elements. One term, much used in the past, but less so nowadays, is **valency** meaning 'strength'. The more useful measure is **oxidation state**. This is a numerical value associated with atoms of each element in a compound or ion. Some chemists prefer the term **oxidation number** (abbreviated ox. no.). The only difference between this and oxidation state is that we say an atom '*has* an oxidation number of +2' but '*is in* an oxidation state of +2'.

There are rules for determining the values of oxidation states.

- Oxidation states are usually calculated as the number of electrons that atoms lose, gain or share when they form ionic or covalent bonds in compounds.

- The oxidation state of uncombined elements (that is, not in compounds) is always zero. For example, each atom in $H_2(g)$ or $O_2(g)$ or $Na(s)$ or $S_8(s)$ has an oxidation state of zero; otherwise, in a compound the numbers are always given a sign, + or −.

- For a monatomic ion, the oxidation state of the element is simply the same as the charge on the ion. For example:

ion	Na^+	Ca^{2+}	Cl^-	O^{2-}
ox. state	+1	+2	−1	−2

- In a chemical species (compound or ion), with atoms of more than one element, the most electronegative element is given the negative oxidation state. Other elements are given positive oxidation states. (For an explanation of the term 'electronegative', see page 38.) For example, in the compound disulphur dichloride, S_2Cl_2, chlorine is more electronegative than sulphur. The two chlorine atoms each have an oxidation state of −1, and thus the two sulphur atoms each have an oxidation state of +1.

- The oxidation state of hydrogen in compounds is +1, except in metal hydrides (e.g. NaH), when it is −1.
- The oxidation state of oxygen in compounds is −2, except in peroxides (e.g. H_2O_2), when it is −1, or in OF_2, when it is +2.
- The sum of all the oxidation states in a neutral compound is zero. In an ion, the sum equals the overall charge. For example, the sum of the oxidation states in $CaCl_2$ is 0; the sum of the oxidation states in OH^- is −1.

Some examples of determining oxidation states will now be shown:

In CO_2 the ox. state of each O atom is −2, giving a total of −4
CO_2 is neutral
the ox. state of C is +4

In $MgCl_2$ the ox. state of Mg is +2
the ox. state of each Cl is −1

In NO_3^- the ox. state of each O is −2
total for O_3 is −6
the overall charge on the ion is −1
therefore ox. state of N in NO_3^- is +5

SAQ 5.2

What is the oxidation state of: C in CO_3^{2-}; Al in Al_2Cl_6?

Redox: oxidation and reduction

The term **redox** is used for the simultaneous processes of *red*uction and *ox*idation. Originally oxidation and reduction were related only to reactions of oxygen and hydrogen. They now include any reactions in which electrons are transferred.

For example, consider what happens when iron reacts with oxygen and with chlorine.

(i) with oxygen:
$$4Fe(s) + 3O_2(g) \longrightarrow 2Fe_2O_3(s)$$
(ii) with chlorine:
$$2Fe(s) + 3Cl_2(g) \longrightarrow 2FeCl_3(s)$$

In both of these reactions, each iron atom has lost three electrons and changed oxidation state from 0 in Fe(s) to +3 in $Fe_2O_3(s)$ and $FeCl_3(s)$.

$$Fe \longrightarrow Fe^{3+} + 3e^-$$

ox. state   0   +3

This is **oxidation**. In all oxidation reactions, atoms of an element in a chemical species lose electrons and increase their oxidation states.

In reaction (i) above, the oxygen atoms each gain two electrons and change oxidation state from 0 in $O_2(g)$ to −2 in $Fe_2O_3(s)$.

$$O_2 + 4e^- \longrightarrow 2O^{2-}$$

ox. state of atoms   0   −2

Similarly, in reaction (ii), chlorine atoms each gain one electron and change oxidation state from 0 to −1.

$$Cl_2 + 2e^- \longrightarrow 2Cl^-$$

ox. state of atoms   0   −1

These are processes of **reduction**. In all reduction reactions, atoms of an element in a chemical species gain electrons and decrease their oxidation states.

We call reactions, such as (i) and (ii) above, redox reactions, as both oxidation and reduction take place at the same time. Any chemical system in which the oxidised and reduced forms of a chemical species exist is a **redox system**. The chemical that *gains* electrons acts as an **oxidising agent**; the chemical that *loses* electrons acts as a reducing agent.

The reactions of the Group II metals with water

All the Group II metals from magnesium to barium reduce water to hydrogen. **Magnesium** reacts very slowly with cold water. A little hydrogen and magnesium hydroxide are formed over a few days.

$$Mg(s) + 2H_2O(l) \longrightarrow Mg(OH)_2(s) + H_2(g)$$

The aqueous solution is weakly alkaline as magnesium hydroxide is very sparingly soluble. When water, as steam, is passed over heated magnesium, there is a rapid reaction (*figure 5.3a*). Hydrogen is released and magnesium oxide remains.

$$Mg(s) + H_2O(g) \longrightarrow MgO(s) + H_2(g)$$

The reactivity of the elements with water increases down the Group from magnesium to barium (*figure 5.3b*). Unlike magnesium, the metals calcium to barium all react readily with cold water to form a cloudy white precipitate of the hydroxide (which is sparingly soluble). During the

● Figure 5.3

a Apparatus to show the reaction of magnesium with steam. The steam is generated by heating material soaked in water at the left-hand end of the test-tube.

b Barium reacts readily with cold water, producing a rapid stream of bubbles of hydrogen.

reaction with water, the metal atoms lose electrons which are transferred to hydrogen atoms in water molecules. For example:

$$Ca(s) + 2H_2O(l) \rightarrow Ca(OH)_2(s) + H_2(g)$$

Ox. states	Ca: 0	H: +1	Ca: +2	H: 0
		O: −2	O: −2	
			H: +1	

In this example, each calcium atom loses two electrons and changes oxidation state from 0 in $Ca(s)$ to +2 in $Ca(OH)_2(s)$. This is oxidation.

Meanwhile, two hydrogen atoms gain one electron each and change oxidation state from +1 in $H_2O(l)$ to 0 in $H_2(g)$. This is reduction. Notice that two water molecules are required for each calcium atom. Only one of the two hydrogen atoms in a water molecule is reduced, the oxidation state of the second hydrogen atom is unchanged at +1 in $Ca(OH)_2(s)$.

Two electrons are lost from each metal atom in the reaction. Down the Group, the first two ionisation energies decrease from magnesium to barium. Consequently, the reactivity of the metals increase down the Group as less energy is required to remove the two electrons. A similar trend in reactivity is found when the Group II metals react with oxygen.

The reactions of the Group II metals with oxygen

The reactions of these metals with oxygen, once started, are vigorous.

Magnesium metal is normally covered with a layer of its oxide. It burns rapidly in air or oxygen with a brilliant whitish flame (*figure 5.4*). This reaction is much used in fireworks and warning flares. White, crystalline magnesium oxide is formed.

$$2Mg(s) + O_2(g) \longrightarrow 2MgO(s)$$

SAQ 5.3

Some magnesium ribbon (0.2 g) was heated in a crucible until it began to burn. When the burning finished, a white powder remained in the crucible. What is this white powder? Calculate the mass of powder you would expect to find.

● Figure 5.4 Magnesium ribbon burning in air. The reaction was used in the first photographic flash, and is still used in fireworks and flares.

SAQ 5.4

a Write an equation, including state symbols, for the burning of strontium in oxygen.

b Describe what you might observe during this reaction.

c Identify the element which is oxidised and the element which is reduced. Explain your answer in terms of electron transfer and oxidation states.

d Explain the increasing reactivity of the Group II metals.

Formation of salts with hydrochloric acid

The salts of Group II elements are all white, crystalline compounds. They are easily prepared by reaction of the metal, metal oxide or metal carbonate with an acid. For example, magnesium, magnesium oxide or magnesium carbonate all dissolve in hydrochloric acid to form colourless solutions containing aqueous magnesium chloride, $MgCl_2(aq)$. This salt may be obtained as a white crystalline compound by partial evaporation of the solution to the point where a good crop of crystals form on cooling. The crystals may be separated by filtration and dried in air (*figure 5.5*).

■ Reaction of magnesium with hydrochloric acid:
Magnesium ribbon dissolves rapidly in cold dilute hydrochloric acid with rapid evolution of hydrogen gas:
$$Mg(s) + 2HCl(aq) \rightarrow MgCl_2(aq) + H_2(g)$$

■ Reaction of magnesium oxide with hydrochloric acid:
Magnesium oxide dissolves slowly in cold dilute hydrochloric acid. The reaction proceeds more rapidly on warming:
$$MgO(s) + 2HCl(aq) \rightarrow MgCl_2(aq) + H_2O(l)$$

■ Reaction of magnesium carbonate with hydrochloric acid:
Magnesium carbonate dissolves rapidly in cold dilute hydrochloric acid with the evolution of carbon dioxide:
$$MgCO_3(s) + 2HCl(aq) \rightarrow MgCl_2(aq) + H_2O(l) + CO_2(g)$$

SAQ 5.5

a Predict what you might observe when calcium carbonate is added to dilute hydrochloric acid. Write a balanced equation, including state symbols, for any reaction that you have predicted.

b Explain why calcium hydroxide might be added to acidic soil.

c Magnesium hydroxide is used in antacid tablets. They relieve excessive acidity in the stomach by neutralising some of the hydrochloric acid present. Write a balanced equation, including state symbols, for the reaction of magnesium hydroxide with hydrochloric acid.

Chalk and lime chemistry

The white cliffs of Dover are composed of chalk. The cliffs are the sedimentary remains of marine invertebrates. Chemically, they are composed of calcium carbonate, $CaCO_3$. Limestone is a similar sedimentary deposit which also contains calcium carbonate (*figure 5.6*). Limestone and chalk are used in large quantities to manufacture quicklime (calcium oxide) and cement.

● **Figure 5.5** Magnesium chloride crystals after they have been separated from solution and dried in air.

● **Figure 5.6** These limestone cliffs are sedimentary deposits that contain calcium carbonate.

Strong heating of calcium carbonate produces calcium oxide, CaO, and carbon dioxide.

$$CaCO_3(s) \rightarrow CaO(s) + CO_2(g)$$

This type of reaction, where a compound is broken down by heat, is known as a **thermal decomposition** (see also page 147).

Traditionally, chalk or limestone were heated in a lime kiln using fuels such as wood or coal (*figure 5.7*).

Calcium oxide reacts vigorously with water (see page 66) to produce calcium hydroxide, Ca(OH)$_2$ (slaked lime).

$$CaO(s) + H_2O(l) \rightarrow Ca(OH)_2(s)$$

The name 'quicklime' for CaO derives from the vigour of this reaction. Here, 'quick' is used in the sense of 'alive'. During the Black Death, corpses were buried under a layer of quicklime. The quicklime reacted with moisture from the corpses, helping to control the spread of disease. In more recent times, quicklime has also been used in this way, for example following the tragic earthquake in Turkey in 1999.

Further addition of water to calcium hydroxide produces the saturated aqueous solution that we call 'lime water'. Calcium hydroxide is only slightly soluble in water, the saturated solution has a concentration of approximately $1.5 \times 10^{-2}\,mol\,dm^{-3}$. Chemists often describe compounds which are slightly soluble as being 'sparingly soluble'. As the concentration of calcium hydroxide in lime water is low, the solution has a low concentration of hydroxide ion, OH^-. The pH of lime water is about 9–10.

You will probably be familiar with lime water as the reagent used to identify carbon dioxide gas.

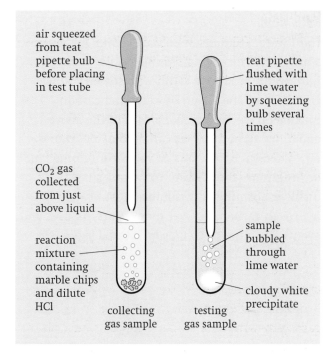

air squeezed from teat pipette bulb before placing in test tube

teat pipette flushed with lime water by squeezing bulb several times

CO_2 gas collected from just above liquid

sample bubbled through lime water

reaction mixture containing marble chips and dilute HCl

cloudy white precipitate

collecting gas sample

testing gas sample

● **Figure 5.8** The lime water test for carbon dioxide.

When a sample of carbon dioxide is bubbled through lime water, a cloudy white precipitate forms. The precipitate is solid calcium carbonate.

$$Ca(OH)_2(aq) + CO_2(g) \rightarrow CaCO_3(s) + H_2O(l)$$

Figure 5.8 shows a straightforward method for performing the lime water test for carbon dioxide.

If we continue to bubble carbon dioxide through lime water after the white precipitate has formed, eventually the mixture turns clear again. The white precipitate of calcium carbonate reacts with water and aqueous carbon dioxide to form a solution of aqueous calcium hydrogen carbonate, Ca(HCO$_3$)$_2$(aq).

$$CaCO_3(s) + H_2O(l) + CO_2(aq) \rightarrow Ca(HCO_3)_2(aq)$$

● **Figure 5.7** Old lime kilns near Agrigento in Sicily.

Precipitates and suspensions

These words have different meanings, although each is used to describe a mixture of a solid with a solvent such as water. A precipitate of calcium carbonate will look very similar to a suspension of calcium carbonate. The difference lies in the way each has been formed. A **suspension** is formed when a finely powdered insoluble solid is shaken with water. A **precipitate** forms following reaction between two soluble compounds.

Hard water

Hard water contains dissolved calcium (or magnesium) ions. The calcium (or magnesium) ions in hard water produce a scum with soap. Hard water is formed by the action of water and carbon dioxide on calcium carbonate (as in the above equation). Rain dissolves carbon dioxide from the air. When such rain falls on rocks containing chalk or limestone, the calcium carbonate slowly dissolves forming very dilute aqueous calcium hydrogen carbonate. Over many years, fissures and eventually large caves may be created (*figure 5.9*).

● **Figure 5.9** The limestone hillside has slowly been eroded by the acidity of rain-water.

SUMMARY

◆ The Group II elements magnesium to barium are typical metals with high melting points and good conductivity of heat and electricity;

◆ Progressing down Group II from magnesium to barium, the atomic radius increases. This is due to the addition of an extra shell of electrons for each element as the Group is descended.

◆ Many of the compounds of Group II elements are commercially important. For example, slaked lime (calcium hydroxide) is used to neutralise acid soil. Magnesium hydroxide is used in antacid tablets to neutralise excess acid in the stomach.

◆ Reactivity of the elements with oxygen or water increases down Group II as the first and second ionisation energies decrease.

◆ The reactions of Group II elements are redox reactions. The elements are powerful reducing agents. Redox reactions may be explained in terms of electron transfer (oxidation is loss of electrons, reduction is gain of electrons) or change of oxidation states (oxidation increases oxidation state; reduction decreases oxidation state).

◆ The Group II elements magnesium to barium react with water to produce hydrogen gas and the sparingly soluble metal hydroxide. As the hydroxide solutions have a pH of 8 or higher, they are called the alkaline earth elements.

◆ The Group II elements magnesium to barium burn in air with characteristic flame colours to form the oxide as a white solid. Flame colours are magnesium white; calcium brick red; strontium red; barium green.

◆ Salts of these metals are readily prepared by reaction of the metal, metal oxide or metal carbonate with an acid. For example, dilute hydrochloric acid reacts with magnesium metal, magnesium oxide or magnesium carbonate to produce magnesium chloride.

◆ Calcium carbonate (as chalk or limestone) may be decomposed by heat to form calcium oxide (quicklime) which reacts violently with water to form calcium hydroxide (slaked lime). Calcium hydroxide is sparingly soluble in water forming lime water.

◆ Lime water produces a milky precipitate with carbon dioxide. This precipitate is calcium carbonate, which will dissolve in excess carbon dioxide to form calcium hydrogencarbonate. It is this reaction which is responsible for the formation of hard water.

Questions

1 The Group II metals magnesium to barium and their compounds are widely used.
   a (i) State the trend in the reactivity of these metals with water.
   (ii) Write an equation for the reaction of one of these metals with water.
   b Suggest one use for each of the following:
   (i) magnesium oxide;
   (ii) calcium hydroxide.

2 Water was gradually added to a Group II metal oxide and a white solid X was formed. X is slightly soluble in water and is used in agriculture.
   a Identify X.
   b Predict the pH of a solution of X in water.
   c Explain why X is used in agriculture.

3 Chalk and limestone provide important sources of calcium carbonate. Calcium carbonate is used to make lime (calcium oxide, CaO) from which hydrated lime (calcium hydroxide, $Ca(OH)_2$) is made. Write balanced equations, including state symbols, for:

   a the conversion of calcium carbonate to calcium oxide;
   b the formation of calcium hydroxide from calcium oxide.

4 The Group II elements all burn fiercely in oxygen.
   a (i) Describe the trend in reactivity down Group II when the elements burn in oxygen.
   (ii) Explain the observed trend in reactivity in terms of ionisation energies.
   b (i) Write a balanced equation for the reaction when magnesium burns in oxygen.
   (ii) Using your equation from (i) and oxidation states, identify the oxidation state changes which take place in this reaction. Identify which element is oxidised and which is reduced. Give your reasons.

CHAPTER 6

The Group VII elements and their compounds

By the end of this chapter you should be able to:

1 explain the trend in the volatilities of chlorine, bromine and iodine in terms of van der Waals' forces;

2 describe the relative reactivity of the elements Cl_2, Br_2 and I_2 in displacement reactions and explain this trend in terms of oxidising power, i.e. the relative ease with which an electron can be captured;

3 describe the characteristic reactions of the ions Cl^-, Br^- and I^- with aqueous silver ions followed by aqueous ammonia (knowledge of complex formulae not required);

4 describe and interpret, in terms of changes in oxidation state, the reaction of chlorine with cold, dilute aqueous sodium hydroxide to form bleach, and the use of chlorine in water purification.

Introduction

The elements of Group VII are called the **halogens**:

fluorine	F	$[He]2s^2\,2p^5$
chlorine	Cl	$[Ne]3s^2\,3p^5$
bromine	Br	$[Ar]3d^{10}\,4s^2\,4p^5$
iodine	I	$[Kr]4d^{10}\,5s^2\,5p^5$
astatine	At	$[Xe]4f^{14}\,5d^{10}\,6s^2\,6p^5$

All the isotopes of astatine are radioactive and so this element will not be considered here. Also, we shall not include fluorine in *all* the discussions on Group VII, because its small size and high electronegativity give it some anomalous properties.

The name 'halogen' is derived from the Greek and means 'salt producing'. It was first used at the beginning of the nineteenth century because chlorine, bromine and iodine are all found in the sea as salts. Nowadays we still use the term, because the halogens are very reactive and readily react with metals to form salts.

The halogens are a family of non-metallic elements with some very similar chemical properties, although there are also clear differences between each element. Their reactivity decreases going down the Group. Their chemical characteristics are caused by the outermost seven electrons – two electrons in the s subshell and five electrons in the p subshell. Therefore only one more electron is needed to complete the outer shell of electrons. As a result the most common oxidation state for the halogens is –1, although other oxidation states do exist, especially for chlorine, which exhibits a range of oxidation states from –1 to +7. In compounds a halogen atom increases its share of electrons from seven to eight (a full outer shell) by either (a) gaining an electron to form a halide (Cl^-, Br^-, I^-) in ionic compounds, or (b) sharing an electron from another atom in a covalent compound.

The halogen elements form **covalent diatomic molecules**. The atoms are joined by a single covalent bond (*figure 6.1*).

Fluorine, chlorine and bromine are poisonous. Their melting and boiling points increase with increasing atomic number: fluorine and chlorine

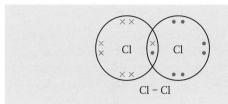

● **Figure 6.1** A dot-and-cross diagram of the covalent bonding in chlorine gas, $Cl_2(g)$.

are gases at room temperature; bromine is a liquid; and iodine is a solid. This decrease in volatility is the result of increasingly strong van der Waals' forces as the number of electrons present in a molecule increases. Halogens form diatomic non-polar molecules, so only instantaneous dipole-induced dipole attractions (see page 43) are present between molecules.

The colour of the elements deepens with increasing atomic number: fluorine is a pale yellow gas; chlorine is a greenish yellow gas; bromine is a dark red liquid giving off a dense red vapour; iodine is a shiny, grey-black crystalline solid which **sublimes** (changes directly from a solid to a gas) to a purple vapour.

The halogens are all oxidising agents, and fluorine is the strongest. The oxidising ability is reflected by the reactivity – fluorine is the most reactive halogen. It is also reflected by the electronegativities – fluorine is the most electronegative element, chlorine the third. Look at *table 6.1* for a summary of the physical properties.

SAQ 6.1

What is the oxidation number of chlorine in Cl_2, $CaCl_2$, Cl_2O_7 and ClO_2?

General properties of the Group VII elements

The general properties of the Group VII elements chlorine, bromine and iodine are as follows:

- They behave chemically in a similar way.
- They are non-metals.
- They all exist as diatomic molecules at room temperature.
- Their melting and boiling points increase with increasing atomic number.
- The colour of the elements deepens with increasing atomic number.
- They are very reactive and readily form salts.
- In compounds a halogen atom increases its share of electrons from seven to eight by ionic or covalent bonding.
- The reactivity of the elements decreases on descending the Group.
- They exhibit a range of oxidation states.
- The electronegativity of the elements decreases on descending the Group.
- Their oxidising ability decreases on descending the Group.

SAQ 6.2

Draw dot-and-cross diagrams of NaCl, showing the ionic bond; and of HCl, showing the covalent bond.

Uses

The commercial and industrial uses of the halogens and their compounds are now outlined.

Chlorine is used in vast quantities for many different processes – twenty-nine million tonnes of chlorine are used worldwide annually. Its main uses are in water purification, as a bleach and in the manufacture of various chemicals such as chloroethene, which is used to make PVC.

One of the classes of organic chemicals made using chlorine is CFCs (*chlorofluorocarbons*). CFCs have been used as aerosol propellants, refrigerants and as foaming agents in polymers. They are currently being

	F	**Cl**	**Br**	**I**
Atomic radius (nm)	0.071	0.099	0.114	0.133
Ionic radius (nm)	0.133	0.180	0.195	0.215
Electronegativity	4.0	3.0	2.8	2.5
Electron affinity (kJ mol^{-1})	−328	−349	−325	−295
Melting point (°C)	−220	−101	−7	114
Boiling point (°C)	−188	−35	59	184

● **Table 6.1** Physical properties of Group VII elements. (The electron affinity is the enthalpy change for the process $X(g) + e^- \longrightarrow X^-(g)$, where X is the halogen.)

withdrawn from many applications because they are pollutants which contribute to the destruction of the ozone layer. However, they are useful in at least two ways – they are used in fire extinguishers because they are inert and non-flammable, and they are vital constituents of artificial blood.

Solvents containing chlorine, such as *di-chloromethane*, CH_2Cl_2, are widely used to dissolve fats and oils.

Chlorine is a good germicide, and is used to kill bacteria in drinking water and swimming pools. Some environmental campaigners are trying to have chlorine banned due to worries over traces of organo-chlorine compounds in water. The danger of this was demonstrated when Peru banned its use in drinking water in 1993. Over a million Peruvians contracted cholera, with 10 000 deaths.

Chlorine and some of its compounds are used as domestic and commercial bleaches. In the First World War chlorine and mustard gas ($ClCH_2CH_2SCH_2CH_2Cl$) were used with devastating effect as poison gases. Chlorine is produced by the electrolysis of brine (see page 32).

Fluorine is used, like chlorine, in CFCs. It is also used to make PTFE (polytetrafluoroethene), which is used as a lubricant, as a coating for non-stick cooking pans, as electrical insulation and in waterproof clothing.

Fluoride ions help to prevent tooth decay. Some children are given fluoride tablets (*box 6A*); many toothpastes contain tin fluoride (SnF_2); and some water supplies are fluoridated with sodium fluoride.

Hydrofluoric acid (HF) is used to etch glass.

Bromochlorodifluoromethane ($CClBrF_2$) is used in fire extinguishers.

Silver bromide is used in photographic film.

Iodine is an essential part of our diet, and an imbalance can cause thyroid problems.

A solution of *iodine in alcohol* is sometimes used as an antiseptic.

The reactivity of the halogens: displacement reactions

The electron affinity of the halogens is shown in *table 6.1*. The more negative the electron affinity,

Box 6A The fluoride controversy

Automatic fluoridation of the water we drink has caused some controversy. Many people feel that it is a good thing, as it is one of the factors linked to a reduction in the number of fillings in children's teeth. However, too much fluoride discolours teeth permanently, and can cause liver damage. So some people feel that water supplies should not be fluoridated, but that the freedom to choose to take fluoride supplements or not should be left to the individual (*figure 6.2*).

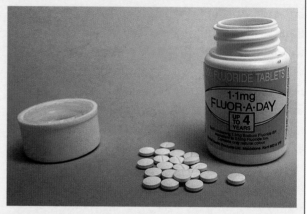

● **Figure 6.2** Fluoride tablets may be taken if drinking water is not fluoridated, to improve dental health.

the greater the ease with which a halogen can capture an electron and the greater the oxidising power of the halogen. Electron affinity becomes less negative from chlorine to iodine so oxidising power of the elements decreases down Group VII.

In most of their oxidising reactions the halogens react as X_2 molecules (X represents a halogen) and form hydrated halide ions, $X^-(aq)$. As the oxidising ability decreases from chlorine to iodine, any halogen can displace another lower in the Group. This means that, if each halogen is reacted with a halide ion in aqueous solution, a series of displacement reactions occurs.

■ Chlorine displaces bromine and iodine:
$$Cl_2(aq) + 2Br^-(aq) \longrightarrow 2Cl^-(aq) + Br_2(aq)$$
$$Cl_2(aq) + 2I^-(aq) \longrightarrow 2Cl^-(aq) + I_2(aq)$$

■ Bromine displaces iodine:
$$Br_2(aq) + 2I^-(aq) \longrightarrow 2Br^-(aq) + I_2(aq)$$

■ Iodine does not displace either chlorine or bromine.

One of the problems with doing these displacement reactions is being able to see if a reaction has taken place – the halide ion solutions are all colourless and very dilute solutions of the halogens can also appear colourless. To avoid this problem, an organic solvent such as cyclohexane is added to the mixture, which forms a separate layer. The halogens are more soluble in organic solvents than in aqueous solution, so they are taken up by the cyclohexane and the colour is much more apparent (*figure 6.3*). For instance, bromine is a strong orange-yellow colour in cyclohexane, and iodine is purple. So if aqueous bromine is mixed with cyclohexane, the bromine dissolves in the cyclohexane, which turns orange. Then if aqueous potassium iodide is added, the cyclohexane turns purple, which shows us that bromine has become bromide ion and displaced iodine from solution (*table 6.2*).

SAQ 6.3

From your knowledge of the structure and bonding of the halogens, explain why they are more soluble in organic solvents than in aqueous solution.

SAQ 6.4

Bromine water (aqueous bromine, Br_2) was shaken with a small volume of cyclohexane, and then the following aqueous solutions were added to separate portions:

a aqueous sodium iodide,
b aqueous chlorine,
c aqueous sodium astatide, NaAt.

Each mixture was shaken again. Describe what you would expect to see. Write equations for any reactions that would occur.

The oxidising ability of the halogens means that they are useful in many ways. Chlorine and its aqueous solution, known as chlorine water, are often used as oxidising agents (chlorine water contains chlorine and chloric(I) acid, HClO). Chlorine is also used in industry as a bleach; it oxidises

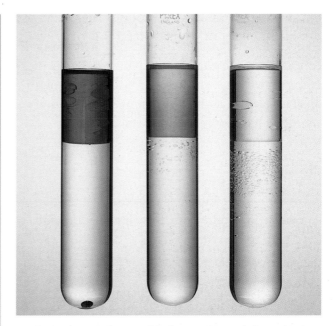

● **Figure 6.3** Colours of halogens in cyclohexane (upper layer) and water (lower layer).

large organic molecules to colourless compounds. In recent years controversy has arisen over the use of chlorine for bleaching paper – although very white paper pulp can be produced, the process results in the formation of dioxins, which are poisonous and can accumulate in living organisms, as dioxins do not break down easily. Nowadays ozone is often used to bleach paper that does not have to be pure white, such as tissues, nappies and toilet paper.

The strong oxidising ability of chlorine is also used by the water industry to treat drinking water. Chlorine is added to water from reservoirs to kill any bacteria, and small amounts of chlorine remain in the water piped to consumers to prevent bacterial contamination. Chlorine is also used to keep water in swimming pools free from contamination.

Fluorine is rarely used as an oxidising reagent as it is difficult to handle.

| Halogen | Halide ion | | |
	Chloride, Cl^-	Bromide, Br^-	Iodide, I^-
Chlorine, Cl_2		orange-yellow bromine released	purple iodine released
Bromine, Br_2	no reaction		purple iodine released
Iodine, I_2	no reaction	no reaction	

● **Table 6.2** Displacement reactions of halogens in aqueous solution (the colours refer to the colours of the halogens in cyclohexane, see *figure 6.3*).

Which halide?

Halides (ions of Group VII elements) are extremely common, so a test to identify which halide is present is very useful. This test is based on the colour of silver halides and the different solubilities of the silver halides in ammonia solution.

- Acidify the unknown halide solution with dilute nitric acid.
- Add aqueous silver nitrate
  caution: silver nitrate is poisonous
  a white precipitate of silver chloride forms if $Cl^-(aq)$ is present
  a cream precipitate of silver bromide forms if $Br^-(aq)$ is present
  a yellow precipitate of silver iodide forms if $I^-(aq)$ is present
- Identification by colour is not completely reliable, so aqueous ammonia is added:
  white silver chloride dissolves in dilute aqueous ammonia forming a colourless solution; cream silver bromide dissolves in concentrated aqueous ammonia forming a colourless solution; yellow silver iodide does not dissolve in concentrated aqueous ammonia.

The colours of the silver halide precipitates are shown in *figure 6.4*.

The equation for the precipitation of silver chloride is:

$$Ag^+(aq) + Cl^-(aq) \longrightarrow AgCl(s)$$

You will not be asked to write equations for the reactions of silver halide precipitates with ammonia for AS level chemistry.

● **Figure 6.4** Colours of silver halide precipitates.

Disproportionation reactions of chlorine

The reaction of chlorine with sodium hydroxide

The way in which chlorine reacts with aqueous sodium hydroxide depends on the temperature.

With *cold* (15 °C) dilute aqueous sodium hydroxide a mixture of halide (Cl^-) and halate(I) (ClO^-) ions is formed:

$$Cl_2(g) + 2NaOH(aq)$$
$$\longrightarrow NaCl(aq) + NaClO(aq) + H_2O(l)$$

This is an interesting reaction because it demonstrates **disproportionation** – a particular type of redox reaction in which one species is oxidised and reduced at the same time. This happens to the chlorine – the ionic equation shows that the oxidation state of chlorine in the products of the reaction are both lower and higher than chlorine itself:

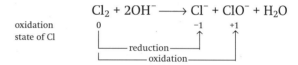

This reaction is used commercially to produce bleach, which is known as HClO, chloric(I) acid or hypochlorous acid. You can see this name on some bleach products. Household bleach is an aqueous solution of sodium chloride and sodium chlorate(I), NaClO, in a one-to-one mole ratio.

The purification of drinking water

When chlorine is used to purify drinking water, disproportionation again occurs to form hydrochloric acid and chloric(I) acid:

$$Cl_2 + H_2O \longrightarrow HCl + HClO$$
oxidation state of Cl   0   -1   +1

The bacteria in water are killed by reactive oxygen atoms which are produced by a slow decomposition of the chloric(I) acid:

$$HClO \longrightarrow HCl + O$$

SUMMARY

◆ The halogens chlorine, bromine and iodine are covalent diatomic molecules at room temperature. They become increasingly less volatile and more deeply coloured on descending Group VII. The volatility decreases as van der Waals' forces increase.

◆ The halogens have many characteristics in common. They are all reactive, and this reactivity decreases on descending the Group.

◆ The halogens all have important industrial uses, especially chlorine, which is used in the manufacture of many other useful products. Possibly the most important use of chlorine is in the prevention of disease by chlorination of water supplies.

◆ All the halogens are good oxidising agents. Chlorine is the strongest oxidising agent of the three halogens studied.

◆ The order of reactivity can be determined by displacement reactions. A halogen can displace another which has a less negative electron affinity.

◆ The identification of a halide ion in solution is made after adding silver nitrate solution and then aqueous ammonia.

◆ Chlorine reacts with cold hydroxide ions in a disproportionation reaction. This reaction produces commercial bleach.

Questions

1 Sodium chlorate (I), found in bleach, decomposes slowly, releasing oxygen, $O_2(g)$.
 a Write the equation for this decomposition.
 b Identify which element has been oxidised and which has been reduced.

2 The relative reactivities of the halogens can be shown by displacement reactions.
 a Copy and complete the table below to show the products of the reaction of each halogen with halide ions. If the reagents do not react, write *no reaction*.
 b Write an equation for the reaction between chlorine and aqueous sodium astatide, NaAt.

3 The colours of silver halides and their reactions with aqueous ammonia may be used to identify aqueous halide ions. Describe tests which use this information to identify an unknown solution that contains either sodium chloride or sodium bromide or sodium iodide.

4 Chlorine is used in the manufacture of bleach, which is widely used as a disinfectant. Bleach is produced by passing chlorine gas up a tower, down which aqueous sodium hydroxide is flowing. The equation for the reaction which takes place in the tower is as follows:
$Cl_2(g) + 2NaOH(aq)$
$\rightarrow NaClO(aq) + NaCl(aq) + H_2O(l)$
Using oxidation states, identify the oxidation state changes which take place in this reaction. Identify which element is oxidised and which is reduced. Give your reasons.

Reagents	Aqueous sodium chloride, NaCl(aq)	Aqueous sodium bromide, NaBr(aq)	Aqueous sodium iodide, NaI(aq)
Chlorine, Cl_2			
Bromine, Br_2			
Iodine, I_2			

● Table for Question 2a

Part 2
Chains and Rings

CHAPTER 7

Basic concepts in organic chemistry

By the end of this chapter you should be able to:

1 interpret and use the terms nomenclature, molecular formula, general formula, structural formula, displayed formula, skeletal formula, homologous series and functional group;

2 describe and explain structural isomerism in compounds with the same molecular formula but different structural formulae, and *cis–trans* isomerism in alkenes in terms of restricted rotation about a double bond;

3 determine the possible structural and/or *cis–trans* isomers of an organic molecule of given molecular formula;

4 perform calculations, involving use of the mole concept and reacting quantities, to determine the percentage yield of a reaction.

Chains and Rings seeks to provide you with a framework for the study of *organic* chemistry. Organic chemistry includes the study of compounds containing carbon and hydrogen *only* (that is, hydrocarbons) and of compounds containing other elements *in addition* to carbon and hydrogen. Such compounds were originally described as organic as they were all believed to be derived from living organisms. Although this idea was dispelled by the synthesis of urea from an inorganic compound, ammonium cyanate, (by the German chemist Friedrich Wöhler in 1828, *figure 7.1*) we still use the term 'organic'.

Organic chemistry is a large subject, mainly because one of its 'essential ingredients', carbon, forms a much greater number and variety of compounds than any other element. Over 90% of known compounds contain carbon, despite the existence of several elements with much greater natural abundance.

Reasons for the greater number and variety of carbon compounds include the following:

■ Carbon readily bonds to itself and to most other elements, including metals.
■ Carbon can bond in a variety of ways giving rise to chains, rings and even cages of carbon atoms.

● **Figure 7.1** Friedrich Wöhler made the organic compound urea from an inorganic source. This dispelled the theory that all organic compounds originated from living organisms.

Compounds that contain only carbon and hydrogen atoms are known as hydrocarbons (*figure 7.2*). Organic chemistry includes the study of hydrocarbons and of compounds containing other elements as well as carbon and hydrogen. As single carbon–carbon and carbon–hydrogen bonds are relatively unreactive, the reactions of these compounds are typically those involving particular functional groups (*table 7.2*).

Organic compounds are also classified as either aliphatic or aromatic. **Aromatic** compounds contain one or more arene rings (see page 85). They are called aromatic compounds as they have distinctive, usually pleasant, smells. All other organic compounds are **aliphatic**. Hence alkanes and alkenes are aliphatic compounds, whilst benzene is an aromatic compound.

Colour	Atom/electron cloud
white	hydrogen
dark grey	carbon
red	oxygen
blue	nitrogen
yellow-green	fluorine
green	chlorine
orange-brown	bromine
brown	phosphorus
violet	iodine
pale yellow	sulphur
yellow ochre	boron
pink	lone-pair electron clouds
green	π-bond electron clouds

● **Table 7.1** Colours used in molecular modelling in this text.

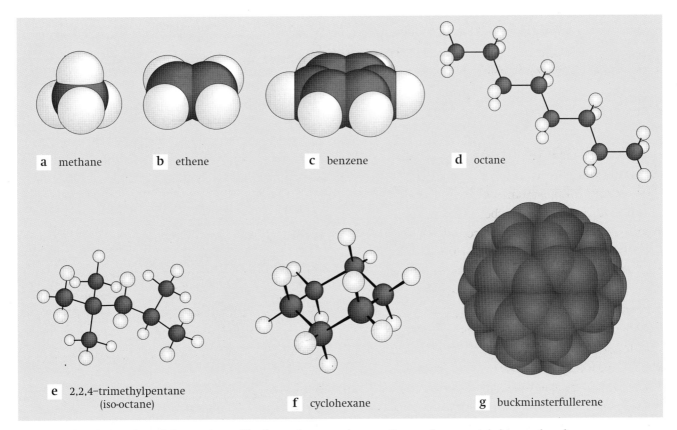

| **a** methane | **b** ethene | **c** benzene | **d** octane |

| **e** 2,2,4–trimethylpentane (iso-octane) | **f** cyclohexane | **g** buckminsterfullerene |

● **Figure 7.2** Examples of the variety of hydrocarbons and one other carbon-containing molecule. Chemists use various types of models for different purposes. The colours used in modelling of molecules are shown in *table 7.1*.

a-c These hydrocarbons are shown as space-filling models. Such models show the region of space occupied by the atoms and the surrounding electrons.

d-f These hydrocarbons are shown as ball-and-stick models, which enable bonds between atoms to be clearly seen.

g Buckminsterfullerene is not a hydrocarbon but an allotrope of carbon (diamond and graphite are other allotropes), a spherical C_{60} molecule named after the architect who designed geodesic domes.

Types of formulae

As well as using different types of models to help visualise molecules, chemists also use different formulae. These include the following.

■ *Molecular formula*

This simply shows the number of atoms of each element present in the molecule, e.g. the molecular formula of hexane is C_6H_{14}.

■ *General formula*

A general formula may be written for each series of compounds. For example, the general formula for the alkanes is C_nH_{2n+2} (where n is the number of carbon atoms present).

■ *Structural formula*

This shows how the atoms are joined together in a molecule. The structural formula of hexane is $CH_3CH_2CH_2CH_2CH_2CH_3$. More information is conveyed. Hexane is seen to consist of a chain of six carbon atoms; the carbon atoms at each end are joined to one carbon and three hydrogen atoms; the carbon atoms between the two ends are joined to two hydrogen and two carbon atoms.

■ *Displayed formula*

This shows all the bonds and all the atoms. The displayed formula of hexane is:

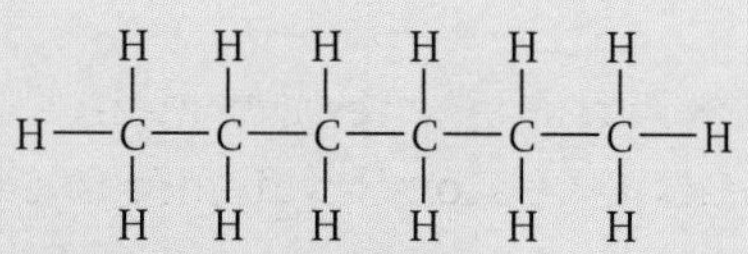

Displayed formulae are also called full structural formulae. One of their disadvantages is that they are a two-dimensional representation of molecules which are three-dimensional. Compare the displayed formula for hexane with the model in *figure 7.6a*.

■ *Skeletal formula*

This shows the carbon skeleton only. Hydrogen atoms on the carbon atoms are omitted. Carbon atoms are not labelled. Other types of atom are shown as in a structural formula. Skeletal formulae are frequently used to show the structures of cyclic hydrocarbons. The skeletal formula of hexane is: ∕∖∕∖∕

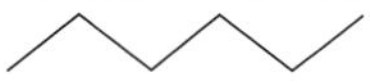

■ *Three-dimensional formula*

This formula gives the best representation of the shape of a molecule.

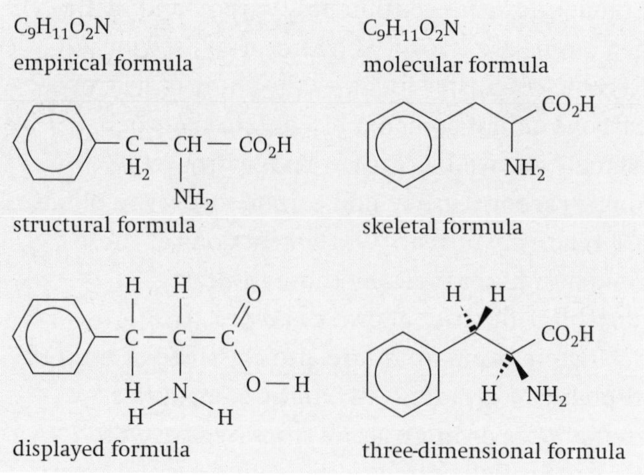

● **Figure 7.3** Different types of formulae for phenylalanine. Note that the skeletal form of the phenyl ring ($-C_6H_5$) is acceptable in all of these formulae.

Examples of the different types of formulae for the amino acid phenylalanine are shown in *figure 7.3*. Phenylalanine is a common, naturally occurring amino acid.

Functional groups

Organic chemistry can be studied in a particularly structured and systematic manner because each different group of atoms that becomes attached to carbon has its own characteristic set of reactions. Chemists refer to these different groups of atoms as **functional groups**. The functional groups that you will meet in the following chapters are shown in *table 7.2*.

Table 7.2 provides you with the classes and structures of these functional groups. An example is also provided of a simple molecule containing each functional group. Each functional group gives rise to a **homologous series** (molecules with the same functional group but different length carbon chains). For example, the alcohol functional group gives rise to the homologous series of alcohols. The first four of these are methanol (CH_3OH), ethanol (CH_3CH_2OH), propan-1-ol ($CH_3CH_2CH_2OH$) and butan-1-ol ($CH_3CH_2CH_2CH_2OH$). The members of a homologous series all have similar chemical properties.

A **general formula** may be written for each homologous series. For example, the general formula of the aliphatic alcohols is $C_nH_{2n+1}OH$ (where n is the number of carbon atoms present).

Class of functional group	Structure of functional group	Name of example	Structural formula of example
alkenes	$\begin{array}{c}\diagdown \quad \diagup\\ C = C\\ \diagup \quad \diagdown\end{array}$	ethene	$CH_2=CH_2$
arenes	⬡	benzene	⬡
halogenoalkanes	$-X$, where $X = F, Cl, Br, I$	chloromethane	CH_3Cl
alcohols	$-OH$	methanol	CH_3OH
aldehydes	$\begin{array}{c}\quad\quad O\\ \quad\quad \parallel\\ -C\\ \quad \diagup\\ H\end{array}$	ethanal	CH_3CHO
ketones	$\begin{array}{c}\diagdown \quad\quad O\\ \quad\quad \parallel\\ -C-C\\ \diagup \quad\quad \diagdown\\ \quad\quad\quad C-\\ \quad\quad \diagup\end{array}$	propanone	CH_3COCH_3
carboxylic acids	$\begin{array}{c}\quad\quad O\\ \quad\quad \parallel\\ -C\\ \quad \diagdown\\ \quad\quad OH\end{array}$	ethanoic acid	CH_3COOH
esters	$\begin{array}{c}\quad\quad O\\ \quad\quad \parallel\\ -C\\ \quad \diagdown\\ \quad\quad O-C-\\ \quad\quad\quad \diagup\end{array}$	ethyl ethanoate	$CH_3COOC_2H_5$
amines	$-NH_2$	methylamine	CH_3NH_2

● **Table 7.2** Functional groups you will meet in the following chapters.

Molecular modelling

Figure 7.4 shows a range of naturally occurring molecules. They are computer-produced images of ball-and-stick molecular models. In such models, atoms are shown as spheres with radii proportional to the atomic radii of the elements involved. A single bond is represented by a rod and a double bond by two rods. Different elements are distinguished by colour, as shown in *table 7.1*.

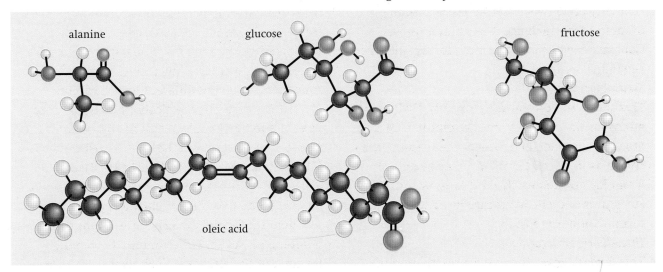

alanine

glucose

fructose

oleic acid

● **Figure 7.4** Ball-and-stick models of some naturally occurring molecules.

SAQ 7.1

Draw the structural formulae for the molecules shown in *figure 7.4*. Identify and label the functional groups present.

Various computer-produced images of molecular models will be used where appropriate throughout this book. Another type that will be used is a space-filling model. In space-filling models, atoms are shown including the space occupied by their electron orbitals. As their orbitals overlap significantly, a very different image to the ball-and-stick image results. *Figure 7.5* shows these two types of model for alanine.

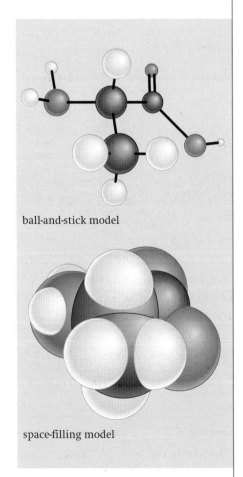

ball-and-stick model

space-filling model

● **Figure 7.5** Different model types for alanine.

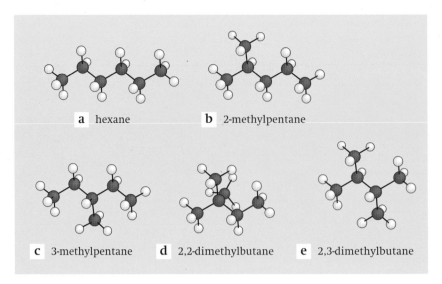

a hexane   **b** 2-methylpentane

c 3-methylpentane   **d** 2,2-dimethylbutane   **e** 2,3-dimethylbutane

● **Figure 7.6** Models and systematic names of C_6H_{14}.

Naming organic compounds

The names given in *figure 7.6* are the systematic names for the **structural isomers** of hexane (see page 88 for more about isomerism). Such names precisely describe the structure of a molecule and enable chemists to communicate clearly. International rules have been agreed for the systematic naming of most compounds. The basic rules for naming hydrocarbons are as follows:

1 The number of carbon atoms in the longest chain provides the stem of the name. Simple alkanes consist entirely of unbranched chains of carbon atoms. They are named by adding -ane to this stem as shown in *table 7.3*.

2 Branched-chain alkanes are named in the same way. The name given to the longest continuous carbon chain is then prefixed by the names of the shorter side-chains. The same stems are used with the suffix -yl. Hence CH_3- is methyl (often called a methyl

Molecular formula	Number of carbon atoms in longest chain	Stem	Name
CH_4	1	meth-	methane
C_2H_6	2	eth-	ethane
C_3H_8	3	prop-	propane
C_4H_{10}	4	but-	butane
C_5H_{12}	5	pent-	pentane
C_6H_{14}	6	hex-	hexane
C_7H_{16}	7	hept-	heptane
C_8H_{18}	8	oct-	octane
C_9H_{20}	9	non-	nonane
$C_{10}H_{22}$	10	dec-	decane
$C_{20}H_{42}$	20	eicos-	eicosane

● **Table 7.3** Naming simple alkanes.

group). In general, such groups are called alkyl groups. The position of an alkyl group is indicated by a number. The carbon atoms in the longest carbon chain are numbered from one end of the chain. Numbering starts from the end that produces the lowest possible numbers for the side-chains. For example

$$CH_3CHCH_2CH_2CH_3$$
$$|$$
$$CH_3$$

is 2-methylpentane, not 4-methylpentane.

3 Each side-chain must be included in the name. If there are several identical side-chains, the name is prefixed by di-, tri-, etc. For example 2,2,3-trimethyl- indicates that there are three methyl groups, two on the second and one on the third carbon atom of the longest chain. Note that numbers are separated by commas, whilst a number and a letter are separated by a hyphen.

4 Where different alkyl groups are present, they are placed in alphabetical order as in 3-ethyl-2-methylpentane.

5 Compounds containing a ring of carbon atoms are prefixed by cyclo-. Cyclohexane is represented as:

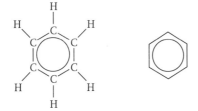

displayed formula   skeletal formula

6 Hydrocarbons may contain alkene or arene groups. These are represented as follows:

alkene: ethene

arene: benzene

displayed formulae   skeletal formulae

Hydrocarbons containing one double bond are called alkenes. The same stems are used but are followed by -ene. The position of an alkene double bond is indicated by the lower number of the two carbon atoms involved. This number is placed between the stem and -ene. Hence $CH_3CH=CHCH_3$ is but-2-ene.

7 The simplest arene is benzene. When one alkyl group is attached to a benzene ring, a number is not needed because all the carbon atoms are equivalent. Two or more groups will require a number. For example:

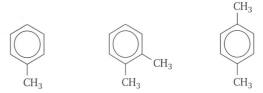

methylbenzene   1,2-dimethylbenzene   1,4-dimethylbenzene

8 Halogeno compounds are named in the same way as alkyl-substituted alkanes or arenes:

$$CH_3CH_2CHBrCH_3$$

2-bromobutane

9 Aliphatic alcohols and ketones are named in a similar way to alkenes:

$$CH_3CH_2CH_2OH \qquad CH_3CH_2COCH_2CH_3$$
propan-1-ol   pentan-3-one

10 Aliphatic aldehyde and carboxylic acid groups are at the end of a carbon chain, so they do not need a number. There is only one possible butanoic acid, $CH_3CH_2CH_2COOH$, or butanal, $CH_3CH_2CH_2CHO$. The names of ketones, aldehydes and carboxylic acids include the carbon atom in the functional group in the stem. Hence CH_3COOH is ethanoic acid.

11 Amines are named using the alkyl- or aryl-prefix followed by -amine. Hence $CH_3CH_2NH_2$ is ethylamine.

SAQ 7.2

Represent the compound 2-chloro-2-methylpropane by means of the following types of formulae:
a displayed, b structural, c skeletal, d molecular, e three-dimensional.

SAQ 7.3

a Name the following compounds:

A $CH_3CH_2CH_2CH_2CH_2CH_2CH_3$

B

C

D

E

F

G

b Draw structural formulae for the following compounds: (i) propanal; (ii) propan-2-ol; (iii) 2-methylpentan-3-one; (iv) propylamine.

SAQ 7.4

Draw displayed formulae for the following compounds:
a 2,2,3-trimethylbutane; **b** cyclobutane; **c** 3-ethylpent-2-ene; **d** ethylbenzene.

Isomerism

Most organic compounds have a molecular formula that is the same as one or more other compounds. This property is called isomerism. **Isomers** have the same molecular formula but the atoms are arranged in different ways. Isomerism arises for a number of reasons, including the ability of carbon to bond to itself and to most other elements in the Periodic Table. The atoms present in a given molecular formula may be treated rather like Lego®, in that a given number of different pieces may be put together in a variety of ways.

Structural isomerism

Structural isomerism describes the situation where chemicals of the same formula behave differently because the structures are different.

For example, the atoms of butane, C_4H_{10}, can be put together in two different ways. Try building models of these two isomers (or use a molecular modelling program on a computer). The two isomers behave in a very similar way chemically. The most noticeable difference in their properties is their boiling points. One isomer is more compact. This reduces the intermolecular forces as the molecules cannot approach each other so closely. This isomer has a boiling point of $-11.6\,°C$. The isomer which is less compact has a boiling point of $-0.4\,°C$. The displayed formulae and the names of these two structural isomers are:

butane

methylpropane

SAQ 7.5

Copy the displayed formulae of the structural isomers of butane. Label each isomer with its appropriate boiling point.

The molecular formula C_2H_6O provides a very different example of structural isomerism. It has two isomers: ethanol, C_2H_5OH, and methoxymethane, CH_3OCH_3. Molecular models of these two isomers are shown in *figure 7.7*. Ethanol is an alcohol whilst methoxymethane is the simplest member of the homologous series of ethers, which are characterised by a $-COC-$ group. As they contain different functional groups, they have very different chemical and physical properties. Ethanol is able to form intermolecular hydrogen bonds; methoxymethane has weaker dipole–dipole

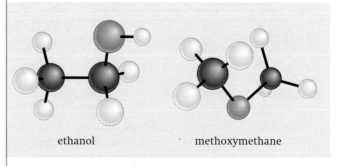

ethanol   methoxymethane

● **Figure 7.7** Structural isomers of C_2H_6O.

intermolecular forces. Consequently the boiling point of ethanol (78.5 °C) is considerably higher than that of methoxymethane (−25 °C). Alcohols take part in many different reactions. Ethers, apart from being highly flammable, are relatively inert.

It is quite easy to mistake the flexibility of molecular structures for isomerism. For example, if you build a model of pentane, C_5H_{10}, you will find it is very flexible (*figure 7.8* shows three of the possibilities). The flexibility of a carbon chain arises because atoms can rotate freely about a carbon–carbon single bond. You should be careful when drawing displayed formulae of isomers. The following structures are not isomers. They are actually the same molecule:

These are all the same molecule; compare the displayed formula with the models in *figure 7.8*. Displayed formulae give a false impression of these structures. Remember that there is a tetrahedral arrangement of atoms round each carbon atom (with bond angles of 109.5°, not 90° as in displayed formulae).

SAQ 7.6
Draw the displayed formulae for all the structural isomers of hexane.

Stereoisomerism

In stereoisomerism, the same atoms are joined to each other in different spatial arrangements. Geometric and optical isomerism are two types of this stereoisomerism. Optical isomerism is studied in Chemistry 2.

Geometric (or *cis–trans*) isomerism

Whilst atoms on either side of a carbon–carbon single bond can rotate freely, those either side of a carbon–carbon double bond cannot. Try making models of but-2-ene, $CH_3CH=CHCH_3$. Two geometric (or *cis–trans*) isomers are possible. You should obtain models similar to those shown in *figure 7.9*. (In *cis*-but-2-ene, the methyl groups are on the *same* side of the double bond. In *trans*-but-2-ene, they lie *across* the double bond.)

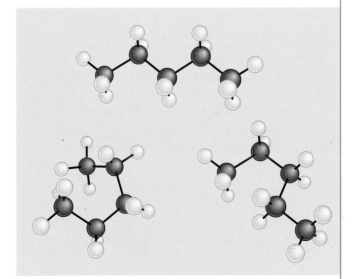

● **Figure 7.8** Models showing the flexibility of pentane. These forms are the same molecule, they are not isomers. The flexibility is due to the free rotation about the C–C single bond.

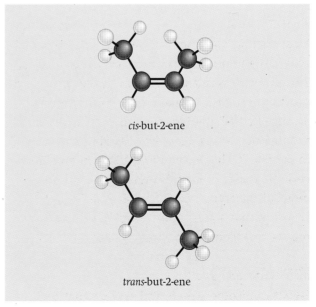

cis-but-2-ene

trans-but-2-ene

● **Figure 7.9** Geometric or *cis–trans* isomers of but-2-ene.

SAQ 7.7

a Draw the geometric isomers of 1,2-dichloroethene, CHCl=CHCl, and label them as *cis* or *trans*.

b Copy the following structures and indicate which can exhibit geometric isomerism by drawing the second isomer and labelling the two isomers as *cis* or *trans*.

$$\begin{array}{cc} \text{Br} & \text{Br} \\ \diagdown & \diagup \\ \text{C}=\text{C} \\ \diagup & \diagdown \\ \text{H} & \text{H} \end{array} \qquad \begin{array}{cc} \text{Br} & \text{H} \\ \diagdown & \diagup \\ \text{C}=\text{C} \\ \diagup & \diagdown \\ \text{H} & \text{H} \end{array}$$

$$\begin{array}{cc} \text{Br} & \text{CH}_3 \\ \diagdown & \diagup \\ \text{C}=\text{C} \\ \diagup & \diagdown \\ \text{H} & \text{H} \end{array} \qquad \begin{array}{cc} \text{Br} & \text{CH}_3 \\ \diagdown & \diagup \\ \text{C}=\text{C} \\ \diagup & \diagdown \\ \text{H} & \text{CH}_3 \end{array}$$

Determination of empirical formulae of organic compounds

The determination of the empirical formula of an organic compound involves **combustion analysis**. A known mass of the compound is burned completely in an excess of oxygen. The carbon dioxide and water produced are collected by absorption onto suitable solids, and the masses of these products are measured. From

● **Figure 7.10** Fermentation vessels in the Carlsberg brewery.

these results we can determine the masses of carbon and of hydrogen in the known mass of the compound. If oxygen is present this is found by subtracting the masses of the other elements present.

If the compound contains nitrogen, a second sample of known mass is reduced using a mixture of reducing agents. Subsequent treatments drive the nitrogen off as ammonia, the quantity of which is determined by titration with acid. This method was named after Kjeldahl (pronounced Keldale) who used it in 1883 for the analysis of the grain for Carlsberg lager (*figure 7.10*).

Let us now look at how the empirical formula of an amino acid is determined. We shall assume, for example, that 0.10000 g of an amino acid produced 0.11710 g of carbon dioxide and 0.05992 g of water, and that in a Kjeldahl determination of nitrogen, a second 0.10000 g of the amino acid produced 0.02264 g of ammonia. To determine the empirical formula of the amino acid, we first calculate the masses of carbon, hydrogen and nitrogen in 0.10000 g of the amino acid:

As 12 g of carbon are present in 1 mol (= 44 g) CO_2,

mass of carbon in 0.11710 g of CO_2 $= \dfrac{12}{44} \times 0.11710\,\text{g}$
$= 0.03194\,\text{g}$
= mass of carbon in the amino acid

As 2 g of hydrogen are present in 1 mol (= 18 g) H_2O,

mass of hydrogen in 0.05992 g of H_2O $= \dfrac{2}{18} \times 0.05992\,\text{g}$
$= 0.00666\,\text{g}$
= mass of hydrogen in the amino acid

As 14 g of nitrogen are present in 1 mol (= 17 g) NH_3,

mass of nitrogen in 0.02264 g of NH_3 $= \dfrac{14}{17} \times 0.02264\,\text{g}$
$= 0.01864\,\text{g}$

The remaining mass of the amino acid must consist of oxygen. Hence:

mass of oxygen in the amino acid $= (0.10000 - 0.03194 - 0.00666 - 0.01864)\,\text{g}$
$= 0.04276\,\text{g}$

	C	H	O	N
Mass (g)	0.03194	0.00666	0.04276	0.01864
Amount (mol)	0.03194/12 $= 2.66 \times 10^{-3}$	0.00666/1 $= 6.66 \times 10^{-3}$	0.04276/16 $= 2.67 \times 10^{-3}$	0.01864/14 $= 1.33 \times 10^{-3}$

Divide by the smallest amount to give whole numbers:

Atoms (mol)	2	5	2	1

Hence the empirical formula is $C_2H_5O_2N$.

SAQ 7.8

A 0.2000 g sample of an organic compound, **W**, was analysed by combustion analysis. 0.4800 g of carbon dioxide and 0.1636 g of water were obtained. A second 0.2000 g sample of **W** produced 0.0618 g of ammonia in a Kjeldahl analysis. Use this data to show that **W** contains only carbon, hydrogen and nitrogen and calculate the empirical formula of **W**.

Practical techniques

Many organic reactions proceed slowly. They often require heating for a period of time. As the reaction mixtures required often contain volatile reactants or solvent, the heating must be carried out under **reflux**: a condenser is placed in the neck of the reaction flask so that the volatile components are condensed and returned to the flask. *Figure 7.11* illustrates the arrangement together with a cross-section diagram (of the type you might reproduce in an examination answer). Note that the water flows into the condenser at the lower (hotter end). This provides the most rapid cooling of the vapour back to liquid. The liquid which is returned to the flask is still close to its boiling point.

The time required for the reflux period will depend on the rate of the reaction. Many reactions require a short period of reflux (perhaps 10 to 30 minutes). Some reactions may require as long as 24 hours. The use of thermostatically controlled heating mantles (shown in the cross-section diagram in *figure 7.11*) allows long refluxes to be carried out safely overnight.

After reflux, the reaction mixture is likely to consist of an equilibrium mixture containing both reactant and product molecules. These may usually be separated by a simple **distillation**. A photograph of distillation apparatus appears in *figure 7.12*. Compare the water flow with the flow for the reflux apparatus. For distillation, although the cold water enters at the lower end of the condenser (as with reflux), this entry point is further from the flask. The water not only condenses the vapour, but also cools the liquid to bring it close to room temperature.

After distillation, further purification may require washing the impure product with water

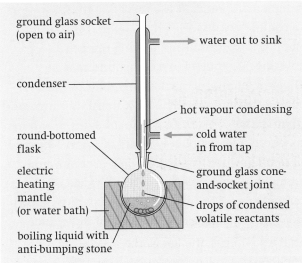

● **Figure 7.11** The apparatus for carrying out a reaction under reflux.

● **Figure 7.12** The apparatus for a distillation.

in a separating funnel (*figure 7.13*). This enables the separation of immiscible liquids. After washing in a separating funnel, the liquid may require drying. It is placed in a stoppered flask together with an anhydrous (containing no water) salt such as calcium chloride. This absorbs excess water. After drying, the liquid will require filtering and redistilling.

Where the product is a solid, distillation is inappropriate. Solid products may crystallise in the reaction flask or may be precipitated on pouring the reaction mixture into water. Rapid separation of the solid is achieved by vacuum filtration (*figure 7.14*).

After separation, the solid is purified by recrystallisation from a suitable solvent. The aim of recrystallisation is to use just enough hot solvent to completely dissolve all the solid. On cooling, the product crystallises, leaving impurities in solution. The purity of a compound may be checked by finding its melting point. A pure compound will usually have a sharp melting point (that is, the point from where it begins to soften to where it is completely liquid is a narrow range of temperature (1 or 2 °C)), whereas an impure compound will melt over a larger range of temperature. The melting-point apparatus shown in *figure 7.15* enables the melting of individual crystals to be seen.

● **Figure 7.13** A separating funnel enables the pink organic layer to be separated from the aqueous layer.

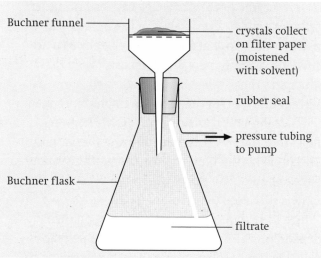

● **Figure 7.14** The apparatus required for a vacuum filtration.

Criteria for checking purity

Determination of the melting point of a solid is one method for checking the purity of a product. The boiling point of a liquid may also give some indication of purity. In addition, there are many modern techniques for establishing purity. Amongst these methods, the techniques of thin-layer chromatography, gas–liquid chromatography and high-performance liquid chromatography are widely used. Paper chromatography and electrophoresis are also used.

Many of these methods are coupled to spectroscopic techniques. Gas–liquid chromatography is often followed by mass spectrometry of the separated components. High-performance liquid chromatography and electrophoresis may be

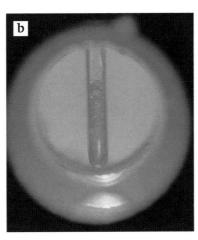

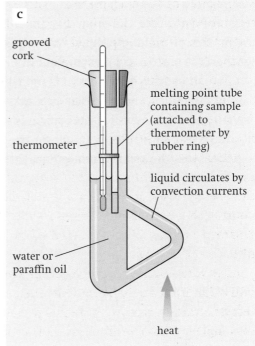

grooved cork

melting point tube containing sample (attached to thermometer by rubber ring)

thermometer

liquid circulates by convection currents

water or paraffin oil

heat

● **Figure 7.15**
a A simple apparatus used to determine melting point.
b Close-up of crystals melting in the apparatus.
c Diagram of a Thiele tube apparatus, also used to determine melting point.

followed by ultraviolet or visible spectroscopy of each component. A capillary electrophoresis apparatus is shown in *figure 7.16*, together with a sample print of results showing the spectra of the components using a three-dimensional graph.

Calculation of percentage yields

Organic reactions often give yields much less than 100%. This is hardly surprising when the product is subjected to recrystallisation or distillation. Material is lost each time the product is transferred from one piece of equipment to another. In addition to this problem, many reactions produce equilibrium mixtures.

In order to find the yield of the product, you first calculate the maximum mass of product that you could obtain from the starting material. This may involve a preliminary calculation to decide if

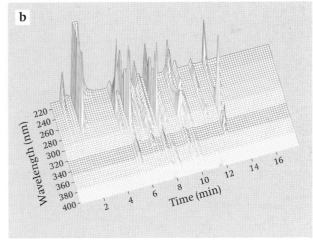

● **Figure 7.16**
a Capillary electrophoresis equipment.
b Capillary electrophoresis enables the separation of organic molecules to take place under the influence of a high voltage. This electrophoretogram shows the retention times for compounds in a mixture; different compounds pass through the capillary tube at different rates. As each compound emerges from the capillary tube, its ultraviolet spectrum is also recorded. The vertical axis shows the absorption of ultraviolet radiation for each compound at certain wavelengths.

one or more of the reagents is in excess. If a reagent is in excess, the other reagent will limit the maximum yield of product. We will use the synthesis of aspirin as an example.

2.0 g of 2-hydroxybenzoic acid is refluxed with 5.5 g of ethanoic anhydride. The products are aspirin and ethanoic acid. The aspirin is easily separated as a solid. The equation for the reaction, together with the relative molecular masses of the compounds, is:

2-hydroxybenzoic acid $M_r = 138$
ethanoic anhydride $M_r = 102$
aspirin $M_r = 180$

$$\text{Amount of 2-hydroxybenzoic acid used} = \frac{2.0}{138} = 0.0145 \text{ mol}$$

$$\text{Amount of ethanoic anhydride used} = \frac{5.5}{102} = 0.54 \text{ mol}$$

As 0.0145 mol of 2-hydroxybenzoic acid requires only 0.0145 mol of ethanoic anhydride, a large excess of ethanoic anhydride has been used.

The reaction equation shows us that one mole of 2-hydroxybenzoic acid produces one mole of aspirin.

Hence maximum yield of aspirin

$$= \frac{180}{138} \times 2.0 = 2.6 \text{ g}$$

A student making aspirin whilst studying this module prepared 1.2g of recrystallised aspirin. His percentage yield was thus

$$\frac{1.2}{2.6} \times 100 = 46\%$$

SAQ 7.9

A student prepared a sample of 1-bromobutane, C_4H_9Br, from 10.0 g of butan-1-ol, C_4H_9OH. After purification she found she had made 12.0 g of 1-bromobutane. What was the percentage yield?

Organising organic reactions

There are several ways of organising the study of organic reactions. In this book the information is organised by functional group, so that subsequent chapters provide you with details of the typical reactions of the functional groups. Before you study these reactions, you need to know a little about the general types of reaction that occur.

You should be familiar with **acid–base** and reduction–oxidation (**redox**) reactions. Organic compounds frequently exhibit both these types of reaction. For example, ethanoic acid behaves as a typical acid, forming salts when reacted with alkalis such as aqueous sodium hydroxide:

$$CH_3COOH(aq) + NaOH(aq) \longrightarrow CH_3COONa(aq) + H_2O(l)$$

As with other acid–base reactions, a salt (sodium ethanoate) and water are formed.

Ethanol is readily oxidised in air to ethanoic acid (wine or beer soon become oxidised to vinegar if left exposed to the air):

$$CH_3CH_2OH(aq) + O_2(g) \longrightarrow CH_3COOH(aq) + H_2O(l)$$

In this redox reaction, oxygen is reduced to water.

There are several other types of reaction. These are substitution, addition, elimination and hydrolysis.

- **Substitution** involves replacing an atom (or a group of atoms) by another atom (or group of atoms). For example, the bromine atom in bromoethane is substituted by the –OH group to form ethanol on warming with aqueous sodium hydroxide:

$$CH_3CH_2Br(l) + OH^-(aq) \longrightarrow CH_3CH_2OH(aq) + Br^-(aq)$$

- **Addition** reactions involve two molecules joining together to form a single new molecule. If ethene and steam are passed over a hot phosphoric acid catalyst, ethanol is produced:

$$CH_2{=}CH_2(g) + H_2O(g) \longrightarrow CH_3CH_2OH(g)$$

- **Elimination** involves the removal of a molecule from a larger one. The addition of ethene to steam may be reversed by passing ethanol vapour over a hot catalyst such as pumice. A water molecule is eliminated:

$$CH_3CH_2OH(g) \longrightarrow CH_2{=}CH_2(g) + H_2O(g)$$

■ **Hydrolysis** reactions involve breaking covalent bonds by reaction with water. The substitution of the bromine atom in bromoethane (above) by hydroxide is also a hydrolysis. The reaction proceeds much more slowly in water:

$$CH_3CH_2Br(l) + H_2O(l) \\ \longrightarrow CH_3CH_2OH(aq) + HBr(aq)$$

What is a reaction mechanism?

A balanced chemical equation shows the reactants and the products of a chemical change. It provides no information about the reaction pathway. The **reaction pathway** will include details of intermediate chemical species (molecules, radicals or ions) which have a transient existence between reactants and products. The **activation energy** for a reaction is the energy required to form these transient species (*figure 7.17a*). You will learn more about activation energy in chapter 14. **Catalysts** are frequently used in reactions to increase the rate of reaction. They do this by providing an alternative reaction pathway with a lower activation energy (*figure 7.17b*).

If a reaction pathway with a lower activation energy is found, more molecules will have sufficient kinetic energy to react. Catalysts take part in the reaction mechanism, but they are recovered unchanged at the end of the reaction. Hence the catalyst does not appear in the balanced chemical equation for the reaction.

The mechanism is described using equations for the steps involved. You will meet the following organic mechanisms in this book:
■ free-radical substitution (page 114);
■ electrophilic addition (page 121);
■ nucleophilic substitution (page 138).
The following mechanisms are studied in Chemistry 2:
■ electrophilic substitution;
■ nucleophilic addition.
The terms free radical, electrophilic and nucleophilic refer to the nature of the attacking

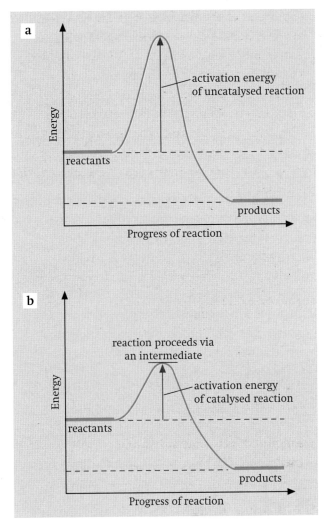

● **Figure 7.17** Activation energy diagrams for a reaction:
a without a catalyst;
b with a catalyst.

species (the reactant that starts a reaction by 'attacking' a bond on another reactant) in the reaction. These terms will be explained in the next section.

Breaking bonds in different ways

A covalent bond consists of a pair of electrons lying between the nuclei of two atoms. The negatively charged electrons attract both nuclei, binding them together. Such a bond may be broken in two different ways. We will consider these possibilities for hydrogen chloride. The dot-and-cross diagram for hydrogen chloride is:

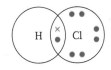

The bond may be broken so that each element takes one of the covalent bond electrons:

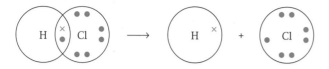

Each element now has a single unpaired electron. (In this example they have also become atoms.) Atoms (or groups of atoms) with unpaired electrons are known as **free radicals**. When a covalent bond is broken to form two free radicals, the process is called **homolytic fission**. If a bond breaks homolytically, the energy is usually provided by ultraviolet light or high temperature.

Unpaired electrons are represented by a dot. Using dots for the unpaired electrons, the homolytic fission of bromomethane to form a methyl radical and a bromine radical may be represented as follows:

$$H_3C - Br \longrightarrow CH_3\cdot + Br\cdot$$

Alternatively, a covalent bond may be broken so that one element takes both covalent bond electrons. Hydrogen chloride would form hydrogen ions and chloride ions:

Notice that the more electronegative element takes both electrons. When a covalent bond is broken to form two oppositely charged ions, the process is called **heterolytic fission**. The bond in hydrogen chloride breaks heterolytically when the gas dissolves in water to form hydrochloric acid.

The movement of *two* electrons from the bond to the same atom is sometimes shown by a curly arrow. Using curly arrows, the heterolytic fission of bromomethane to form a positive methyl ion and a bromide ion may be represented as follows:

$$H_3C - Br \longrightarrow CH_3^+ + Br^-$$

Positively charged ions that contain carbon, such as CH_3^+, are known as **carbocations**. (A negatively charged ion such as CH_3^- is known as a **carbanion**.)

Free radicals, carbocations and carbanions are all highly reactive species. They react with molecules, causing covalent bonds to break and new covalent bonds to form.

Carbocations and carbanions are examples of reagents known as electrophiles and nucleophiles respectively. An **electrophile** (electron-lover) is an electron-pair acceptor which is attracted to an electron-rich molecule, leading to the formation of a new covalent bond between the electrophile and the molecule under attack. Electrophiles must be capable of accepting a pair of electrons. A **nucleophile** (nucleus-lover) is an electron-pair donor which is attracted to an atom with a partial positive charge, leading to the formation of a new covalent bond between the nucleophile and the atom under attack. Nucleophiles must possess a lone-pair of electrons for this new bond.

SAQ 7.10

Draw dot-and-cross diagrams for the following species: $Br\cdot$, Cl^-, CH_3^+, CH_3^-, $CH_3\cdot$, NH_3, BF_3. Classify them as free radicals, electrophiles or nucleophiles. What do you notice about the outer electron shells of free radicals, electrophiles and nucleophiles?

SUMMARY

◆ All organic compounds contain carbon and hydrogen. Most organic compounds also contain other elements, such as oxygen, nitrogen and chlorine.

◆ Chemists use a wide variety of formulae to represent organic molecules. These include general, empirical, molecular, structural, skeletal, displayed and three-dimensional formulae.

◆ Functional groups, which have their own characteristic reactions, are attached to the hydrocarbon framework of an organic molecule. Alkenes, arenes, halogen atoms, alcohols, aldehydes and ketones, carboxylic acids, esters and amines are examples of functional groups.

- Various types of molecular models (ball-and-stick, space-filling) are used to visualise organic molecules.

- Organic molecules are named in a systematic way, related to their structures.

- Organic molecules with the same molecular formula but with different structures are called isomers. Two common types of isomerism are structural and cis–trans (or geometrical). Structural isomers have different structural formulae and cis–trans isomers have different displayed formulae.

- The empirical formula of an organic compound is found by combustion analysis.

- Practical techniques used in the preparation of organic compounds include reflux, distillation, vacuum filtration, separation of immiscible liquids in a separating funnel and recrystalisation.

- Most organic preparations involve equilibrium reactions and/or lead to losses of product during separation and purification. The percentage yield indicates the proportion of the maximum yield that has been obtained.

- The study of organic reactions is traditionally organised by functional group. Each functional group has its own characteristic reactions.

- Reactions may also be studied by type or by mechanism. Organic compounds may show the following types of reaction: acid–base, redox, substitution, addition, elimination or hydrolysis.

- Reaction mechanisms may involve electrophiles, nucleophiles or free radicals. Each of these reagents is capable of forming a new covalent bond to the atom attacked. Electrophiles are electron-pair acceptors. Nucleophiles are electron-pair donors. Free radicals are highly reactive, attacking any atom with which they are capable of forming a bond.

- Covalent bonds may be broken homolytically to form two free radicals, each with an unpaired electron. Polar bonds will frequently break heterolytically to form one cation and one anion.

- Curly arrows show the movement of two electrons in a reaction mechanism.

Questions

1 a Explain the following terms and give an example of each:
   (i) electrophile;
   (ii) nucleophile;
   (iii) free radical.
  b Write balanced equations to illustrate:
   (i) electrophilic addition;
   (ii) nucleophilic substitution;
   (iii) free-radical substitution.

2 a Explain, using examples, the following terms used in organic chemistry:
   (i) general formula;
   (ii) homologous series.
  b The Cl–Cl bond can be broken either by homolytic fission or by heterolytic fission. Explain, with the aid of suitable equations, what you understand by the terms **homolytic fission** and **heterolytic fission**.

3   a   An organic compound of bromine, **X**, has a molecular mass of 137 and the following percentage composition by mass: C, 35.0%; H, 6.6%; Br, 58.4%.

(i) Calculate the empirical formula of compound **X**.

(ii) Show that the molecular formula of **X** is the same as the empirical formula.

b   (i) Draw displayed formulae for all the possible structural isomers of **X**.

(ii) Name the structural isomers that you have drawn in (i).

(iii) Draw the skeletal formulae for the isomers that you have drawn in (i).

CHAPTER 8

Hydrocarbons: fuels

By the end of this chapter you should be able to:

1 explain the use of crude oil as a source of hydrocarbons (separated by fractional distillation) which can be used directly as fuels or for processing into petrochemicals;

2 state that branched alkanes, cycloalkanes and arenes are used in petrol to promote efficient combustion;

3 describe the use of *cracking* to obtain more useful alkanes and alkenes;

4 describe the use of *reforming* to obtain cycloalkanes and arenes;

5 describe the use of *isomerisation* to obtain branched alkanes;

6 describe and explain how the combustion reactions of alkanes lead to their use as fuels in industry, in the home and in transport;

7 outline the value to society of fossil fuels in relation to needs for energy and raw materials, the non-renewable nature of fossil fuel reserves and the need to develop renewable fuels, for example biofuels, which do not further deplete finite energy resources.

Sources of hydrocarbons

The fossil deposits of crude oil and natural gas have been the primary sources of alkanes throughout the twentieth century. Much of the wealth of the industrialised world can be ascribed to this exploitation of a natural resource. The vast majority of these deposits have been used to provide fuel for heating, electricity generation and transport. Smaller, but significant, proportions have been used to produce lubricants and to provide a source of hydrocarbons for the chemical process industry. In the UK, the chemical and petrochemical industries are by far the biggest contributors towards a positive balance in the value of manufacturing trade with the rest of the world. The UK chemical industry employs approximately 250 000 people and, in 1996 produced about 11% of total industrial output. *Figure 8.1* shows just how dependent the UK is on its chemical industry for the size of manufacturing exports.

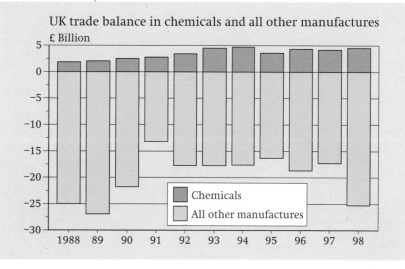

● **Figure 8.1** UK trade balance in chemicals and all other manufactures. The chemical industry is UK manufacturing's number one exporter. With exports of £22.5bn and imports of £18.1bn it earned a trade surplus of £4.4bn in 1998.

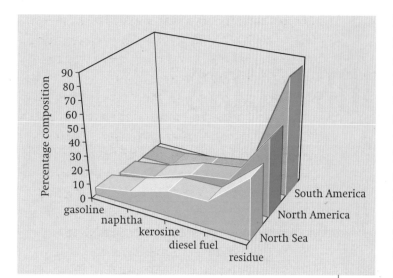

● **Figure 8.2** Breakdown of compositions of oils by oil fractions. North Sea oil contains a higher proportion of the gasoline and naphtha fractions than oils from North or South America.

Crude oil is a complex mixture of hydrocarbons. The composition of oil from different places varies considerably (*figures 8.2* and *8.3*). Three main series of hydrocarbons are present: arenes, cycloalkanes and alkanes. Arenes are hydrocarbons containing one or more benzene rings (see page 87). At a given boiling point, the densities of these decrease in the order arenes > cycloalkanes > alkanes. This provides a method for comparing the compositions of different oils.

Separating the hydrocarbons in crude oil

Crude oil must be refined so that use can be made of the wide variety of hydrocarbons present. In general, chemists separate mixtures of similar

● **Figure 8.3** Californian crude is rich in cycloalkanes!

liquids by **fractional distillation**. This technique relies on differences in boiling points of the different molecules in the liquid. Fractional distillation can be successful even where differences in boiling point are small. As crude oil is such a complex mixture, it is first broken down into **fractions**. Each fraction consists of a mixture of hydrocarbons with a much narrower range of boiling points than the full range of hydrocarbons in crude oil. This separation into fractions is known as fractional distillation. Further distillation processes in an oil refinery enable separation of the hydrocarbons in a fraction where this is desired. We shall consider fractional distillation in more detail by looking at one type of column for such a distillation.

Prior to entering a fractional distillation column (*figure 8.4*), the crude oil must be

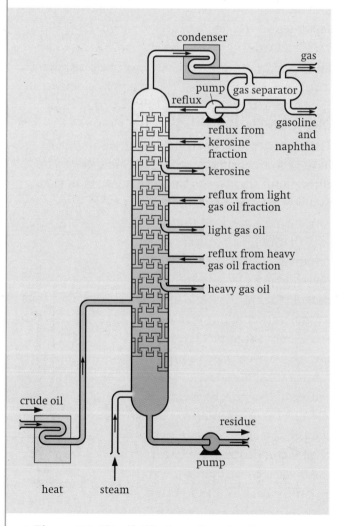

● **Figure 8.4** The distillation of crude oil.

vaporised. This is achieved by passing the crude oil through pipes in a furnace where the oil is heated to 650 K. The resulting mixture of liquid and vapour is fed into the distillation column at a point above the bottom. The column (which may be up to 100 m in height) is divided by a number of steel 'trays' (40 to 50 in a 100 m column). Vapour passes up the column through the trays via holes (*figure 8.5*). Each tray is like a sieve. Liquid flows down the column from tray to tray over a 'weir'.

There is a temperature gradient between the (hot) bottom of the column and the (cool) top of the column. When vapour passes through a tray, the hot vapour comes into contact with a slightly cooler liquid. Some of the hydrocarbon molecules in the vapour will condense, causing more volatile hydrocarbons in the liquid to evaporate. An individual tray will contain a liquid mixture of hydrocarbons with a narrow range of boiling points.

By the time 40 to 50 such condensations and evaporations have taken place, the crude oil has separated into fractions. The most volatile hydrocarbons (with the lowest boiling points) are now at the top of the column. The least volatile hydrocarbons (with the highest boiling points) are at the bottom of the column. From the bottom to the top of the column, increasingly volatile hydrocarbons will be found.

Once operating, a column may be kept in a **steady state** by maintaining the input of crude oil at a flow rate which balances the total of the flow rates at which the fractions are removed. You can create a similar steady state when you are taking a bath! If you continue to run hot water when the bath is full, the bath water will not overflow the sides providing you adjust the flow of hot water to be the same as the flow down the overflow pipe. When a steady state exists, the compositions of the liquid and vapour at any one tray do not vary. This enables the various fractions to be drawn from the column at appropriate points. An individual tray will contain a mixture of hydrocarbons with quite a narrow range of boiling points.

A fractional distillation column is designed to separate crude oil into the following fractions: refinery gases, gasoline and naphtha, kerosine, gas (diesel), oil, and residue. The refinery gases consist of simple alkanes containing up to four carbon atoms. They are used as fuels or as a source (or feedstock) for building other molecules. Gasoline contains alkanes with five to ten carbon atoms and is used as petrol. Naphtha is the fraction of crude oil which is the most important source of chemicals (or feedstock) for the chemical process industry. Other fractions and natural gas are of lesser importance. Kerosine is used for jet fuels and for domestic heating. Gas oil is used as diesel fuel and as a feedstock for catalytic cracking. The residue is used as a source of lubricating oils and waxes and bitumen. Bitumen mixed with crushed stone is the tarmac used to surface roads. *Figure 8.6* shows a distillation column in a modern oil refinery.

Further treatment

After distillation, the different hydrocarbon fractions are treated in a variety of different ways. These include processes such as vacuum distillation

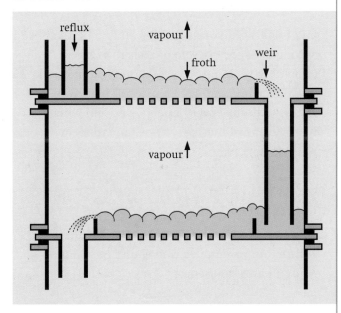

● **Figure 8.5** Trays in a fractionating column.

● **Figure 8.6** The skyline of an oil refinery is dominated by fractional distillation columns.

(to separate out less volatile components such as lubricating oils and waxes from the residue), desulphurisation (to remove sulphur) and cracking (to produce more gasoline and alkenes). There is insufficient gasoline and naphtha fractions from the primary distillation to satisfy the demand for petrol, so higher boiling fractions are cracked to produce more gasoline and naphtha. Modern petrol engines require higher proportions of branched-chain alkanes, cycloalkanes and arenes to promote efficient combustion. These are produced by reforming and isomerisation.

Cracking involves heating the oil fraction with a catalyst. Under these conditions, high-molecular-mass alkanes are broken down into low-molecular-mass alkanes as well as alkenes. Both C–C and C–H bonds are broken in the process. As the bond-breaking is a random process, a variety of products, including hydrogen, are possible and some of the intermediates can react to produce branched-chain alkane isomers. For example, a possible reaction equation for decane is:

$$CH_3CH_2CH_2CH_2CH_2CH_2CH_2CH_2CH_2CH_3$$
decane

$$\longrightarrow CH_3CH_2CH=CH_2 \quad + \quad H_3C-\overset{\overset{\displaystyle H}{|}}{\underset{\underset{\displaystyle CH_3}{|}}{C}}-CH_2CH_2CH_3$$
but-1-ene 2-methylpentane

The chemical industry uses alkenes such as ethene for a variety of products (for example, poly(ethene) from ethene). 2, 2, 4-trimethylpentane is an important component of petrol.

SAQ 8.1

Write balanced equations showing the structural formulae for all the possible products formed on cracking pentane.

In the catalytic cracker (*figure 8.7*) the hot, vaporised oil fraction and the catalyst behave as a fluid. The seething mixture is called a **fluidised bed**. Some of the hydrocarbon mixture is broken down to carbon, which blocks the pores of the catalyst. The fluidised bed of the catalyst is pumped into a regeneration chamber, where the carbon coke is burnt off in air at a high temperature, allowing the catalyst to be recycled.

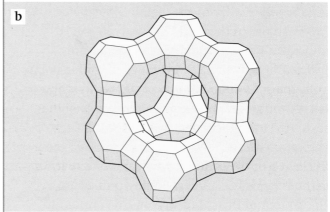

● **Figure 8.7**
a A catalytic cracker occupies the bulk of the central part of this photograph.
b A computer graphic showing the framework of zeolite Y, a modern catalyst used to crack hydrocarbons.

Reforming involves the conversion of alkanes to cycloalkanes, or of cycloalkanes to arenes. Reforming reactions are catalysed by bimetallic catalysts. For example, a cluster of platinum and rhenium atoms is very effective at removing hydrogen from methylcyclohexane to form methylbenzene:

A catalyst containing clusters of platinum and iridium atoms enables conversion of straight-chain alkanes to arenes:

$$CH_3CH_2CH_2CH_2CH_2CH_3 \quad \longrightarrow \quad \bighexagon \quad + \quad 4H_2$$

These metal clusters are between 1 and 5nm in diameter and are deposited on an inert support such as aluminium oxide. The rhenium and iridium help prevent the build-up of carbon deposits, which reduce the activity of the catalysts.

Isomerisation involves heating the straight-chain isomers in the presence of a platinum catalyst:

$$CH_3CH_2CH_2CH_2CH_2CH_3 \longrightarrow H_3C - \overset{\overset{\displaystyle CH_3}{|}}{\underset{\underset{\displaystyle CH_3}{|}}{C}} - CH_2CH_3$$

The resulting mixture of straight- and branched-chain isomers then has to be separated. This is done by using a molecular sieve, which is another type of zeolite that has pores through which the straight-chain isomers can pass (*figure 8.8*). The branched-chain isomers are too bulky and thus are separated off; the straight-chain molecules are recycled to the reactor.

Fuels

Many substances burn in reactions with oxygen, with transfer of energy to the surroundings (*figure 8.9*). Only those used on a large scale, however, are properly described as fuels. Oxidation of chemicals in the fuels coal, petroleum and gas provides over 90% of the energy used in most industrialised countries; hydroelectricity and nuclear power together supply about 9%.

What makes a good fuel?

The essential reaction for any chemical fuel is:

fuel + oxygen (or other oxidiser)
$\rightarrow$ oxidation products + energy transfer

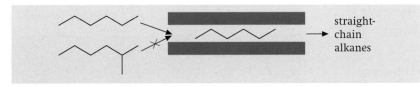

● **Figure 8.8** Shape selectivity by a zeolite catalyst – separation of isomers by a molecular sieve.

Fuel	Formula	Relative molecular mass	Energy released per mole ($kJ\,mol^{-1}$)	Energy released per kilogram ($kJ\,kg^{-1}$)
Carbon (coal)	$C(s)$	12	−393	−32 750
Methane	$CH_4(g)$	16	−890	−55 625
Octane	$C_8H_{18}(l)$	114	−5512	−48 350
Methanol	$CH_3OH(l)$	32	−715	−22 343
Hydrogen	$H_2(g)$	2	−286	−143 000

● **Table 8.1** Comparison of fuels in terms of energy released.

● **Figure 8.9** Gases from oilfields are often disposed of by being burnt as controllable 'flares'. This is a waste of gas but the costs of collection, storage and transportation are higher than the income available from selling the gas for other uses.

SAQ 8.2

Write balanced equations for the complete combustion of the fuels shown in *table 8.1*.

Though different fuels are needed for different purposes the ideal characteristics include the following.

■ *A fuel should react with an oxidiser to release large amounts of energy*

It is interesting to compare fuels on the basis of energy per unit amount of material (mole) and energy per unit mass (kilogram) (*table 8.1*). Remember that fuels are usually purchased in kilograms or tonnes, not in moles.

SAQ 8.3

From the data in *table 8.1*, compare hydrogen with methane. Why are the values for the energy released per kilogram so different when compared with the energy released per mole?

■ *A fuel must be oxidised fairly easily, ignite quickly and sustain burning without further intervention*
Gaseous or easily vaporised fuels usually perform well, as they mix easily and continuously with air/oxygen, which helps the reaction. Solid fuels (coal) are sometimes powdered for use in large industrial furnaces.

■ *A fuel should be readily available, in large quantities and at a reasonable price*
The availability and price of oil, for example, affect national economies so much that governments can fall and countries go to war when these change. The price of any fuel includes many factors: the costs of finding it; extraction, refining and transportation; all the company overheads, such as buildings, salaries and advertising; fuel taxes levied by governments; and the capital costs of the equipment needed to burn it. During the 1960s Britain changed the main gas supply from 'coal gas' (mainly hydrogen and carbon monoxide) to 'natural gas' (methane). This required a large-scale and expensive programme of adapting gas burners in industries and homes to suit the slower burning rate of methane. The advantages were that large supplies of methane were becoming available from gas-fields near to the British coast and that methane was thought to be a much 'cleaner' and safer fuel than the coal gas produced in dirty gas-works in most towns (*figure 8.10*).

■ *A fuel should not burn to give products that are difficult to dispose of, or are unpleasant or harmful*
This is a considerable problem for most fuels (see below), as hydrogen is the only fuel with a safe, non-polluting product from its oxidation reaction to water.

■ *A fuel should be convenient to store and transport safely and without loss*
Over the ages, people have tackled many problems of fuel storage, from how to keep wood dry to how to keep liquid oxygen extremely cold

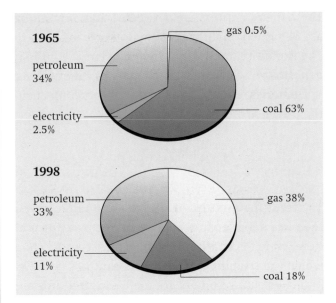

● **Figure 8.10** Changing use of fuel in Britain, 1965–98. Use of coal has greatly declined as methane gas is used for domestic and industrial energy supply, and many more gas-fuelled power stations for generating electricity are built.

and safe for space flight (*figure 8.11*). If gases such as methane and hydrogen are to be used as alternatives to petrol in vehicles, the problems of storage of large amounts of gas must be solved. People are worried about storing these gases under high pressure in cylinders. Scientists are developing some interesting ways, however, of storing hydrogen as its solid compounds, such as the hydrides of metals: $FeTiH_2$ or $LaNi_5H_7$ or $MgNiH_4$. These hydrides release hydrogen when warmed gently and they may enable safe hydrogen-fuelled motor transport.

● **Figure 8.11** A space shuttle is propelled by fuels including liquid oxygen. Note the spherical storage tank for fuel on the right-hand side of the picture.

SAQ 8.4

a Why is oxygen transported into space in liquid form instead of as gas?

b Why are large quantities of liquid or gaseous fuels often stored in spherical tanks?

Problems with chemical fuels

Reliance upon the main chemical fuels coal, oil and gas is increasingly a matter of worldwide concern.

These fuels are 'fossil fuels', formed over millions of years. They are, in effect, non-renewable resources, yet we are consuming them extremely quickly. It is predicted that most of the Earth's oil reserves will be depleted over the next hundred years. Britain's oil- and gas-fields will disappear long before that, if used at the present rate.

The fossil fuels also happen to be the raw materials that supply the feedstock for most of our chemical industry. They may be processed by distillation, cracking and re-forming to yield the carbon-based compounds which are made into the polymers, medicines, solvents, adhesives, etc., that modern society would find difficult to replace (see chapter 6). For how long can we afford to carry on burning the feedstock?

Oxidation of the carbon-based compounds in fuels produces vast amounts of carbon dioxide (CO_2). At one time carbon dioxide was considered to be a relatively harmless gas. Now it is known to be a major contributor to the 'greenhouse effect', which causes an increase in atmospheric temperatures. Some governments are so concerned about this effect, which could bring about disastrous climatic change, that many means of reducing carbon dioxide levels in the atmosphere are being considered. Britain has set a target of reducing CO_2 emissions by 35% of the 1992 levels by the year 2000. The simplest solution would be an outright ban on the use of coal, oil and methane. Governments are understandably reluctant to take such drastic action, as national economies have become so dependent on these fuels. However, we may see increasing 'carbon taxes' (extra taxes levied upon use of carbon-compound fuels) and other means of restricting their use.

Spillage of fuel often causes great damage to local environments (figure 8.12). This damage

● **Figure 8.12** The oil tanker *Braer* broke open and spilled large amounts of oil around the Shetland Islands in 1993.

ranges from streams and ponds polluted by leaky fuel tanks to major disasters when oil tankers break open. There can be immense loss of animal and plant life and enormous costs of cleaning up.

Inefficient burning of carbon-based fuels in defective furnaces and domestic gas fires and in poorly tuned engines produces the very poisonous gas, carbon monoxide. Instead of:

$$C(s) + O_2(g) \longrightarrow CO_2(g)$$

partial oxidation gives:

$$2C(s) + O_2(g) \longrightarrow 2CO(g)$$

Inhalation of carbon monoxide may cause death, as it interferes with the transport of oxygen in the bloodstream. Other dangerous gases produced by the burning of fuels include nitrogen oxides and sulphur oxides, which form strongly acidic solutions in water (hence 'acid rain') (figure 8.13). A large variety of compounds, including

● **Figure 8.13** These trees in Germany were killed by the effects of acid rain, caused mainly by the sulphur oxides produced from burning coal.

● **Figure 8.14** Acidic gases, such as sulphur dioxide are removed by reaction with calcium oxide. The calcium sulphate produced is used to make plasterboard. The 'smoke' is actually water vapour.

carcinogens, appear in the smoke from burning coal and wood (*figure 8.14*).

SAQ 8.5

What are the reactions of nitrogen(IV) oxide (NO_2) and the sulphur oxides (SO_2 and SO_3) with water? Write equations for these reactions.

Alternatives to fossil fuels

Biofuels

Plants can be grown to be used *directly* as fuels, e.g. wood. Plants can also be grown for *conversion* into fuels, e.g. sugar from sugar cane is easily fermented into ethanol. This can be used directly as an alternative to petrol or mixed with petrol. There is increasing use of natural oils, such as rapeseed or sunflower oil, as part of diesel fuels.

Plants convert atmospheric carbon dioxide by photosynthesis to cellulose and other plant material. If crops are used either directly as, or for conversion into, a fuel, the carbon dioxide released to the atmosphere simply replaces that removed during plant growth. Scientists working for Shell are exploring the potential for growing forests of fast cropping trees and using the biomass (plant material) as a renewable energy source. The biomass is dried and chipped before being converted to gas and bio-oil by heating in the absence of air. The gas or bio-oil is then used to fuel a gas turbine to generate electricity.

Greater overall efficiency results when the biomass is first converted to gas and bio-oil.

Waste products Large municipal landfill sites produce significant quantities of biogas by anaerobic decay of biological materials. In the past, this gas often seeped into the atmosphere where it can form an explosive mixture with air. Now, it is collected in pipes and often flared for safe disposal. Biogas is mainly composed of methane which has a much greater greenhouse effect than its combustion product carbon dioxide. In a few cases, the collection and combustion of biogas from landfill sites is being used to generate electricity.

■ *Advantages*: renewable; helps to reduce waste; used with simple technology.
■ *Disadvantages*: not large enough supply to replace fossil fuels at present rates of use.

Methanol (CH_3OH)

This simple alcohol can be made quite cheaply from methane. It is often used in racing cars (*figure 8.15*).

■ *Advantages*: methanol burns cleanly and completely; little carbon monoxide is produced.
■ *Disadvantages*: methanol is more toxic than ethanol; it provides much less energy per litre than petrol; mixtures of methanol and petrol absorb water and car engines may corrode; methanol and petrol tend to separate into layers; combustion of methanol produces the carcinogenic aldehyde methanal when there is insufficient air.

● **Figure 8.15** This 'ChampCar', driven by Juan Montoya, is fuelled by methanol.

Nuclear fuels

Fission: Energy is released when the nuclei of atoms of isotopes of uranium U-235 undergoes fission (splitting) in a chain reaction (*figure 8.16*). Very large amounts of energy are available from this process. The energy is normally used in power stations to heat water to drive electricity-generating steam turbines.

■ *Advantages*: no carbon, nitrogen or sulphur oxides as polluting by-products.

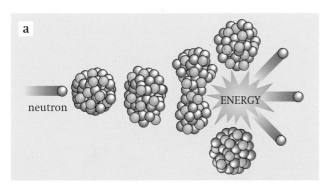

● **Figure 8.16** Nuclear energy.
a Nuclear fission: a neutron colliding with a uranium nucleus causes fission and the release of energy and more neutrons.
b Fuel rods containing uranium-235 being loaded into a nuclear reactor. The top of the reactor core is kept under 11 metres of water to protect the workers from the intense radiation.

■ *Disadvantages*: radioactive waste products are difficult to store and treat; safety systems to contain radioactivity are very costly.

Fusion: Energy is released when deuterium and tritium 'fuse' to form helium:

$$^2_1\text{H} + ^3_1\text{H} \longrightarrow ^4_2\text{He} + ^1_0\text{n}$$

■ *Advantages*: potentially almost limitless as an energy supply as the 'fuels' come from water.

■ *Disadvantages*: no fusion reactors are yet producing energy at economic rates; they are extremely costly.

Moving air: wind

The energy of moving air is transferred into the motion of windmills and wind turbines (*figure 8.17*). Much science and technology is being devoted to improving the efficiency of the wind machines, and they soon may provide over 10% of the UK energy needs.

■ *Advantages*: renewable; pollution- and waste-free; can be used in locality where energy is needed.

■ *Disadvantages*: high initial expense for large-scale generation of electricity; not a reliable source in calm weather; large 'wind-farms' have environmental impact: both noise and visual.

Moving water

Hydroelectricity: Water stored behind dams or from waterfalls can be released through turbines and generate electricity or be used directly to turn wheels in mills (*figure 8.18a*). Hydroelectricity is a major source of power in many countries.

● **Figure 8.17** This wind-farm in Spain includes many wind turbines for generating electricity.

● **Figure 8.18**
a A hydroelectric power station is sited below the storage lake and dam.
b This device, on a sea inlet in Islay, uses the motion of waves to generate electricity. Other wave motion devices are used out at sea.

Waves: The motion of waves is used to cause oscillating motion in various devices and to generate electricity (*figure 8.18b*).

Tides: Incoming tides in river estuaries fill up large water stores behind barrages across the river. The water can be released through turbines to generate electricity.

■ *Advantages*: renewable; quite predictable; pollution- and waste-free; can be used on large scale.

■ *Disadvantages*: costly to install; environmental impact of dams and barrages.

Sunlight: solar heating and photovoltaics

Solar panels, which are panels of solar heat collectors, are used to heat water in parts of the world where sunshine is plentiful (*figure 8.19a*).

Photovoltaic cells convert light into electricity (*figure 8.19b*). In future, large satellites may generate electricity and beam energy by microwave to Earth:

■ *Advantages*: renewable; pollution-free with no waste products.

■ *Disadvantages*: low sunlight levels in UK; none at night; photovoltaics have high initial costs; very large arrays needed for large-scale production of electricity.

● **Figure 8.19**
a Solar water heaters on a roof top in Kathmandu, Nepal.
b A lighthouse in Shetland that uses photovoltaic cells to charge storage batteries.

Geothermal: hot rocks

Some distance below the surface of the Earth, the temperature is high (about 85 °C at 2 km below). Water pumped into wells in the hot rock zone is

● **Figure 8.20** Geothermal power stations are widely used in Iceland where hot rocks are near the surface. The four wells in this station provide enough steam to drive a power plant producing 100 megawatts of thermal energy and 2.7 megawatts of electricity. The steam is also used to heat cold water, which is then piped to the capital, Reykjavik, for heating and washing.

heated; the extracted hot water can be used to heat buildings (*figure 8.20*).

■ *Advantages*: almost unlimited source.

■ *Disadvantages*: not widely available; expensive initially; technological problems.

Hydrogen

Many scientists believe that we should run a 'hydrogen economy'. Hydrogen can be extracted quite cheaply from water by electrolysis. Much scientific and technological effort is being spent on effective storage and transport systems.

■ *Advantages*: no pollution, as water is the only waste product from burning hydrogen in air (*figure 8.21*); available in large quantities.

● **Figure 8.21** A prototype hydrogen-powered car.

● **Figure 8.22** The fate of the airship *Hindenburg* in 1937. Hydrogen was not used as fuel but to keep the airship buoyant. This and similar tragedies have made people very cautious about the use of hydrogen as a fuel for transport, but with careful planning it can be used at least as safely as petrol.

■ *Disadvantages*: regarded as too dangerously explosive by many people (*figure 8.22*); difficult to store and use for transport or in domestic situations.

Electricity from chemical cells

Cells work by using oxidation and reduction reactions (redox systems) in which electrons are transferred. Cells act as convenient stores of electricity (*figure 8.23a*). There is much research into batteries (collections of cells) that will provide energy in sufficient quantities to power cars and lorries. The familiar lead–acid batteries, used in many delivery vans in towns, may be replaced in the future by other batteries using, for example, sodium and sulphur.

Fuel cells are of great interest (*figure 8.23b*). In these, redox reactions between hydrogen and oxygen, or alcohols and oxygen, take place over

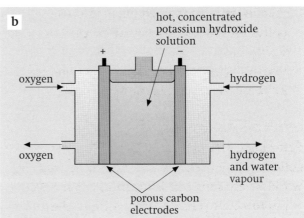

● **Figure 8.23**

a This vehicle is powered by a number of rechargeable lead–acid batteries, seen underneath.

b A simple fuel cell using the hydrogen–oxygen reaction. The gases must be supplied continuously to the electrodes, so a fuel cell is not a 'store' of electricity. This cell provides a voltage of 1.23 V and can be designed to give 70% efficiency in converting the energy of the reaction to electricity.

catalysts. Fuel cells are very clean and efficient, and are used in small spacecraft. They have not yet been developed for very large-scale generation of electricity.

SUMMARY

- Currently, natural gas and crude oil are our major sources of hydrocarbons. The majority of hydrocarbons release large amounts of energy on combustion and are used as fuels for electricity generation, industry, homes or transport.

- A significant proportion of these hydrocarbons are converted into a wide range of chemical products.

- Cracking of the less useful fractions from crude oil produces a range of more useful alkanes and alkenes. The branched-chain alkanes are suitable for petrol and the alkenes are used to make polymers and other chemical products such as anti-freeze.

- Isomerisation converts straight chain alkanes into more of the branched-chain alkanes. Re-forming converts alkanes to cycloalkanes or arenes. Branched-chain alkanes, cycloalkanes and arenes all improve the efficiency of combustion in modern petrol engines.

- Our reserves of fossil fuels such as gas and oil are limited; once these reserves are exhausted, alternative sources of energy will be needed by society. In the search for alternatives, chemists and other scientists are now working to develop renewable fuel sources such as biofuels.

Questions

1 Give an account of what is meant by the term **cracking**. Illustrate your answer by reference to the cracking of decane and the variety of products obtained. Comment on the importance of the cracking process.

2 Various processes are carried out in an oil refinery to provide sufficient petrol of the appropriate quality for modern car engines. Three of these reactions are illustrated below:

Cracking, for example:
Reaction 1

$$CH_3(CH_2)_{10}CH_3 \rightarrow \underset{B}{H_3C-\overset{\overset{\displaystyle CH_3}{|}}{\underset{\underset{\displaystyle CH_3}{|}}{C}}-\overset{\overset{\displaystyle H}{|}}{\underset{\underset{\displaystyle H}{|}}{C}}-\overset{\overset{\displaystyle CH_3}{|}}{\underset{\underset{\displaystyle H}{|}}{C}}-CH_3} + \underset{C}{H_2C=CHCH_2CH_3}$$

A

Isomerisation, for example
Reaction 2
$$CH_3CH_2CH_2CH_2CH_3 \rightarrow D$$

Reforming, for example
Reaction 3
$$\underset{E}{C_6H_{12}} \rightarrow \underset{F}{C_6H_6} + G$$

a Name the compounds **A**, **B** and **C** in reaction 1.

b Suggest a structure for compound **D** in reaction 2.

c (i) Draw skeletal formulae for compounds **E** and **F** in reaction 3.

   (ii) Name the product **G** in reaction 3. Write a balanced equation for this reaction.

CHAPTER 9

Hydrocarbons: alkanes

By the end of this chapter you should be able to:

1 state that alkanes are *saturated* hydrocarbons;

2 explain, in terms of van der Waals' forces, the variations in boiling points of alkanes with different carbon chain length and branching;

3 describe the lack of reactivity of alkanes in terms of the non-polarity of C–H bonds;

4 describe the chemistry of alkanes, typified by methane, its combustion and its substitution by chlorine and by bromine to form halogenoalkanes;

5 describe how *homolytic fission* leads to the mechanism of *free-radical substitution* in alkanes, typified by methane and chlorine, in terms of *initiation*, *propagation* and *termination* reactions.

Physical properties of alkanes

The homologous series (see page 84) of alkanes has the general formula C_nH_{2n+2}. Alkanes are non-polar molecules containing only C–H and C–C covalent bonds. As all the C–C bonds are single bonds, alkanes are described as saturated hydrocarbons. Unsaturated hydrocarbons, such as the alkenes (chapter 10), contain one or more double bonds between carbon atoms.

The atoms in alkanes are held together by σ orbitals. A σ **orbital** lies predominantly along the axis between two nuclei. It may be regarded as being formed by the overlap of two atomic σ orbitals. The two electrons in the orbital attract both nuclei, binding them together in a σ bond. The geometry of alkane molecules is based on the tetrahedral arrangement of four covalent σ bonds round each carbon atom. The σ bonds lie between a carbon atom and either a hydrogen atom or another carbon atom. All bond angles are 109.5°. The molecules can rotate freely about each carbon–carbon single bond. This freedom to rotate allows a great degree of flexibility to alkane chains. The σ bonds in ethane are shown in *figure 9.1*.

The physical states of alkanes at room temperature and pressure change from gases to liquids to

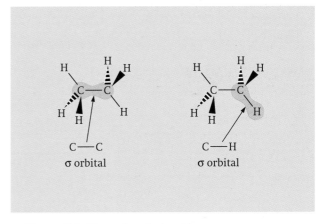

● **Figure 9.1** The σ bonds in ethane.

solids as the number of carbon atoms in the alkane molecule increases. We say that the **volatility** of the alkanes decreases with increasing number of carbon atoms in the alkane molecule. Volatility is the ease with which a liquid turns to vapour. We can examine this trend by plotting graphs of the melting or boiling points of alkanes against the number of carbon atoms present. *Figure 9.2* shows such a graph of the melting points for the **straight-chain** alkanes, butane to dodecane and eicosane. The term straight-chain indicates no branching is present in the molecule's carbon chain.

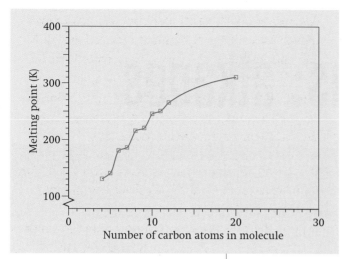

● **Figure 9.2** Melting points of straight-chain alkanes.

SAQ 9.2

Volatility is determined by the strength of the intermolecular forces between alkane molecules.

a Name the type of intermolecular forces found in alkanes. Give a reason for your answer, and

b explain the trends in the melting and boiling points of the alkanes in terms of these intermolecular forces.

Table 9.2 shows the boiling points for pentane and isomers of pentane. 2-methylbutane has one methyl group as a branch, 2,2-dimethyl-propane has two methyl group branches.

Again, a trend is apparent. As the number of branches in the chain increases, the boiling point decreases. The isomers all have the same number of carbon and hydrogen atoms, so we cannot explain the trend in terms of an increasing number of electrons. Look at the space filling models for these isomers, also shown in the table.

As the isomers become more branched, the overall shape of the molecule changes from that of a flexible long balloon (pentane) to one resembling a spherical balloon (2,2-dimethylpropane). The long balloon shape of pentane molecules allows them to pack more closely together than the spherical shape of 2,2-dimethylpropane. The intermolecular forces increase when the molecules approach more closely so the boiling point of pentane is higher than that of 2,2-dimethylpropane. The boiling point of 2-methylbutane, with only one branching point in the carbon chain, lies between the other two isomers.

SAQ 9.1

a *Table 9.1* contains the boiling points of the first twelve alkanes, and eicosane, $C_{20}H_{42}$. Plot these boiling points on the vertical axis of a graph against the number of carbon atoms present. Compare the shape of your graph with the melting point graph (*figure 9.2*).

Alkane	Molecular formula	Boiling point (K)
methane	CH_4	109
ethane	C_2H_6	185
propane	C_3H_8	231
butane	C_4H_{10}	273
pentane	C_5H_{12}	309
hexane	C_6H_{14}	342
heptane	C_7H_{16}	372
octane	C_8H_{18}	399
nonane	C_9H_{20}	424
decane	$C_{10}H_{22}$	447
undecane	$C_{11}H_{24}$	469
dodecane	$C_{12}H_{26}$	489
eicosane	$C_{20}H_{42}$	617

● **Table 9.1** The boiling points of straight-chain alkanes.

Alkane	Structural formula	Boiling point (K)	Space filling model
pentane	$CH_3CH_2CH_2CH_2CH_3$	309	
2-methylbutane	$CH_3CHCH_2CH_3$ with CH_3 above	301	
2,2-dimethylpropane	CH_3CCH_3 with CH_3 above and CH_3 below	283	

● **Table 9.2** The boiling points of pentane and its isomers.

Chemical properties of alkanes

Combustion in air

Alkanes make excellent fuels. Complete combustion in an excess of air produces carbon dioxide and water. For example, butane is used as a fuel in camping gas stoves. The equation for the combustion of butane is:

$$C_4H_{10}(g) + 6\tfrac{1}{2}O_2(g) \rightarrow 4CO_2(g) + 5H_2O(l)$$

Natural gas, used for cooking and heating in many homes (*figure 9.3*), is predominantly methane. Whether using natural gas or butane camping gas, it is important to ensure a good supply of air. If there is insufficient oxygen, incomplete combustion will occur, with the formation of carbon monoxide instead of carbon dioxide. For example, with methane the equation for complete combustion is:

$$CH_4(g) + 2O_2(g) \rightarrow CO_2(g) + 2H_2O(l)$$

The equation for incomplete combustion and formation of carbon monoxide is:

$$CH_4(g) + 1\tfrac{1}{2}O_2(g) \rightarrow CO(g) + 2H_2O(l)$$

Carbon monoxide is a poisonous gas which bonds to the iron of haemoglobin in the blood in preference to oxygen. Carbon monoxide is colourless and odourless, so its presence is not noticed. Early symptoms of poisoning by carbon monoxide include the skin flushing red, headache and nausea. Many deaths result from the use of faulty gas fires in poorly ventilated rooms. It is important to have all gas equipment serviced annually and checked for carbon monoxide emissions. In the UK, legislation now requires adequate ventilation wherever there are gas installations. Property landlords are required by law to have their gas equipment checked annually.

● **Figure 9.3** In a gas boiler the complete combustion of natural gas produces carbon dioxide and water.

SAQ 9.3

A principal component of petrol is an isomer of octane (C_8H_{18}).

a Write balanced equations for the combustion of octane: (i) in a limited supply of air with the formation of carbon monoxide and water and (ii) in a supply of air which ensures complete combustion with the formation of carbon dioxide and water.

b Using your equations from part **a**, calculate: (i) the additional number of moles of oxygen required to prevent the formation of carbon monoxide on combustion of one mole of octane and (ii) the additional volume of air required (assume one mole of a gas occupies $24.0\,dm^3$ and that air contains 20% oxygen).

The substitution reaction of alkanes

Alkanes are remarkably inert compounds. A reason for the inertness of alkanes arises from their lack of polarity. As carbon and hydrogen have very similar electronegativities, alkanes are non-polar molecules. Consequently, alkanes are not readily attacked by common chemical reagents. Most reagents that you have met are highly polar compounds. For example, water, acids, alkalis and many oxidising and reducing agents (see page 68) are polar, and they usually initiate reactions by their attraction to polar groups in other compounds. Such polar reagents do not react with alkanes.

Some non-polar reagents will react with alkanes. The most important of these are the halogens, which, in the presence of ultraviolet light, will *substitute* hydrogen atoms in the alkane with halogen atoms. For example, when chlorine is mixed with methane and exposed to sunlight, chloromethane is formed and hydrogen chloride gas is evolved:

$$CH_4(g) + Cl_2(g) \longrightarrow CH_3Cl(g) + HCl(g)$$

Because the reaction requires ultraviolet light, it is called a photochemical reaction.

Further substitution is possible, in turn producing dichloromethane, trichloromethane and tetra-chloromethane. Other halogens, such as bromine, produce similar substitution products. With hexane, for example, bromine produces bromohexane (*figure 9.4*):

$$C_6H_{14}(l) + Br_2(l)$$
$$\longrightarrow C_6H_{13}Br(l) + HBr(g)$$

● **Figure 9.4** The reaction of bromine with hexane in ultraviolet light.

The substitution mechanism

The overall equation for a reaction gives no clue as to the stages involved between reactants and products. The sequence of stages is known as the **mechanism** of a reaction. For example, the energy of ultraviolet light is sufficient to break the Cl–Cl bond. Absorption of light energy causing a bond to break is known as **photodissociation**. Homolytic fission (page 96) occurs and two chlorine atoms are formed, each having seven electrons in their outer shell. The chlorine atoms each have one unpaired electron and are thus free radicals (page 96). Free radicals react very rapidly with other molecules or chemical species. As **homolytic fission** of a chlorine molecule must occur before any chloromethane can be formed, it is known as the **initiation step**.

$$Cl–Cl(g) \xrightarrow{\text{UV light}} Cl\cdot(g) + Cl\cdot(g)$$

The reaction of a chlorine free radical with a methane molecule produces hydrogen chloride and a $CH_3\cdot$ (methyl) free radical. The dot indicates the unpaired electron. The carbon atom in this $CH_3\cdot$ fragment also has seven electrons in its outer shell. A methyl free radical can react with a chlorine molecule to produce chloromethane and a new chlorine free radical:

$$Cl\cdot(g) + H–CH_3(g) \longrightarrow Cl–H(g) + CH_3\cdot(g)$$

$$CH_3\cdot(g) + Cl–Cl(g) \longrightarrow CH_3Cl(g) + Cl\cdot(g)$$

These two steps enable the reaction to continue. In the first step, a chlorine free radical is used up. The second step releases a new chlorine free radical, which allows repetition of the first step. The reaction will continue for as long as there is a supply of methane molecules and undissociated chlorine molecules. The two steps constitute a **chain reaction** and are known as the **propagation steps** of the reaction.

The reaction to form chloromethane and hydrogen chloride ceases when the supply of reagents is depleted. There is a variety of possible termination steps. These include recombination of chlorine free radicals to form chlorine molecules. Alternatively, two methyl free radicals can combine to form an ethane molecule:

$$Cl\cdot(g) + Cl\cdot(g) \longrightarrow Cl_2(g)$$

$$CH_3\cdot(g) + CH_3\cdot(g) \longrightarrow CH_3CH_3(g)$$

These, or any other, **termination step** will remove free radicals and disrupt the propagation steps, thus stopping the chain reaction.

The four steps (initiation, two propagation steps and one of two termination steps) involved in the formation of chloromethane and hydrogen chloride from methane and chlorine constitute the mechanism of this reaction. As the reaction is a substitution involving free radicals, it is known as a **free-radical substitution**.

SAQ 9.4

a Which of the following reagents are likely to produce free radicals in ultraviolet light?

$HCl(aq)$, $Br_2(l)$, $NaOH(aq)$, $Cl_2(g)$, $KMnO_4(aq)$.

b Write balanced equations for the reactions of butane with those reagents that produce free radicals.

SUMMARY

◆ Alkanes are saturated hydrocarbons with the general formula C_nH_{2n+2}. At room temperature the alkanes from methane to butane are gases; pentane to $C_{16}H_{34}$ are liquids; $C_{17}H_{36}$ and above are waxy solids.

◆ The melting and boiling points of alkanes increase with the length of the hydrocarbon chains. The increase may be explained in terms of increasing attraction between the non-polar alkanes with increasing chain length. The intermolecular forces are instantaneous dipole-induced dipole (or van der Waals') forces.

◆ For a given straight-chain alkane, the boiling points of its branched chain isomers are lower because the branched molecules cannot approach as closely.

◆ Alkanes are relatively unreactive as they are non-polar. Most reagents are polar and do not usually react with non-polar molecules.

◆ Alkanes burn completely to carbon dioxide and water and are widely used as fuels.

◆ Chlorine or bromine substitute for hydrogen atoms in alkanes in the presence of ultraviolet light producing halogenoalkanes.

◆ The Cl–Cl or Br–Br bond is broken in a photodissociation reaction producing reactive Cl· or Br· free radicals. This process is described as homolytic fission as each free radical retains one electron from the covalent bond. The initiation step of free-radical substitution is followed by propagation steps involving a chain reaction which regenerates the halogen free radicals. Termination of the reaction may occur, for example, when two free radicals combine.

Questions

1 a Petrol is a mixture of alkanes containing 6 to 10 carbon atoms per molecule. Some of these alkanes are isomers of one another.

   (i) Explain the term **isomers**.

   (ii) State the molecular formula of an alkane present in petrol.

b The major hydrocarbon in camping gas is butane. Some camping gas was reacted with chlorine to form a mixture of isomers.

   (i) What conditions are required for this reaction to take place?

   (ii) Two isomers, A and B, were separated from this mixture. These isomers had a molar mass of $92.5\,g\,mol^{-1}$. Deduce the molecular formula of these two isomers.

   (iii) Draw the displayed formulae of A and B and name each compound.

2 Alkanes burn readily and react rapidly with free radicals produced by the action of ultraviolet light on chlorine, Cl_2, or bromine, Br_2, molecules. However, they are remarkably unreactive with common laboratory acids or alkalis such as concentrated sulphuric acid, H_2SO_4, or aqueous sodium hydroxide, NaOH.

a Write a balanced equation for the complete combustion of heptane, $C_7H_{16}(l)$. Include state symbols in your equation.

b (i) Describe the formation of bromine free radicals, $Br\cdot$, from bromine molecules in ultraviolet light.

(ii) Describe, using balanced equations, the reaction steps involved in the substitution reaction of bromine free radicals with hexane, C_6H_{14}, to form bromohexane, $C_6H_{13}Br$.

CHAPTER 10

Hydrocarbons: alkenes

By the end of this chapter you should be able to:

1 state that alkenes are *unsaturated* hydrocarbons;

2 state and explain the bonding in alkenes in terms of the overlap of adjacent p orbitals to form a π bond;

3 state and explain the shape of ethene and other related molecules;

4 describe the chemistry of alkenes, for example by certain *addition reactions* of ethene and propene;

5 define an *electrophile* as an *electron pair acceptor*;

6 describe how *heterolytic fission* leads to the mechanism of *electrophilic addition* in alkenes, typified by bromine and ethene to form 1,2-dibromoethane;

7 describe the *addition polymerisation* of alkenes, for example ethene and propene;

8 deduce the repeat unit of a *polymer* obtained from a given *monomer*;

9 identify, in a given section of polymer, the monomer from which it was obtained;

10 outline the use of alkenes in the industrial production of organic compounds;

11 outline the difficulties in disposing of polymers, for example non-biodegradability or toxic combustion products;

12 outline, for polymers, the movement towards recycling, the combustion of waste for energy production and their use as a feedstock for cracking in the production of useful organic compounds;

13 outline the role of chemists in minimising damage to the environment.

A number of biologically important molecules are alkenes. Many of these are based on the simple diene, isoprene (2-methylbuta-1,3-diene):

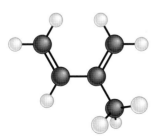

Some trees can be tapped for their latex or natural rubber (*figure 10.1*). Latex is a polymer of isoprene. The natural oil, limonene, present in the

● **Figure 10.1** Scraping the bark off a rubber tree in this way causes the liquid rubber to accumulate at one point, where it can be collected.

rind of oranges and lemons is derived from two isoprene units:

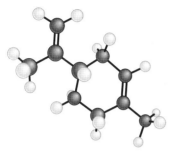

Alkenes are used to make many chemicals that feature prominently in modern life. Some examples of these chemicals are shown in *figure 10.2*.

Physical properties of alkenes

Simple alkenes are **hydrocarbons** that contain one carbon–carbon double bond. The simplest alkene is ethene, $CH_2=CH_2$. The general formula of the homologous series of alkenes is C_nH_{2n}.

SAQ 10.1

Draw a dot-and-cross diagram for ethene. Predict the shape of the molecule and give estimates of the bond angles.

● **Figure 10.2** A range of products produced from alkenes, including poly(chloroethene) window frames, ethane-1,2-diol (used in antifreeze) and industrial methylated spirits (mainly ethanol with methanol added to avoid alcohol tax – used as a solvent).

Bonding in alkenes: σ and π bonds

Electrons in molecules occupy σ and π molecular orbitals. A π orbital (or π bond) lies predominantly in two lobes, one on each side of a σ bond. Overlap of two atomic π orbitals produces a π molecular orbital or π **bond**. To ensure maximum overlap, ethene must be a planar molecule. A single covalent bond, such as C–C or C–H, consists of a σ bond. Double bonds such as C=C consist of one σ bond and one π bond.

overlap of p orbitals produces
π molecular orbitals

Compounds which contain π bonds, such as ethene, are called unsaturated compounds. The term **unsaturated** indicates that the compound will combine by *addition* reactions with hydrogen or other chemicals, losing its multiple bonds.

Saturated compounds contain only *single* carbon–carbon bonds. The terms 'saturated' and 'unsaturated' are often used in connection with oils and fats. The molecules in vegetable oils contain several double bonds – they are described as **polyunsaturated**. In hard margarine, hydrogen has been added to these double bonds so the margarine is now saturated. However, several of the fatty acids which are essential to our diet are polyunsaturated and so, to ensure that these fatty acids are retained, much modern margarine is only partially saturated.

Cis-trans isomerism

Many alkenes exhibit *cis–trans* isomerism; we shall consider an example. Natural rubber is a polymer of 2-methylbuta-1,3-diene (or isoprene, page 117). The repeating unit contains a carbon–carbon double bond. All the links between the isoprene units are on the same side of this double bond. This arrangement is described as the *cis* isomer:

cis-poly(2-methylbuta-1,3-diene): natural rubber

Natural rubber is the familiar material used for balloons, rubber gloves and condoms.

Another possible arrangement has the links between each 2-methylbuta-1,3-diene unit on alternate sides of the double bond. As they lie across the double bond, this is the *trans* isomer. It is found naturally as gutta-percha, which is a grey, inelastic, horny material obtained from the percha tree in Malaysia. It is used in the manufacture of golf balls.

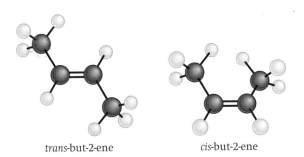

trans-poly(2-methylbuta-1,3-diene): gutta-percha

Both *cis*- and *trans*-2-methylbuta-1,3-diene can be manufactured from 2-methylbuta-1,3-diene using appropriate Ziegler–Natta catalysts. Such catalysts were developed by the German chemist Karl Ziegler and the Italian chemist Giulio Natta, and are based on triethylaluminium and titanium(IV) chloride. Ziegler and Natta made a substantial contribution to the development of polymers and were jointly awarded the Nobel prize for chemistry in 1963.

Cis–trans isomerism is frequently encountered in alkenes, and arises because rotation about a double bond cannot occur unless the π bond is broken. In addition to a double bond, the molecule must have two identical groups, one on each of the two carbon atoms involved in the double bond. The other two groups must be different to this identical pair. But-2-ene is the simplest alkene to show *cis–trans* isomerism:

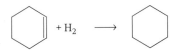

trans-but-2-ene   cis-but-2-ene

In the *cis* isomer, two methyl groups are on the same side of the double bond; in the *trans* isomer they are on opposite sides.

SAQ 10.2

Consider the following:

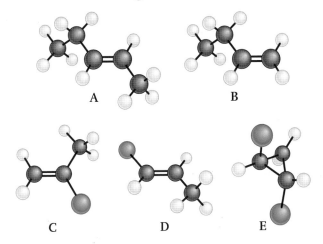

a Which, apart from **A**, can exist as *cis–trans* isomers?

b Draw and name the structural formulae for the pair of *cis–trans* isomers for **A**.

Characteristic reactions of alkenes

Most alkene reactions involve breaking the π bond. This is weaker than the C–C σ bond and reacts with a variety of reagents.

Addition reactions to the double bond

The characteristic reaction of an alkene involves a simple molecule (such as hydrogen, water or bromine) joining across the double bond to form a single product. Such reactions are called **addition reactions**. Addition reactions are the second important type of organic reactions that you will meet.

Addition of hydrogen

This converts the unsaturated alkene to a saturated alkane. Hydrogen gas and a gaseous alkene are passed over a finely divided nickel catalyst supported on an inert material. The equation for the addition of hydrogen to cyclohexene is:

$$\text{(hexagon with double bond)} + H_2 \longrightarrow \text{(hexagon)}$$

Another example is the manufacture of margarine from vegetable oil over a nickel catalyst at a temperature of about 450 K and a hydrogen pressure of up to 1000 kPa (*figure 10.4*).

The molecules of sight

The molecule that is responsible for initiating the signal to our brain, which allows us to see, is called retinal. This molecule is present in the rod and cone cells of the eye. One of its isomers is responsible for the absorption of light. Each double bond is locked into position, preventing rotation. When this isomer absorbs light, one of the two electron-pairs in a double bond is split apart. This allows the retinal molecule to change its shape by rotating around the single bond left behind. After bond rotation, the two electrons that were split apart by the absorption of light come together, fixing the molecule in its new shape and preventing further rotation. This is shown in the reaction sequence in *figure 10.3*. The dramatic change of shape affects the shape of the protein to which the retinal is attached. This causes a signal to be sent via the optic nerve to the brain. The new *trans*-retinal isomer breaks away from the protein and is converted back to *cis*-retinal, ready for further light absorption.

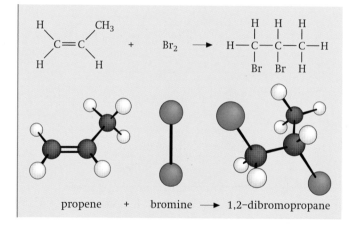

only one of the double bonds (labelled A here) is broken by the absorption of light energy, *hf*

● **Figure 10.3** The change of shape of a retinal molecule by rotation about the single bond that results from absorption of light.

In the *cis* isomer, two methyl groups are on the same side of the double bond; in the *trans* isomer, they are on opposite sides. The breaking of one of the bonds in a double bond by light absorption is not a usual reaction for alkenes.

Addition of halogens

When an alkene such as propene is bubbled through a solution of bromine at room temperature, the bromine solution is rapidly decolourised from its characteristic orange colour (*figure 10.5*). Unlike free-radical substitution on an alkane, this reaction does not require ultraviolet light and will occur in total darkness. The bromine joins to the propene to form 1,2-dibromopropane:

$$CH_3CH{=}CH_2 + Br_2 \longrightarrow CH_3CHBrCH_2Br$$

propene + bromine ⟶ 1,2–dibromopropane

● **Figure 10.4** A hydrogenation vessel for making margarine.

● **Figure 10.5** The reaction of ethene with a solution of bromine. This characteristic reaction provides a test for an alkene (*table 10.1*).

Test	Observation if an alkene is present
shake alkene with bromine water	orange bromine water is decolourised

● **Table 10.1** Simple test for an alkene.

Chlorine and iodine produce similar addition products. Fluorine is too powerful an oxidant and tends to ignite hydrocarbons!

Addition of hydrogen halides

Hydrogen halides also add readily to alkenes. Ethene produces chloroethane on bubbling through concentrated aqueous hydrochloric acid at room temperature:

$$CH_2=CH_2(g) + HCl(aq) \longrightarrow CH_3CH_2Cl(l)$$

The reactivity of the hydrogen halides increases from HF to HI, following the order of decreasing bond energy. Hydrogen fluoride will react with an alkene only under pressure. Alkenes such as propene can give rise to two different products:

$$CH_3CH=CH_2 + HBr \longrightarrow CH_3CHBrCH_3 \text{ or}$$
$$CH_3CH_2CH_2Br$$

The normal product is 2-bromopropane, $CH_3CHBrCH_3$.

Addition of steam

This is a route to making alcohols. Industrially, steam and a gaseous alkene are passed over a solid catalyst. A temperature of 600 K and a pressure of 6 MPa are used in the presence of a phosphoric acid H_3PO_4 catalyst. The addition of steam to ethene produces ethanol:

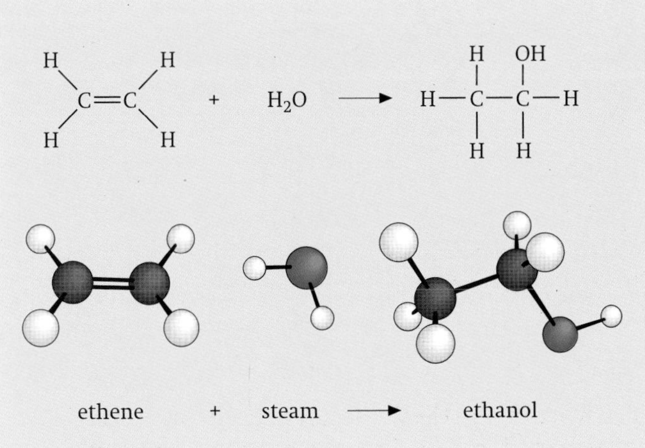

ethene + steam ⟶ ethanol

The mechanism of addition

Although bromine and ethene are non-polar reagents, the bromine molecule becomes polarised when close to a region of negative charge such as the ethene π bond. The π bond then breaks, with its electron-pair forming a new covalent bond to the bromine atom, which carries a partial, positive charge. At the same time, the bromine molecule undergoes heterolytic fission (page 96). Heterolytic fission involves both electrons in the bond moving to the same atom. These changes produce a bromide ion and a positively charged carbon atom (a **carbocation**) in the ethene molecule (*figure 10.6*).

Carbocations are highly reactive and the bromide ion rapidly forms a second carbon–bromine covalent bond to give 1,2-dibromoethane.

In this mechanism, the polarised bromine molecule has behaved as an electrophile. An **electrophile** is a reactant which is attracted to an electron-rich centre or atom, where it accepts a pair of electrons to form a new covalent bond. The reaction is an example of one which proceeds by an **electrophilic addition** mechanism.

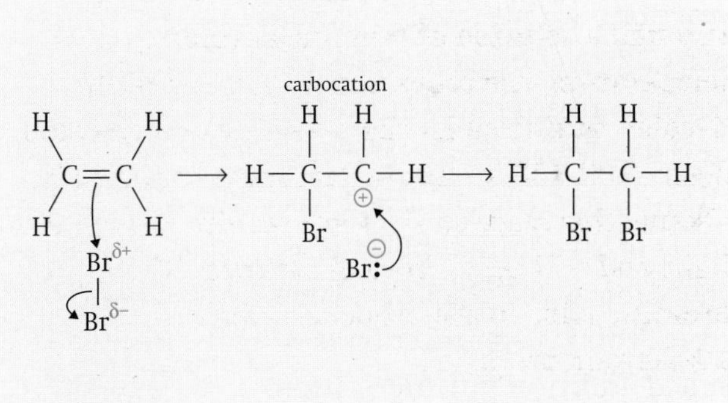

● **Figure 10.6** The formation of a carbocation in the bromination of ethene.

SAQ 10.3

a Draw a dot-and-cross diagram of the carbocation formed in an electrophilic addition to ethene. How many electrons are there on the positively charged carbon atom? Explain how this atom completes its outer electron shell when it combines with a bromide ion.

b Suggest a mechanism for the addition of hydrogen chloride to ethene.

c If the reaction of bromine with ethene is carried out in ethanol containing some lithium chloride, a second, chlorine-containing, product is formed, as well as 1,2-dibromoethane. Suggest a structure for this second product.

d Which of the following are likely to behave as electrophiles: $Cl_2(g)$, $Na^+(aq)$, $F^-(aq)$, $H_2(g)$, $SO_3(g)$, $ICl(g)$? Give an explanation in each case.

Polymerisation of alkenes

During polymerisation, an alkene undergoes an addition reaction to itself. As one molecule joins to a second, a long molecular chain is built up. The reactions are initiated in various ways and the initiator may become incorporated at the start of the polymer chain. Ignoring the initiator, the empirical formula of an addition polymer is the same as the alkene it comes from. This type of reaction is called **addition polymerisation**. Many useful polymers are obtained via addition polymerisation of different alkenes.

Poly(ethene) was first produced accidentally by two scientists (Eric Fawcett and Reginald Gibson) in 1933. The reaction involves ethene adding to itself in a chain reaction. It is a very rapid reaction, chains of up to 10 000 ethene units being formed in one second. The product is a high-molecular-mass straight-chain alkane. It is a polymer and is a member of a large group of materials generally known as plastics. The alkene from which it is made is called the **monomer** and the section of polymer that the monomer forms is called the **repeat unit** (often shown within brackets in structural formulae):

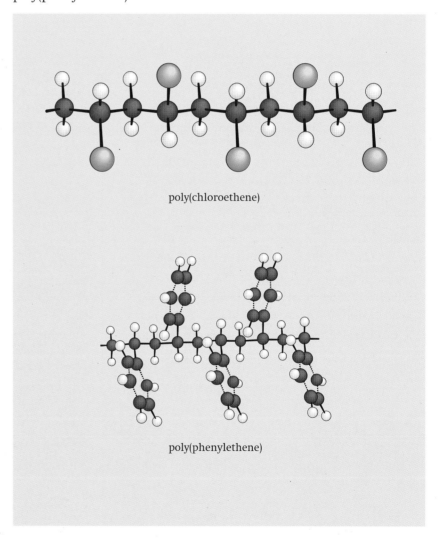

n is very large, e.g. up to 10 000

Other important poly(alkene)s include poly(chloroethene) and poly(phenylethene).

poly(chloroethene)

poly(phenylethene)

They are more commonly known as PVC and polystyrene respectively. Note how the systematic name is derived by putting the systematic name of the alkene in brackets, and prefixing this with 'poly'.

The skeletal formulae of the monomers, chloroethene (traditionally vinyl chloride) and phenylethene (styrene), are as follows:

chloroethene   phenylethene

Note that when a benzene ring becomes a group attached to an alkene its name changes to phenyl (from 'phene', an old name for benzene). The phenyl group may also be written as C_6H_5-.

SAQ 10.4

a Write balanced equations for the formation of poly(chloroethene) and poly(phenylethene) using displayed formulae. Show the repeat unit in brackets.

b A polymer which is often used to make plastic boxes for food storage has the structure:

CH₃   CH₃   CH₃   CH₃

Draw displayed formulae to show (i) the repeat unit of this polymer and (ii) the monomer from which it is made. Label your diagrams with the appropriate systematic names.

We now have several methods for the addition polymerisation of alkenes. These methods provide the wide variety of poly(alkene)s for the many applications of these versatile materials. *Figure 10.7* shows some examples of these uses. The use of poly(alkene)s has created a major problem when we wish to dispose of them. *Figure 10.8* is a sight

● **Figure 10.7** Some products made from poly(alkene)s.

● **Figure 10.8** A beach littered with poly(alkene) waste products, on Holy Island, near the coast of Anglesey in Wales.

familiar to us all. As they are alkanes, they break down very slowly in the environment. They are resistant to most chemicals and to bacteria (they are non-biodegradable). It might seem desirable to collect waste poly(ethene), sort it and recycle it into new products (as in *figure 10.9*).

Some praiseworthy attempts at recycling are being made, mostly of manufacturing waste. However, the current costs of recycling in terms of the energy used in collecting and reprocessing domestic waste plastic is often greater than that used in making new material. A second option is to burn the poly(ethene) to provide energy. The energy released on its combustion is about the same as the energy used in its production. It is potentially a good fuel as it is a hydrocarbon and would reduce the amount of oil or other fossil

● **Figure 10.9** Recycling poly(alkene)s into a new product. Different types of polymers must be separated if the plastics are to be recycled. A mixture of polymers will produce a very inferior plastic.

fuels burned. It could be burnt with other combustible household waste. This would save considerable landfill costs and provide a substantial alternative energy source. Modern technology is such that the waste could be burnt cleanly and with less pollution than from traditional fossil-fuel power stations. The carbon dioxide produced would not add to the total emissions of this greenhouse gas but replace emissions from burning other fossil fuels. Other pollutant gases, such as hydrogen chloride from PVC, can be removed by the use of gas scrubbers. In a gas scrubber, acidic gases are dissolved and neutralised in a spray of alkali. European Union legislation requires household waste incinerators to use gas scrubbers. *Figure 10.10* shows a modern waste incinerator in Vienna.

A third option is feedstock recycling. In view of the limitations of mechanical recycling, BP (British Petroleum) developed a method for processing mixed and contaminated plastics. They have now built a pilot plant at their refinery site in Grangemouth, Scotland. In the plant the polymers are cracked (see page 102) to produce a mixture of hydrocarbons. The mixture contains alkanes, alkenes and arenes which provide additional feedstock for the main refinery. Alkenes, once separated, may once again be made into polymers such as poly(ethene) or poly(propene).

● **Figure 10.10** The incinerator in Vienna is not only clean, it is also a tourist attraction!

SUMMARY

♦ The homologous series of alkenes has the general formula C_nH_{2n}. Alkenes are unsaturated hydrocarbons with one carbon–carbon double bond consisting of a σ bond and a π bond.

♦ Ethene is a planar molecule, other alkenes are planar of the double bond and the four adjacent atoms. Many alkenes have cis–trans isomers which arise because rotation about the double bond is prevented.

♦ Alkenes are more reactive than alkanes because they contain a π bond. The characteristic reaction of the alkene functional group is addition, which occurs across the π bond. For example ethene produces: ethane with hydrogen over a nickel catalyst; 1,2-dibromoethane with bromine at room temperature; chloroethane with hydrogen chloride at room temperature; ethanol with steam in the prescence of H_3PO_4.

♦ The mechanism of the reaction of bromine with ethene is electrophilic addition. Electrophiles accept a pair of electrons from an electron-rich atom or centre, in this case the π bond. A carbocation intermediate is formed after the addition of the first bromine atom. This rapidly reacts with a bromide ion to form 1,2-dibromoethane.

Alkenes produce many useful polymers by addition polymerisation. For example, poly(ethene) from $CH_2=CH_2$, poly(propene) from $CH_3CH=CH_2$, poly(chloroethene) from $CH_2=CHCl$ and poly(tetrafluoroethene) from $CF_2=CF_2$ (see chapter 12, page 140).

The disposal of polymers are difficult as they are chemically inert and non-biodegradable. When burnt, they may produce toxic products such as hydrogen chloride from PVC (poly(chloroethene)). Whilst much manufacturing waste plastic is recycled, the costs of collecting and sorting most domestic waste plastic are too high to make recycling worthwhile. Use of the energy released on combustion (for heating buildings) is a better option for domestic waste, but treatment of flue gases is required to remove toxic pollutants. A third option is feedstock recycling where the polymers are cracked to form alkenes. The alkenes are separated and used as feedstock to make new polymers.

Questions

1   The following diagrams show the structures of four isomers of molecular formula C_4H_8.

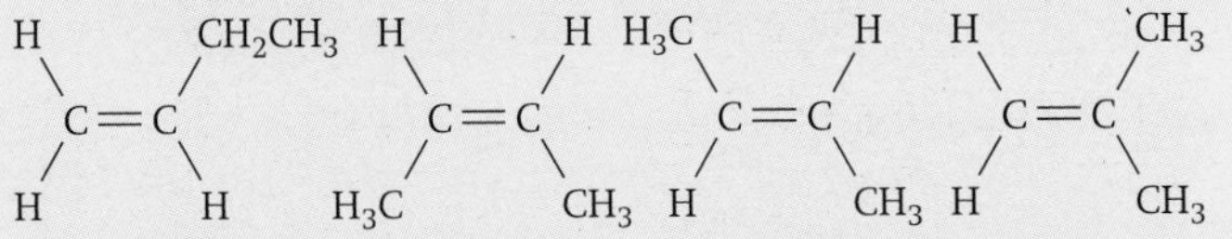

A   B   C   D

a   (i) To which class of compounds do the four isomers belong?
   (ii) Which two diagrams show compounds that are *cis–trans* isomers?

b   Compound A reacts with hydrogen bromide.
   (i) Draw the displayed formulae of the two possible products and give their systematic names.
   (ii) What type of reaction has taken place?
   (iii) What type of mechanism is involved?

c   Compound D produces one product with steam in the presence of phosphoric acid.
   (i) What type of reaction has occurred?
   (ii) Draw the structural formula for this product and label it with its systematic name.

2   Chlorine can react with ethene and with methane. It reacts readily with ethene in the dark but does not react with methane unless sunlight or another source of UV light is present. For each reaction, write a balanced equation, describe the mechanism and state clearly whether or not the chlorine undergoes homolytic fission or heterolytic fission.

3   Cracking of the unbranched compound E, C_6H_{14}, produced the saturated compound F and an unsaturated hydrocarbon G (M_r, 42). Compound F reacted with bromine in UV light to form a monobrominated compound H and an acidic gas I. Compound G reacted with hydrogen bromide to form a mixture of two compounds J and K.

a   Use this evidence to suggest the identity of each of compounds E to K. Include equations for the reactions in your answer.

b   Oil companies often 'reform' compounds such as E. Explain why this is done and suggest two organic products of the reforming of E.

c   Predict the structure of the polymer that could be formed from compound G.

CHAPTER 11

Alcohols

By the end of this chapter you should be able to:

1 explain, in terms of hydrogen bonding, the water solubility and relatively low *volatility* of alcohols;

2 describe and explain the industrial production of ethanol by the reaction of steam with ethene in the presence of H_3PO_4, and fermentation from sugars, for example glucose;

3 outline the use of ethanol in alcoholic drinks;

4 describe the chemistry of alcohols, typified by the reactions of ethanol;

5 describe the classification of alcohols into primary, secondary and tertiary alcohols;

6 describe the oxidation of primary alcohols to form aldehydes and carboxylic acids, the oxidation of secondary alcohols to form ketones, and the resistance to oxidation of tertiary alcohols;

7 outline the use of ethanol as a fuel and methanol as a petrol additive;

8 identify, from an *infrared spectrum*, an alcohol, a *carbonyl compound* and a carboxylic acid.

The homologous series of aliphatic alcohols has the general formula $C_nH_{2n+1}OH$. They are named by replacing the final '-e' in the name of the alkane with '-ol'. The position of the alcohol group is indicated by a number. For example, $CH_3CH_2CH(OH)CH_3$ is butan-2-ol.

Physical properties of alcohols

Miscibility with water

Miscibility is a measure of how easily a liquid mixes; it is the equivalent of solubility for solids. The miscibility of alcohols may be understood in terms of their ability to form hydrogen bonds to water. Methanol and ethanol are freely miscible in water in all proportions. When water and ethanol

mix, some of the hydrogen bonds between the molecules in the separate liquids are broken. These are replaced by hydrogen bonds between water and ethanol. There is no significant gain or loss in energy. *Figure 11.1* shows a molecular model of hydrogen bonds between water and ethanol.

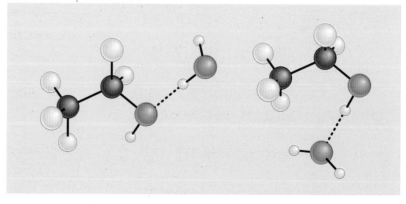

● **Figure 11.1** Hydrogen bonding between ethanol and water (the hydrogen bonds are represented by dotted lines). The bonds form between an oxygen lone-pair and a hydrogen atom.

The miscibility of alcohols in water decreases with increasing length of the hydrocarbon chain. Although the hydroxyl group can still form hydrogen bonds to water, the long hydrocarbon chain disrupts hydrogen bonding between other water molecules. The hydrocarbon chains do not form strong intermolecular bonds with water molecules, because the hydrocarbon chains are essentially non-polar and only exert weak van der Waals' forces.

Volatility of alcohols

Hydrogen bonding between alcohol molecules reduces their **volatility** considerably. Volatility is the ease with which a liquid turns to vapour. The intermolecular forces are significantly stronger in alcohols than in alkanes of comparable size and shape. *Table 11.1* shows the boiling points of some alcohols together with the boiling points of comparable alkanes. To allow for the atoms in the –OH group, each alcohol is compared to the alkane with one more carbon atom. The higher the boiling point, the less volatile the liquid.

All the alcohols in *table 11.1* have boiling points significantly above those of the comparable alkanes.

Industrial production of ethanol

Industrial methylated spirit is a widely used solvent. Methylated spirit is ethanol which is adulterated with methanol. Methanol is poisonous and so it is dangerous to drink methylated spirit. The coloured methylated spirit sold in hardware shops contains a purple dye with a foul taste as a further deterrent. The adulteration means that methylated spirit does not carry the high taxes imposed on alcoholic drinks.

Most industrial ethanol is made by the addition reaction of steam with ethene in the presence of a phosphoric acid catalyst.

$$CH_2=CH_2(g) + H_2O(g) \rightarrow CH_3CH_2OH(g)$$

Production of ethanol by fermentation and distillation

Ethanol has been known to humans in the form of alcoholic drinks for many thousands of years. If ripe fruit is harvested and left, **fermentation** of the sugar in the fruit will soon commence, producing ethanol and other compounds. Fermentation involves yeasts, which occur naturally on the skins of many ripening fruits such as grapes. It is quite probable that early humans, as hunters and gatherers, consumed alcohol by eating partially fermented fruit. It would have been quite a short step forward to allowing fruit (or partially germinated grain) to ferment in a container to form an alcoholic liquor. Such liquors would have a wide range of compounds present and would probably have given many of those people drinking them very sore heads!

Fermentation has become increasingly sophisticated (*figure 11.2*). The process is an exothermic reaction which provides yeast with energy for its metabolism. Glucose (a sugar) is converted to ethanol and carbon dioxide by enzymes in the yeast:

$$C_6H_{12}O_6(aq) \longrightarrow 2C_2H_5OH(aq) + 2CO_2(g)$$

The reaction does not require oxygen (it is an **anaerobic** process), so fermentation is carried out with air excluded to prevent the oxidation of the ethanol to undesirable compounds such as aldehydes, which affect the flavour of the product and may cause headaches.

In the 1980s and 1990s, there have been some major improvements in wine making. One key improvement has been that the fermentation can be carried out at a lower temperature under nitrogen. These conditions can help to preserve the flavour of the fruit and have led to the production of many good quality wines at reasonable prices.

Alcohol	Boiling point (K)	Intermolecular forces	Alkane	Boiling point (K)	Intermolecular forces
ethanol	352	hydrogen bonds	propane	231	van der Waals'
propan-1-ol	371	hydrogen bonds	butane	273	van der Waals'
butan-1-ol	390	hydrogen bonds	pentane	309	van der Waals'

● **Table 11.1** Boiling points of alcohols and alkanes of comparable size and shape.

● **Figure 11.2** Stainless steel fermentation vessels at a modern winery.

Fermentation stops when the ethanol concentration reaches about 15% by volume. This is because ethanol kills the yeast at this concentration. The higher concentration of alcohol found in spirits is produced by distillation of the fermented liquor (see page 91).

The use and abuse of alcoholic drinks

Alcoholic drinks provide us with valuable nutrients, such as minerals and vitamins, as well as a source of energy. It has been estimated that almost 25% of dietary intake of energy (for both children and adults!) in seventeenth-century Britain came from alcoholic drinks.

The ethanol in these drinks also affects our behaviour, and when drunk in excess may cause liver damage or even death. Whilst death may result from long-term alcohol abuse, it may also be caused from excessive short-term consumption, for example half a bottle of spirits drunk all at once. One reason people consume alcoholic drinks is because it makes them feel more relaxed and able to cope with stress. They generally feel more cheerful, less anxious and less tense. These effects are produced by the ethanol depressing the activity of the central nervous system.

Even small quantities of alcohol affect our ability to concentrate when driving motor vehicles or operating machinery. It has been shown that the intake of only one unit of alcohol may be sufficient to affect us. A unit of alcohol is a rough measure of the quantity of alcohol consumed. It is approximately:

■ half a pint of beer;
■ a glass of wine;
■ a single measure of spirits.

The number of units required to raise the blood alcohol concentration (BAC) over the legal limit depends on a number of factors such as sex, body weight, age and how quickly it is consumed. As the driving ability of people is affected well before this limit is achieved it is clearly very unwise to consume anything containing ethanol before driving. The BAC can remain above the legal limit until the morning after drinking or even longer.

The reactions of alcohols

Alcohol reactions may be divided into groups, according to which bonds are broken. The bonds present in a typical alcohol such as ethanol are shown in *table 11.2*, together with their average bond enthalpies (see page 148).

SAQ 11.1

When a bond is broken, is the energy absorbed or released? Place the bonds in *table 11.2* in order of increasing strength.

Although the O–H bond is the strongest, it is also the most polar. The atoms involved in polar bonds are more susceptible to attack by polar reagents, so the O–H bond is not necessarily the most difficult bond to break in ethanol.

SAQ 11.2

a Apart from the O–H bond, which other bond in an alcohol is very polar?

b Why are this bond and the O–H bond so polar?

c Polar reagents include electrophiles and nucleophiles. Explain what is meant by each of these terms.

Bond	Bond enthalpy (kJ mol^{-1})
C–C	350
C–H	410
C–O	360
O–H	460

● **Table 11.2** Bonds and bond enthalpies in ethanol.

We shall now look at the reactions of alcohols in order, according to which bonds are broken.

Reactions in which the O-H bond is broken

Reaction with sodium

Metallic sodium reacts more gently with ethanol than with water, producing a steady stream of hydrogen. As ethanol is less dense than sodium, the metal sinks in ethanol, rather than floating as it does on water. The resulting solution turns phenolphthalein indicator pink (*figure 11.3*) and produces a white solid on evaporation. The white solid is the ionic organic compound called sodium ethoxide, $CH_3CH_2O^-Na^+$. The equation for the reaction is:

$$2CH_3CH_2OH(l) + 2Na(s)$$
$$\longrightarrow 2CH_3CH_2O^-Na^+(alcoholic) + H_2(g)$$

The $CH_3CH_2O^-$ ion is an ethoxide ion. In general, aliphatic alcohols produce alkoxide ions with sodium. This reaction may be compared to the reaction of sodium with water, in which one of the O-H bonds in a water molecule is broken, leaving a hydroxide ion:

$$2H_2O(l) + 2Na(s) \longrightarrow 2Na^+OH^-(aq) + H_2(g)$$

As sodium reacts more gently with ethanol than with water, industrial methylated spirit is used to safely destroy small quantities of sodium. You will find that industrial methylated spirit is used in

● **Figure 11.3** Sodium reacting with ethanol. Phenolphthalein indicator has also been added. The pink colour shows that the alkaline ethoxide ion, $CH_3CH_2O^-$, has been formed.

school and college laboratories rather than pure ethanol. Pure ethanol is much more expensive and is subject to strict Customs and Excise control.

The reactivity of other aliphatic alcohols with sodium decreases with increasing length of the hydrocarbon chain. All reactions between aliphatic alcohols and sodium produce hydrogen and an ionic product. The organic anions formed have the general name alkoxide ions.

The formation of esters

When ethanol is warmed with ethanoic acid in the presence of a strong acid catalyst, an ester, ethyl ethanoate, is formed. During this reaction the O-H bond in ethanol is broken. Ethyl ethanoate smells strongly of pears. Other esters of aliphatic alcohols and carboxylic acids also have characteristic fruity odours. Many of these esters are found naturally in fruits. The equation for the formation of ethyl ethanoate is:

$$CH_3CH_2OH + H_3C-\overset{\overset{\displaystyle O}{\|}}{C}-OH \rightleftharpoons H_3C-\overset{\overset{\displaystyle O}{\|}}{C}-OCH_2CH_3 + H_2O$$

Concentrated sulphuric acid is usually used as the acid catalyst and the mixture is refluxed (page 91). The impure ester is obtained from the reaction mixture by distillation. The reaction mixture contains an equilibrium mixture of reactants and products.

Esters may also be prepared by reaction of an alcohol with an acyl chloride (**acylation**). Acyl chlorides react very vigorously and exothermically with alcohols, releasing hydrogen chloride gas. No catalyst is required and the reaction mixture may require cooling to slow down the reaction. The equation for the reaction of ethanol with ethanoyl chloride is:

$$CH_3CH_2OH + H_3C-\overset{\overset{\displaystyle O}{\|}}{C}-Cl \rightleftharpoons H_3C-\overset{\overset{\displaystyle O}{\|}}{C}-OCH_2CH_3 + HCl$$

Reactions in which the C-O bond is broken

Substitution to form halogenoalkanes

When ethanol is heated with concentrated sulphuric acid and solid sodium (or potassium) bromide, bromoethane is formed. This method provides a standard route to other halogenoalkanes from the corresponding alcohols. You should bear in mind that halogenoalkanes are important intermediates in the formation of many other compounds. You will learn more about halogenalkanes in the next chapter.

Concentrated sulphuric acid and sodium bromide react to produce hydrogen bromide and sodium hydrogen sulphate. In the absence of an alcohol, the hydrogen bromide would escape as a gas:

$$NaBr(s) + H_2SO_4(l) \longrightarrow NaHSO_4(s) + HBr(g)$$

When ethanol is present, the hydrogen bromide acts as a nucleophile, substituting a bromine atom for the hydroxyl, $-OH$, group on the alcohol:

$$C_2H_5OH(l) + HBr(g) \longrightarrow C_2H_5Br(l) + H_2O(l)$$

Note that this reaction is the reverse of the hydrolysis of a halogenoalkane (page 138). Bromoethane distils from the hot liquid. The product is usually collected under water. Excess hydrogen bromide dissolves in the water. *Figure 11.4* shows the apparatus used to produce a small sample of bromoethane in the laboratory.

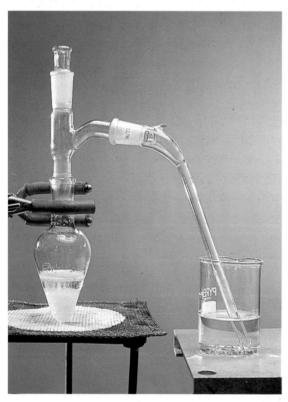

● **Figure 11.4** Bromoethane forms when a mixture of ethanol, concentrated sulphuric acid and sodium bromide crystals is heated. The product distils from the reaction mixture and collects as oily droplets under water.

SAQ 11.3

a Draw a dot-and-cross diagram of hydrogen bromide.

b Indicate the polarity of the hydrogen bromide on your diagram.

c Draw the displayed formula for ethanol and indicate the polarity of the carbon–oxygen bond.

d Using curly arrows, draw diagrams to show the replacement of the hydroxyl group by a bromine atom.

e Complete your reaction scheme by showing the formation of water.

SAQ 11.4

Compare the conditions for the hydrolysis of bromoethane with those for the reverse reaction. Explain how the different conditions enable the reaction to be reversed.

Reactions that may also involve breaking C–C or C–H bonds

Mild oxidation

Like halogenoalkanes (page 137), aliphatic alcohols may be classed as primary, secondary or tertiary.

■ In a **primary alcohol**, the $-OH$ group is on a carbon atom which is bonded to only *one* other carbon atom. Ethanol is a primary alcohol.

■ In a **secondary alcohol**, the $-OH$ group is on a carbon atom which is bonded to *two* other carbon atoms.

■ In a **tertiary alcohol**, the $-OH$ group is on a carbon atom which is bonded to *three* other carbon atoms.

Examples of primary, secondary and tertiary alcohols are:

$$H_3C - CH_2 - CH_2 - OH$$

propan-1-ol
primary alcohol

$$H_3C - \overset{\overset{\displaystyle CH_3}{|}}{\underset{\underset{\displaystyle H}{|}}{C}} - OH$$

propan-2-ol
secondary alcohol

$$H_3C - \overset{\overset{\displaystyle CH_3}{|}}{\underset{\underset{\displaystyle CH_3}{|}}{C}} - OH$$

2-methylpropan-2-ol
tertiary alcohol

SAQ 11.5

Molecular models for six isomers of pentanol, $C_5H_{11}OH$, are shown in *table 11.3*. The oxygen atoms are coloured red. Draw and label the structural formulae for these isomers. Name those without names and classify each of the alcohols as primary, secondary or tertiary.

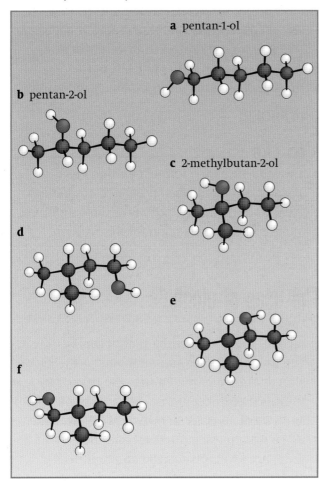

a pentan-1-ol

b pentan-2-ol

c 2-methylbutan-2-ol

d

e

f

● **Table 11.3** Isomers of pentanol.

Primary and secondary aliphatic alcohols are oxidised on heating with acidified aqueous potassium dichromate(VI); tertiary alcohols remain unchanged with this reagent (*figure 11.5*). As primary and secondary alcohols produce different, easily distinguished products, this reaction provides a useful means of identifying an unknown alcohol as primary, secondary or tertiary:

■ Primary alcohols produce aldehydes on gentle heating with acidified dichromate(VI). As aldehydes are more volatile than their corresponding alcohols, they are usually separated by distillation as they are formed. On stronger heating under reflux with an excess of acidified

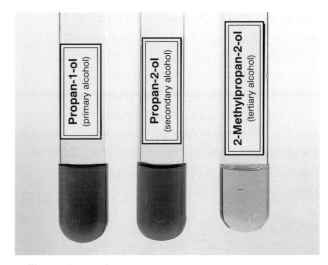

Propan-1-ol (primary alcohol)
Propan-2-ol (secondary alcohol)
2-Methylpropan-2-ol (tertiary alcohol)

● **Figure 11.5** The colour changes that occur when primary, secondary and tertiary alcohols are treated with hot, acidified potassium dichromate(VI).

dichromate(VI), the aldehydes are oxidised to carboxylic acids.

■ Secondary alcohols produce ketones on gentle heating with acidified dichromate(VI).

■ Tertiary alcohols do not react with acidified dichromate(VI).

During the oxidation reactions that occur with primary and secondary alcohols, the orange colour of the dichromate(VI) ion, $Cr_2O_7^{2-}(aq)$, changes to the green colour of the chromium(III) ion, $Cr^{3+}(aq)$.

Ethanol, a primary alcohol, produces the aldehyde ethanal on gentle heating with acidified dichromate(VI). You may prepare a sample of aqueous ethanal by distilling the aldehyde as it is formed when acidified dichromate(VI) is added dropwise to hot ethanol. Simplified equations are frequently used for the oxidation of organic compounds, with the oxygen from the oxidising agent being shown as [O]:

$$CH_3CH_2OH + [O] \longrightarrow H_3C - \overset{\overset{\displaystyle O}{\|}}{C} - H + H_2O$$
ethanal

Ethanal has a smell reminiscent of rotting apples. Further oxidation, by refluxing ethanol with an excess of acidified dichromate(VI), produces ethanoic acid:

$$H_3C - \overset{\overset{\displaystyle O}{\|}}{C} - H + [O] \longrightarrow H_3C - \overset{\overset{\displaystyle O}{\|}}{C} - OH$$
ethanoic acid

You can separate aqueous ethanoic acid from the reaction mixture by distillation after it has been refluxing for 15 minutes. You can detect the ethanoic acid by its characteristic odour of vinegar and by its effect on litmus paper, which turn red.

The secondary alcohol propan-2-ol, on gentle heating with acidified dichromate(vi), produces the ketone propanone. No other products can be obtained even with prolonged refluxing of an excess of the reactants.

$$H_3C - \underset{\underset{H}{|}}{\overset{\overset{CH_3}{|}}{C}} - OH + [O] \longrightarrow H_3C - \underset{\underset{propanone}{}}{\overset{\overset{O}{||}}{C}} - CH_3 + H_2O$$

Typically, ketones have pleasant odours resembling wood and fruit. Heptan-2-one is present in oil of cloves as well as in some fruits.

Complete oxidation: combustion

Ethanol is used as a fuel in the form of methylated spirit; it burns with a pale blue flame, but it is rather volatile and the flame is hard to see in sunlight, so accidents can occur when refilling stoves. Many campers favour it for cooking as it may be carried in lighter containers than those needed for gas. The equation for the complete combustion of ethanol is:

$$C_2H_5OH(l) + 3O_2(g) \longrightarrow 2CO_2(g) + 3H_2O(l);$$
$$\Delta H = -1367.3 \text{ kJ mol}^{-1}$$

C–C and C–H bonds are broken in this reaction, as ethanol is completely oxidised to carbon dioxide and water.

In some countries ethanol is blended with petrol to make a cheaper motor fuel. Methanol is used as a fuel for US ChampCar racing.

Dehydration to alkenes

You can produce alkenes by eliminating hydrogen halide from halogenoalkanes or water from alcohols. For example, if ethanol vapour is passed over a hot, porous ceramic surface, both C–O and C–H bonds are broken producing ethene and water:

$$C_2H_5OH(g) \longrightarrow CH_2{=}CH_2(g) + H_2O(g)$$

The ceramic surface acts as a catalyst; the pores of the ceramic provide a large surface area. The high temperature, catalyst and large surface area all increase the rate of this reaction. The reaction is often referred to as **dehydration**, because a water molecule is removed. *Figure 11.6* shows how you can prepare a small sample of ethene by this method. (Note the similarity to the cracking of an alkane – see page 102.)

An alternative method of dehydrating an alcohol involves heating the alcohol with an excess of concentrated sulphuric acid at about 170 °C. It is important to use an excess of acid, because an excess of ethanol leads to the formation of an ether (ethoxyethane) and water:

$$2C_2H_5OH(l) \longrightarrow C_2H_5OC_2H_5(l) + H_2O(l)$$

SAQ 11.6

a Draw the displayed formula for the organic product produced when propan-2-ol vapour is passed over a heated, porous ceramic surface.

b Write a balanced equation for this reaction.

The uses of alcohols

■ **Fuels**

Alcohols have high enthalpies of combustion. The uses of ethanol and methanol as fuels have already been mentioned (see also page 152). Unleaded petrol contains about 5% of methanol and 15% of an ether known as MTBE (which is made from methanol). The rapid increase in the number of vehicles which can use unleaded

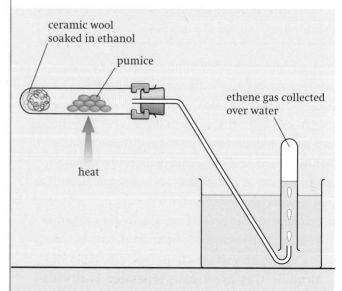

● **Figure 11.6** The dehydration of ethanol.

fuel caused MTBE production to grow faster than that of any other chemical.

■ **Solvents**

As alcohols contain the polar hydroxyl group and a non-polar hydrocarbon chain, they make particularly useful solvents. They will mix with many other non-polar compounds and with polar compounds. Methanol and ethanol will also dissolve some ionic compounds.

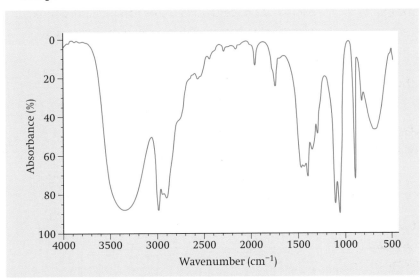

● **Figure 11.7** The infrared spectrum of ethanol.

Functional Group	Location	Wavenumber or cm^{-1}	Absorbance
O–H	alcohols	3200–3600	strong, broad
O–H	carboxylic acids	2500–3500	medium, very broad
C=O	aldehydes, ketones, acids and esters	1680–1750	strong, sharp

● **Table 11.4** Infrared absorption frequencies of some functional groups.

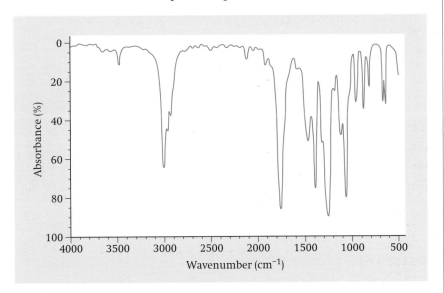

● **Figure 11.8** The infrared spectrum of ethyl ethanoate.

Structural identification using infrared spectroscopy

In a modern infrared spectrometer, a beam of infrared radiation is passed through a sample of the chemical to be identified. Computer analysis enables the absorbance of radiation to be measured at different frequencies. Study of the resulting spectrum enables the presence (or absence) of particular functional groups to be established. *Figure 11.7* shows the infrared spectrum of ethanol. Notice that absorbance increases in a downward direction. An unusual unit is used to measure frequency, the wavenumber or cm^{-1}. *Table 11.4* shows the absorption frequencies which we shall use in this unit.

Look again at the infrared spectrum of ethanol in *figure 11.7*. Most of the absorptions are sharp and some overlap. The absorption of interest is the strong, broad absorption at about 3420 cm^{-1}, which shows the presence of the O–H group. (The O–H absorptions are usually broadened by the effect of hydrogen bonding between molecules.)

If ethanol is warmed with ethanoic acid in the presence of a few drops of concentrated sulphuric acid, ethyl ethanoate (see page 129) is formed:

$$CH_3 - C \overset{\displaystyle O}{\underset{\displaystyle O - CH_2CH_3}{<}}$$

How do we know that the ester is present? The infrared spectrum of a pure sample of ethyl ethanoate is shown in *figure 11.8*.

Note the absence of the strong, broad absorption from the O–H group in ethanol. Instead, there is a strong, sharp absorption at 1720 cm^{-1} which arises from the C=O group.

When ethanol is refluxed with an excess of potassium dichromate and dilute sulphuric acid, ethanoic acid is formed (see page 131). Infrared spectroscopy again helps us to distinguish the product from ethanol. The infrared spectrum of a pure sample of ethanoic acid is shown in *figure 11.9*.

The strong, very broad absorption between 2500 and 3500 cm^{-1} is partly due to the O–H group in the acid. (Although groups containing C–H bonds also absorb in this region, they are of little help in identification as such bonds are present in all organic compounds.) Compare the spectrum of ethanoic acid with that of ethanol. There are clear differences between the two spectra.

SAQ 11.7

a Draw the structural formula of ethanoic acid.

b Apart from the O–H group, which other group can be identified in the spectrum for ethanoic acid? Use *figure 11.9* to record the absorbance and frequency of this bond.

Oxidation of a primary alcohol under milder conditions produces an aldehyde, for example ethanal from ethanol.

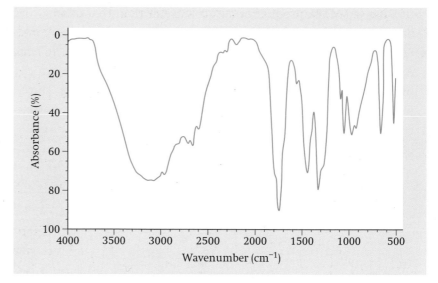

● **Figure 11.9** The infrared spectrum of ethanoic acid.

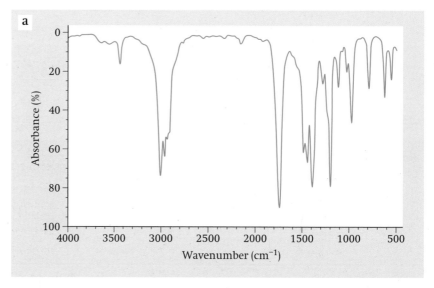

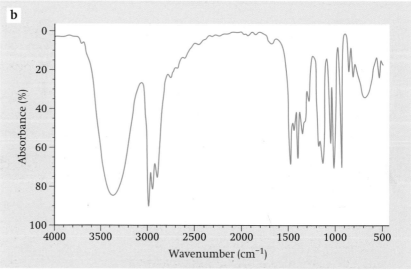

● **Figure 11.10** The infrared spectra of butanone and butan-2-ol, for use with SAQ 11.8.

Oxidation of secondary alcohols produces ketones, for example propanone from propan-2-ol (see page 132).

The infrared spectra of butan-2-ol and butanone are shown in *figure 11.10*.

Identify which of **a** or **b** is butanone. Explain your reasoning.

SUMMARY

- Alcohols are soluble or partly miscible in water because hydrogen bonds can form between water molecules and the –OH group. Hydrogen bonding reduces the volatility of alcohols when compared to hydrocarbon molecules of similar size.

- Industrially, ethanol is produced by the addition reaction of steam to ethene using H_3PO_4 as a catalyst.

- Ethanol has been used by humans for thousands of years in the form of alcoholic drinks, produced by the fermentation of sugar. Whilst alcoholic drinks are a valuable source of nutrients, excessive alcohol consumption may have serious consequences.

- Hydrogen bonding reduces the volatility of alcohols when compared to molecules of similar size.

- Alcohol reactions may be grouped together by the bond(s) broken: the O–H bond, the C–O bond or the C–C and C–H bonds.

- The O–H bond is broken either by sodium to form an alkoxide and hydrogen or by carboxylic acids to form an ester and water.

- The C–O bond is broken by nucleophilic halides in, for example, hydrogen bromide.

- C–C and C–H bonds are broken by oxidation or elimination reactions.

- Oxidation of a primary alcohol occurs in two steps: an aldehyde is formed first and this is oxidised further to a carboxylic acid. Secondary alcohols are oxidised to ketones. Tertiary alcohols are not oxidised under mild conditions. Mild oxidation is usually achieved by heating the alcohol with acidified dichromate(VI).

- Complete oxidation of alcohols occurs on combustion to form carbon dioxide and water.

- Elimination of water from an alcohol produces an alkene; the reaction is a dehydration. Dehydration may be carried out by passing ethanol vapour over a heated porous surface.

- Both methanol and ethanol are useful fuels. Alcohols are also used as solvents.

- Infrared spectroscopy enables identification of alcohols, aldehydes and ketones, carboxylic acids and esters by the presence of O–H and C=O absorption frequencies in the spectra.

Questions

1 An alcohol has a relative molecular mass of 74.0 and has the following composition by mass: C, 64.9%; H, 13.5%; O, 21.6%.

 a Calculate the empirical formula of the alcohol and show that its molecular formula is the same as the empirical formula.

 b Draw the displayed formula of the four possible isomers of this alcohol.

Questions

2 a (i) Explain what is meant by the term **structural isomerism**.

(ii) Draw the displayed formulae for all of the alcohols with the molecular formula $C_4H_{10}O$, classifying each as primary, secondary or tertiary.

b For one primary, one secondary and one tertiary alcohol you identified in **a**, describe its reaction, if any, with acidified aqueous potassium dichromate(VI), naming the organic products of the reaction.

3 Esters are often described as having 'fruity smells'. An ester can be prepared in the laboratory by the reaction of an alcohol and a carboxylic acid in the presence of an acid catalyst.

a Ethanol reacts with 2-methylbutanoic acid to produce an ester which is found in ripe apples.

(i) Draw the displayed formula of 2-methylbutanoic acid.

(ii) When ethanol reacts with 2-methylbutanoic acid, the ester produced has the formula $CH_3CH_2CH(CH_3)CO_2CH_2CH_3$. Write a balanced equation for the formation of this ester.

b The following experiment was carried out by a student:

A 9.2 g sample of ethanol and 20.4 g of 2-methylbutanoic acid were mixed in a flask and 2.0 g of concentrated sulphuric acid was added. The mixture was refluxed for four hours and then fractionally distilled to give 17.4 g of the crude ester. The ester was washed repeatedly with aqueous sodium carbonate until there was no more effervescence. After further washing with distilled water and drying, 15.6 g of pure ester were obtained.

By referring to the experimental procedure above,

(i) explain the meaning of **refluxed**;

(ii) explain why the crude ester was washed repeatedly with aqueous sodium carbonate;

(iii) state which gas was responsible for the **effervescence**.

(iv) Calculate how many moles of each reactant were used. [Ethanol, M_r: 46; 2-methylbutanoic acid, M_r: 102.]

(v) Use your answers to **a**(ii) and to **b**(iv) to calculate the percentage yield of pure ester obtained in the above experiment.

4 An alcohol **A**, C_4H_9OH, is warmed with acidified potassium dichromate(VI). The colour of the reaction mixture changes from orange to green. Distillation of the green mixture produces a colourless liquid containing product **B**. The infrared spectrum of **B** is shown below:

a Use the spectrum above to identify two functional groups present in the product **B**.

b (i) Suggest a structure for the alcohol **A**. Draw a displayed formula of your suggested structure.

(ii) Name the alcohol that you have drawn.

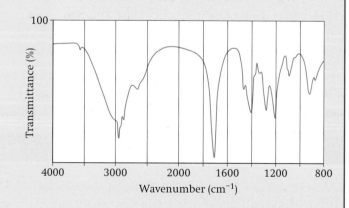

CHAPTER 12

Halogenoalkanes

By the end of this chapter you should be able to:

1 describe substitution reactions of halogenoalkanes, typified by reactions of bromoethane;

2 define the term *nucleophile* as an electron pair donor;

3 describe the mechanism of *nucleophilic substitution* in the hydrolysis of primary halogenoalkanes;

4 explain the rates of hydrolysis of primary halogenoalkanes in terms of the *relative bond enthalpies* of the C–Hal bond (C–F, C–Cl, C–Br and C–I). Aqueous silver nitrate in ethanol can be used to compare these rates;

5 describe the *elimination* of hydrogen bromide from halogenoalkanes, typified by bromoethane, with hot ethanolic sodium hydroxide;

6 outline the uses of fluoroalkanes and fluorohalogenoalkanes, chloroethene and tetrafluroethene, and halogenoalkanes;

7 outline the role of chemists in minimising damage to the environment by, for example, developing alternatives to CFCs in an effort to halt the depletion of the ozone layer.

This chapter deals with the properties and reactions of the simple halogenoalkanes. These have the general formula $C_nH_{2n+1}X$, where X is a halogen atom: one of F, Cl, Br or I. They are named by prefixing the name of the alkane with fluoro, chloro, bromo or iodo and a number to indicate the position of the halogen on the hydrocarbon chain. For example, $CH_3CH_2CHClCH_3$ is 2-chlorobutane.

SAQ 12.1

Name the following compounds: $CH_3CH_2CH_2I$, $CH_3CHBrCH_3$ and $CBrF_2CBrF_2$.

The classification of halogenoalkanes

Halogenoalkanes are classified according to their structures (*figure 12.1*) in a similar way to the

classification of alcohols (see page 130).

- In a **primary halogenoalkane** such as 1-chlorobutane, the halogen atom is covalently bonded to a carbon atom which, in turn, has a covalent bond to just *one* other carbon atom.

- In a **secondary halogenoalkane** such as 2-chlorobutane, the halogen atom is covalently bonded to a carbon atom which, in turn, has covalent bonds to *two* other carbon atoms.

- In a **tertiary halogenoalkane** such as 2-chloro-2-methylpropane, the halogen atom is covalently bonded to a carbon atom which, in turn, has covalent bonds to *three* other carbon atoms.

SAQ 12.2

What type of isomerism is shown by the compounds in *figure 12.1*?

Draw the structural formula of one further isomer of C_4H_9Cl. Is this a primary, a secondary or a tertiary chloroalkane?

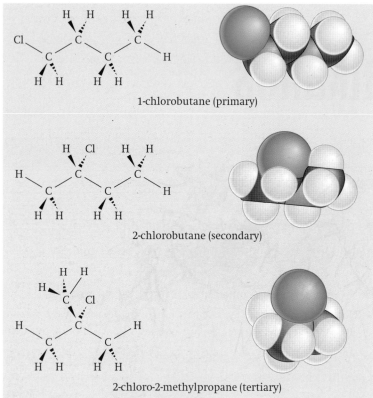

1-chlorobutane (primary)

2-chlorobutane (secondary)

2-chloro-2-methylpropane (tertiary)

● **Figure 12.1** The classification of halogenoalkanes as primary, secondary or tertiary.

Physical properties

Typically, halogenoalkanes and halogenoarenes are volatile liquids that do not mix with water.

SAQ 12.3

a Explain why 1-chloropropane, C_3H_7Cl, is a liquid at room temperature (boiling point = 46.7 °C) whereas butane, C_4H_{10}, is a gas (boiling point = 0 °C).

b Why is it that halogen compounds such as 1-chloropropane do not mix with water?

Nucleophilic substitution

The predominant type of chemical reaction shown by halogenoalkanes involves substitution of the halogen by a variety of other groups. As the halogen atom is more electronegative than carbon, the carbon–halogen bond is polar:

In a substitution reaction, the halogen atom will leave as a halide ion. This means that the atom or group of atoms replacing the halogen atom must possess a lone-pair of electrons. This lone-pair is donated to the slightly positive, δ+, carbon atom, and a new covalent bond forms. A chemical that can donate a pair of electrons, with the subsequent formation of a covalent bond, is called a nucleophile.

The mechanism for the nucleophilic substitution of bromine in bromomethane by a hydroxide ion is:

Nucleophilic attack is followed by loss of the bromine atom as a bromide ion. A new covalent bond between the nucleophile and carbon is formed. Overall a substitution reaction has occurred.

Some nucleophiles possess a net negative charge but this is not necessary for nucleophilic behaviour. Nucleophiles which will substitute for the halogen atom in halogenoalkanes include the hydroxide ion, water and ammonia. The conditions and equations for these reactions follow.

Hydrolysis

As the halogenoalkanes do not mix with water, they are mixed with ethanol before being treated with dilute aqueous sodium hydroxide. Warming the mixture causes a nucleophilic substitution to occur, producing an alcohol. The same hydrolysis reaction will occur more slowly without alkali, if the halogenoalkane is mixed with ethanol and water. The equation for the hydrolysis of bromoethane with alkali is:

$$CH_3CH_2Br + OH^- \longrightarrow CH_3CH_2OH + Br^-$$

The equation for the hydrolysis of bromoethane with water is:

$$CH_3CH_2Br + H_2O \longrightarrow CH_3CH_2OH + HBr$$

SAQ 12.4

Write a balanced equation for the alkaline hydrolysis of 2-bromo-2-methylpropane, using structural formulae for the organic compounds. Name the organic product.

The relative rates of hydrolysis of 1-halogenobutanes

Hydrolysis gets easier as you change the halogen from chlorine to bromine to iodine. At first sight this may seem strange, since the polarity of the carbon–halogen bond decreases from chlorine to iodine. You might expect that a less positively charged carbon atom would react less readily with the nucleophilic hydroxide ion.

However, examination of the carbon–halogen bond enthalpies (table 12.1) shows that the strength of the bond decreases significantly from C–Cl to C–I. This suggests that the ease of breaking the carbon–halogen bond is more important than the size of the positive charge on the carbon atom. A nucleophile may be attracted more strongly to the carbon atom but, unless it forms a stronger bond to carbon, it will not displace the halogen.

The carbon–fluorine bond does not undergo nucleophilic substitution because it is the strongest carbon–halogen bond. Despite its high polarity, no nucleophile will displace it. This accounts for the very high stability of the fluoroalkanes.

You can observe the relative rates of hydrolysis of halogenoalkanes by adding aqueous ethanolic silver nitrate to the reaction mixture and timing the first appearance of a silver halide precipitate (figure 12.2). This will form as soon as sufficient halide ions have been formed by the hydrolysis of the halogenoalkane. For example:

$$Ag^+(aq) + Cl^-(aq) \longrightarrow AgCl(s)$$

- 1-chlorobutane slowly produces a faint white precipitate of silver chloride.
- 1-bromobutane produces a white precipitate of silver bromide rather more rapidly.
- 1-iodobutane produces a yellow precipitate of silver iodide most rapidly.

Reaction with ammonia

If halogenoalkanes are mixed with an excess of ethanolic ammonia and heated under pressure, amines are formed. For example, bromoethane will form ethylamine:

$$CH_3CH_2Br + NH_3 \longrightarrow CH_3CH_2NH_2 + HBr$$

Ethylamine is a primary amine.

SAQ 12.5

Explain why ammonia behaves as a nucleophile in the formation of ethylamine, and suggest a mechanism for this reaction. What will happen to the hydrogen bromide formed?

Bond	Bond enthalpy (kJ mol⁻¹)
C–F	467
C–Cl	340
C–Br	280
C–I	240

● **Table 12.1** Bond enthalpies of carbon–halogen bonds.

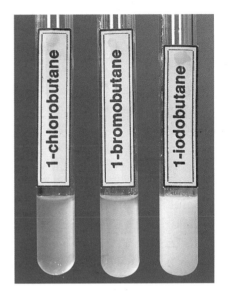

● **Figure 12.2** The hydrolysis of halogenoalkanes by aqueous ethanolic silver nitrate after 15 minutes. The silver nitrate produces an insoluble precipitate of a silver halide.

Elimination reactions

Halogenoalkanes undergo nucleophilic substitution reactions with aqueous alcoholic sodium hydroxide to produce alcohols. However, if halogenoalkanes are refluxed with a purely alcoholic solution of sodium hydroxide, a different reaction occurs. For example, bromoethane will produce ethene:

$$CH_3CH_2Br + NaOH \longrightarrow CH_2=CH_2 + NaBr + H_2O$$

This involves the elimination of hydrogen bromide, leaving an alkene. The hydrogen bromide is neutralised by the alkali. Under these conditions, the rate of the elimination reaction is faster than the rate of the nucleophilic substitution reaction. At lower temperatures, the substitution reaction proceeds at a faster rate.

The uses of halogen compounds

As a functional group, the halogen atom provides chemists with useful routes to the synthesis of other compounds. This is a more important use of organic halogen compounds than their usefulness as products in themselves. For example, the synthesis of a medicine such as ibuprofen requires alkyl groups to be joined to benzene. This is achieved by reactions between halogenoalkanes and benzene. Ibuprofen is an anti-inflammatory medicine that brings relief to many people suffering from rheumatoid arthritis (which causes painful inflammation of the joints).

Halogenoalkanes which do have direct applications include the polymers poly(chloroethene), better known as PVC, and poly(tetrafluoroethene) (*figure 12.3*); several CFCs, for example dichlorodifluoromethane or trichlorofluoromethane, which have been used as refrigerants, aerosol propellants or blowing agents (for producing foamed polymers); CCl_2FCClF_2 as a dry cleaning solvent or degreasing agent for printed circuit boards, and firefighting compounds such as bromochlorodifluoromethane (*figure 12.4*). When combustible

● **Figure 12.3** Poly(tetrafluoroethene), PTFE, is used in the non-stick coating on saucepans and in waterproof clothing.

● **Figure 12.4** Bromochlorodifluoromethane, BCF, is very effective at extinguishing fires. However, it is not now in general use because the breakdown products are poisonous.

materials are ignited, free radicals are generated. These free radicals propagate a seemingly unlimited variety of combustion reaction steps which produce more free radicals. By diverting or terminating these free radical steps we can extinguish the combustion. Bromochlorodifluoromethane (or BCF) is used in some fire extinguishers. The presence of a bromine atom confers flame-retarding qualities on the product. The high temperatures in fires break this compound down, producing free radicals such as Br·(g). These react rapidly with other free radicals produced during combustion, quenching the flames.

Chemists and the environment

Trouble in the ozone layer

Chlorofluorocarbons (CFCs) are regularly blamed for causing damage to our environment. Although they absorb much more infrared radiation per molecule than carbon dioxide, their contribution to the 'greenhouse effect' is very low due to their very low abundance in the atmosphere (carbon dioxide is the main cause of the 'greenhouse

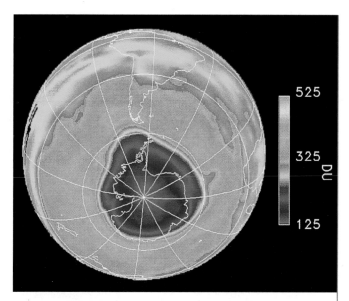

● **Figure 12.5** Representation of satellite measurements of the ozone 'hole' over Antarctica. Ozone concentration is measured in Dobson units (DU). The depletion of ozone reaches a maximum in October, the Antarctic spring, and is probably due mainly to the effects of chlorofluorocarbons (CFCs).

effect'). More importantly, CFCs are responsible for a thinning of the protective ozone layer (*figure 12.5*) in the stratosphere. (Ozone absorbs significant quantities of harmful ultraviolet radiation and thus protects us from skin cancer.) CFCs are still used in air conditioners and were formerly used as refrigerants and aerosol propellants. They were chosen for these purposes as they are gases that liquefy easily when compressed. They are also very unreactive, non-flammable and non-toxic. (Before CFCs were used as refrigerants, highly toxic compounds such as ammonia or sulphur dioxide were used in domestic refrigerators. Leakage of ammonia or sulphur dioxide caused a number of deaths in the 1920s. As a result, some parts of the USA took the drastic measure of banning these early domestic refrigerators.)

The high stability of CFCs has been part of the cause of the problems in the ozone layer. This has enabled concentrations of CFCs to build up in the atmosphere. When they reach the stratosphere, CFCs absorb ultraviolet radiation, which causes **photodissociation** of carbon–chlorine bonds. For example:

$$CF_2Cl_2(g) \xrightarrow{\text{UV light}} CF_2Cl\cdot(g) + Cl\cdot(g)$$

Very reactive chlorine free radicals, $Cl\cdot(g)$, are formed.

These radicals catalyse the decomposition of ozone to oxygen. The overall reaction equation is:

$$2O_3(g) \longrightarrow 3O_2(g)$$

The developments of compounds such as CFCs and BCF illustrate aspects of the work of chemists which benefit society and the environment. Unwanted fires cause considerable economic and environmental damage.

Often, chemists respond to the needs of society by developing new, safer products. This happened in 1928 when Thomas Midgeley (an American engineer) was asked to find a safer alternative to the early refrigerants sulphur dioxide and ammonia. He suggested the use of CF_2Cl_2 and demonstrated its lack of toxicity by inhaling the gas and blowing out a candle!

In recent years, we have learnt that the introduction of CFCs like CF_2Cl_2 were not without environmental consequences. These consequences have been identified by chemists and other scientists. An understanding of the processes involved has also helped in the search for safer replacements, as you will see in chapter 14. Nowadays, chemists are designing new 'ozone-friendly' chemicals to replace the destructive CFCs. The compound 1,1,1,2-tetrafluoroethane, CF_3CH_2F, is now being manufactured as an appropriate alternative. The presence of the hydrogen atoms increases the reactivity of this compound relative to CFCs, so that it is broken down in the lower atmosphere much more rapidly. If it does reach the stratosphere, it does not produce the damaging chlorine free radicals. The use of such alternatives should allow the ozone layer to recover, although the process may well be slow.

SUMMARY

- Halogenoalkanes have the general formula $C_nH_{2n+1}X$, where X is F, Cl, Br or I. They are named by prefixing the name of the alkene with fluoro, chloro, bromo or iodo and a number to indicate the position of the halogen on the hydrocarbon chain.

- Halogenoalkanes react with a wide range of nucleophiles. Nucleophiles possess a pair of electrons, which is donated to the positively charged carbon atom in a C–X bond. The halogen is substituted by the nucleophile, which forms a new covalent bond to the carbon atom attacked.

- Bromoethane produces the following products on reaction with the following nucleophiles:
  - ethanol on warming with water or aqueous alkali;
  - ethylamine on heating under pressure with alcoholic ammonia.

- The reactivities of different halogenoalkanes depends on the relative strengths of the C–X bonds. The C–F bond is very unreactive due to its high bond energy. The rate of hydrolysis of the C–X bond increases from chlorine to iodine as the bond energy decreases.

- On heating bromoethane with a strong base dissolved in ethanol, elimination of hydrogen bromide takes place and ethene is formed.

- Poly(tetrafluoroethene) (a fluoroalkane) is an important polymer valued for its inertness, high melting point and smooth, slippery nature. It is used for non-stick saucepans and electrical insulation. PVC, poly(chloroethene) is a very widely used material.

- Chlorofluoroalkanes have been used extensively as they are inert, non-toxic, non-flammable compounds that have appropriate physical properties for use as propellants, refrigerants, blowing agents or cleaning solvents.

- Chemists play an important role, for example in the development of alternatives to CFCs to provide for the perceived needs of society and to minimise damage to the environment.

- CFCs, which were used extensively in refrigerators and aerosol cans, are very unreactive. Their low reactivity means that they stay in the atmosphere for a long time. They are broken down by ultraviolet radiation to release chlorine free radicals, which have reduced the concentration of ozone in the stratosphere.

- CF_3CH_2F is being introduced as a replacement for various CFCs in refrigerants and aerosols.

- Bromochlorodifluoromethane (BCF), CF_2ClBr, has been used in some fire extinguishers. It is not now in general use because it produces poisonous breakdown products.

Questions

1 There are four isomers of C_4H_9Br. The isomer 2-bromo-2-methylpropane is shown below:

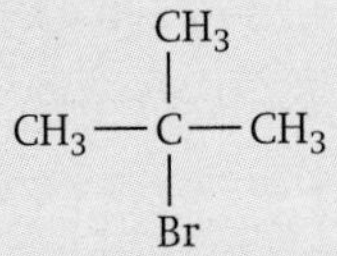

$$CH_3-\underset{\underset{Br}{|}}{\overset{\overset{CH_3}{|}}{C}}-CH_3$$

a Draw the other **three** isomers of C_4H_9Br and classify each as either primary, secondary or tertiary.

b Describe the mechanism of the nucleophilic substitution of 2-bromo-2-methylpropane using aqueous sodium hydroxide.

2 On heating, the compound 1-bromobutane, $CH_3CH_2CH_2CH_2Br$, undergoes reactions, as shown in the scheme below:

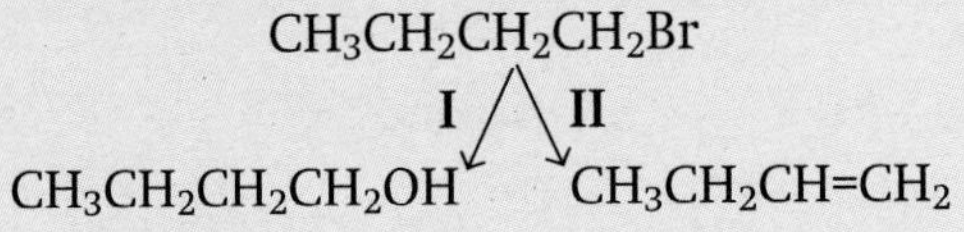

$$CH_3CH_2CH_2CH_2Br$$

I $\diagup$ $\diagdown$ II

$CH_3CH_2CH_2CH_2OH$ $\qquad$ $CH_3CH_2CH=CH_2$

a For each of the two reactions shown, name the reagents and the solvents used.

b If 1-chlorobutane was used in reaction **I** in place of 1-bromobutane, what difference (if any) would you expect in the rate of reaction? Explain your answer.

c If 2-bromo-2-methylpropane was used in reaction **I** in place of 1-bromobutane, what difference (if any) would you expect in the rate of reaction? Explain your answer.

3 Many halogenated carbon compounds are important in industry, but their disposal can cause major environmental problems. Using halogenated solvents and polymers as examples, discuss the problems associated with their disposal and indicate which part of the environment is likely to be affected in each case.

Part 3
How far, how fast?

CHAPTER 13

Enthalpy changes

By the end of this chapter you should be able to:

1 explain that some chemical reactions are accompanied by *enthalpy changes*, principally in the form of heat energy. The enthalpy changes can be *exothermic* (ΔH negative) or *endothermic* (ΔH positive);

2 recognise the importance of oxidation as an exothermic process, for example in the combustion of fuels and the oxidation of carbohydrates such as glucose in respiration;

3 recognise that endothermic processes require an input of heat energy;

4 construct a simple *enthalpy profile* diagram for a reaction to show the difference in enthalpy of the reactants compared with that of the products;

5 explain chemical reactions in terms of enthalpy changes associated with the breaking and making of chemical bonds;

6 explain and use the terms *enthalpy change of reaction*, *standard conditions* and *bond enthalpy*;

7 calculate enthalpy changes from appropriate experimental results, including the use of the relationship: energy change $= mc\Delta T$;

8 use Hess's law to construct *enthalpy cycles* and carry out calculations using such cycles and relevant enthalpy terms.

All chemical reactions involve change. In flames, for example, we can see the changes caused by very fast reactions between the chemicals in burning materials and oxygen from the atmosphere (*figure 13.1*). There are new substances, new colours and changes of state, but the most obvious changes in these reactions are the transfers of energy as light and heating of the surroundings. All life on Earth depends on the transfer of energy in chemical reactions. Plants need the energy from the Sun for the production of carbohydrates by photosynthesis; animals gain energy from the oxidation of their food chemicals.

● **Figure 13.1** The chemical reactions in this fire are releasing large quantities of energy.

Energy transfer: exothermic and endothermic reactions

Most chemical reactions release energy to their surroundings. These reactions are described as **exothermic**. We recognise exothermic reactions most easily by detecting a rise in the temperature of the reaction mixture and the surroundings (the test-tube or beaker, the solvent, air, etc.). Examples of exothermic reactions include:

■ oxidation reactions such as:
the combustion of fuels, respiration in plants and animals (involving oxidation of carbohydrates such as glucose);

■ acids with metals,

■ water with 'quicklime' (calcium oxide) (see page 67).

Some chemical reactions occur only while energy is transferred to them *from* an external source. Reactions, such as these, which require a heat input are **endothermic** reactions. The energy input may come from a flame, electricity, sunlight or the surroundings. Examples of endothermic reactions include:

■ the decomposition of limestone by heating (*figure 13.2*):

$$CaCO_3(s) + energy \longrightarrow CaO(s) + CO_2(g)$$

■ photosynthesis (*figure 13.3*). The energy is supplied to the reactions in the cells by sunlight:

$$CO_2(g) + H_2O(l) + energy$$
$$\longrightarrow carbohydrate\ in\ leaves + O_2(g)$$

● **Figure 13.3** Photosynthesis in green leaves: the most essential chemical reaction of all.

■ dissolving ammonium chloride in water (*figure 13.4*). When the pack is kneaded, water and ammonium chloride crystals mix. As the crystals dissolve, energy is transferred from the surroundings, cooling the injury:

$$NH_4Cl(s) + H_2O(l) + energy \longrightarrow NH_4^+(aq) + Cl^-(aq)$$

● **Figure 13.2** A modern lime kiln. Calcium carbonate, as limestone or chalk, has been converted to calcium oxide (quicklime) for centuries (see page 71), by strong heating in lime-kilns.

● **Figure 13.4** The use of endothermic reactions to treat injuries.

Classify the following processes as exothermic or endothermic: evaporation; crystallisation; making magnesium oxide from magnesium and air; making copper oxide from copper carbonate.

Energy is conserved

It is important to understand that energy is not being created by exothermic chemical reactions and it is not destroyed in endothermic reactions. Energy is transferred from the reacting chemicals to the surroundings or the other way around. The total energy of the whole system of reacting chemicals and the surroundings remains *constant*. This applies to any energy transfer and is summarised in the **law of conservation of energy**: Energy can neither be created nor destroyed.

You may also hear this universal law called the **first law of thermodynamics**, as thermodynamics is the science of transfers of energy.

Enthalpy, and enthalpy changes

Measurements of the energy transferred during chemical reactions must be made under controlled conditions. A special name is given to the energy exchange with the surroundings when it takes place at constant pressure. This name is **enthalpy change**.

Enthalpy is the total energy content of the reacting materials. It is given the symbol H. Enthalpy cannot be measured as such, but it is possible to measure the enthalpy change when energy is transferred to or from a reaction system and changes from one enthalpy to another.

Enthalpy change is given the symbol ΔH (Δ is the upper case of the Greek letter δ, pronounced 'delta', and it is often used in mathematics as a symbol for change). So:

$$\Delta H = H_{products} - H_{reactants}$$

As ΔH is a measure of energy transferred to or from known amounts of reactants, the units are kilojoules per mole ($kJ\,mol^{-1}$).

We can illustrate enthalpy changes by enthalpy profiles (*figure 13.5*). An exothermic enthalpy

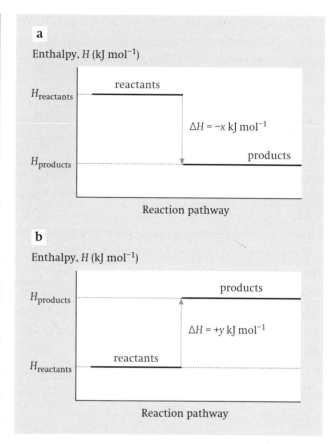

● **Figure 13.5** Enthalpy profiles for **a** an exothermic reaction and **b** an endothermic reaction.

change is always given a negative value, as the energy is lost from the system to the surroundings. It is shown in *figure 13.5a* as:

$$\Delta H = -x\,kJ\,mol^{-1}$$

For example, when methane burns:

$$CH_4(g) + 2O_2(g) \longrightarrow CO_2(g) + 2H_2O(l);$$
$$\Delta H = -890.3\,kJ\,mol^{-1}$$

This means that when one mole of methane burns completely in oxygen, 890.3 kilojoules of energy are transferred to the surroundings (*figure 13.6a*).

An endothermic enthalpy change is always given a positive value, as the energy is gained by the system from the surroundings. It is shown in (*figure 13.5b*) as:

$$\Delta H = +y\,kJ\,mol^{-1}$$

For example, on heating calcium carbonate:

$$CaCO_3(s) \longrightarrow CaO(s) + CO_2(g);$$
$$\Delta H = +572\,kJ\,mol^{-1}$$

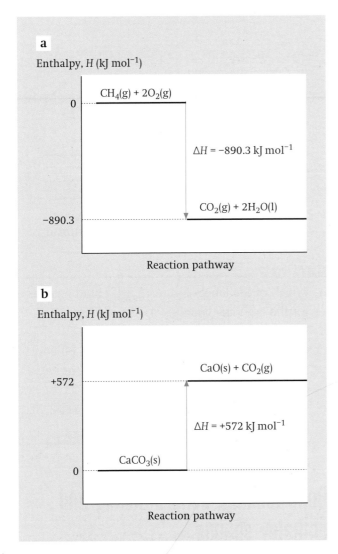

● **Figure 13.6** Enthalpy profiles for **a** the combustion of methane and **b** the decomposition of calcium carbonate.

This means that an input of 572 kilojoules of energy is needed to break down one mole of calcium carbonate to calcium oxide and carbon dioxide (*figure 13.6b*).

Standard enthalpy changes: standard conditions

When we compare the enthalpy changes of various reactions we must use standard conditions, such as known temperatures, pressures, amounts and concentrations of reactants or products. This allows us to compare the standard enthalpy changes for reactions.

A standard enthalpy change for a reaction takes place under these standard conditions:
■ a pressure of 100 kilopascals (10^2 kPa);
■ a temperature of 298 K;

■ the reactants and products must be in the physical states (solid, liquid or gas) that are normal for these conditions;
■ any solutions have a concentration of 1.0 mol dm^{-3}.

The complete symbol for a standard enthalpy change of reaction may be written as, $\Delta H^{\ominus}_{r,298}$, the meanings of the symbols being:
■ $\ominus$ means standard and assumes a pressure of 100 kPa;
■ r is a general symbol for reaction and is changed to f for formation reactions or c for combustion reactions;
■ 298 means all reactants and products are in their physical states at a temperature of 298 K, e.g. carbon dioxide is a gas at 298 K but water is a liquid.

Note that, as values for standard enthalpy changes are usually quoted at 298 K, it is common practice to omit 298 from the symbol.

Standard enthalpy change of reaction $\Delta H^{\ominus}_{r}$

This is defined as: the **standard enthalpy change of reaction** is the enthalpy change when amounts of reactants, as shown in the reaction equation, react together under standard conditions to give products in their standard states.

It is necessary to make clear which reaction equation we are using when we quote a standard enthalpy change of reaction. For example, the equation for the reaction between hydrogen and oxygen can be written in two different ways and there are different values for $\Delta H^{\ominus}_{r}$ in each case.

equation (i)
$$2H_2(g) + O_2(g) \longrightarrow 2H_2O(l);$$
$$\Delta H^{\ominus}_{r} = -572 \text{ kJ mol}^{-1}$$

equation (ii)
$$H_2(g) + \tfrac{1}{2}O_2(g) \longrightarrow H_2O(l);$$
$$\Delta H^{\ominus}_{r} = -286 \text{ kJ mol}^{-1}$$

Note that the value of $\Delta H^{\ominus}_{r}$ in (ii) is half that of $\Delta H^{\ominus}_{r}$ in (i).

Standard enthalpy change of formation $\Delta H^{\ominus}_{f}$

This is defined as: the **standard enthalpy change of formation** is the enthalpy change when one mole of a compound is formed from its elements under standard conditions; both compound and elements are in their standard states.

For example, water is formed in both equations (i) and (ii) above but only in equation (ii) is one mole of water formed. Thus equation (ii) shows that the value of $\Delta H_f^\ominus (H_2O) = -286 \text{ kJ mol}^{-1}$ (*figure 13.7*).

SAQ 13.2

a Write balanced equations for the formation of (i) ethane (C_2H_6) and (ii) aluminium oxide (Al_2O_3). Use a data book to add values for $\Delta H_f^\ominus$ in each case.

b Draw the enthalpy profile for the enthalpy change of formation of ethane. Label your diagram fully.

Standard enthalpy change of combustion $\Delta H_c^\ominus$

The **standard enthalpy change of combustion** is the enthalpy change when one mole of an element or compound reacts completely with oxygen under standard conditions.

For example, the standard enthalpy change of combustion of hydrogen is given by equation (ii) above:

$$H_2(g) + \tfrac{1}{2}O_2(g) \longrightarrow H_2O(l);$$
$$\Delta H_c^\ominus = -286 \text{ kJ mol}^{-1}$$

Another example is shown in *figure 13.8*.

In practice it is not possible to achieve complete combustion under standard conditions. Measurements are taken under experimental conditions; then a value for the enthalpy change is determined and this is corrected to standard conditions through calculations.

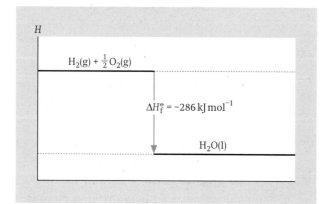

● **Figure 13.7** The standard enthalpy change of formation of water.

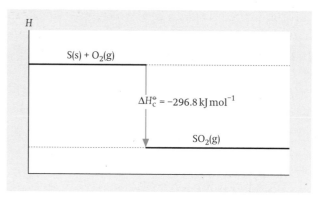

● **Figure 13.8** The standard enthalpy change of combustion of sulphur to form sulphur dioxide.

SAQ 13.3

a Which of the labels $\Delta H_r^\ominus$, $\Delta H_f^\ominus$, $\Delta H_c^\ominus$ could be used for the enthalpy changes shown in *figure 13.6*?

b What are the reaction equations for the combustion of (i) octane (C_8H_{18}) and (ii) ethanol (C_2H_5OH), including the values for $\Delta H_c^\ominus$ (use a data book)?

c Why is the $\Delta H_f^\ominus$ of water the same as the $\Delta H_c^\ominus$ of hydrogen?

Bond making, bond breaking and enthalpy change

A typical combustion reaction, such as the burning of methane, is

$$CH_4(g) + 2O_2(g) \longrightarrow CO_2(g) + 2H_2O(l);$$
$$\Delta H_c^\ominus = -890.3 \text{ kJ mol}^{-1}$$

or, drawing the molecules to show the bonds:

For this reaction to occur, some bonds must break and others form:

- bonds breaking   4 × C–H and 2 × O=O
- bonds forming   2 × C=O and 4 × H–O

The basis of understanding energy transfers during chemical reactions is a fairly simple rule: When bonds break, energy is absorbed (endothermic process). When bonds form, energy is released (exothermic process).

If the energy released by the formation of some bonds is greater than the energy absorbed by the breaking of other bonds, there will be a surplus of energy transferred to the surroundings. The overall reaction will be exothermic.

If the energy released by bond formation is less than the energy absorbed by bond breaking then, overall, energy must be transferred from the surroundings. The reaction will be endothermic.

In the case of the combustion of methane, after all the bond breaking and bond formation, the surplus energy transferred to the surroundings is 890.3 kJ for each mole of methane.

Bond enthalpy

Chemists find that it is useful to measure the amount of energy needed to break a covalent bond, as this indicates the strength of the bond. They call it the **bond enthalpy**. The values are always quoted as bond enthalpy per mole (of bonds broken).

Consider the example of oxygen gas, $O_2(g)$. The bond enthalpy of oxygen is the enthalpy change for the process:

$$O_2(g) \longrightarrow 2O(g); \qquad \Delta H = +498 \text{ kJ mol}^{-1}$$

The symbol E is often used for bond enthalpy per mole. It is related to particular bonds as $E(X-Y)$, where X–Y is a molecule. Thus $E(X-Y)$ is the same as ΔH for the dissociation process

$$X-Y(g) \longrightarrow X(g) + Y(g)$$

Typical values of bond enthalpies per mole are shown in *table 13.1*.

The values quoted in tables for bond enthalpies per mole satisfy the following four conditions.

- They are all positive, as the changes during breaking of bonds are endothermic (energy is absorbed). The same quantities of energy would be released in an exothermic change when the bonds form.
- They are average values. The actual value of the bond enthalpy for a particular bond depends upon which molecule the bond is in. For example, the C–C bond has slightly different strengths in ethane C_2H_6 and in propane C_3H_8, as it is affected by the other atoms and bonds in the molecules. The bond enthalpy quoted in data books for C–C is an average of the values from many different molecules.
- They are compared for bonds in gaseous compounds only.
- They are very difficult to measure directly. They are usually calculated using data from measurements of enthalpy changes of combustion of several compounds.

SAQ 13.4

A book of data gives a value for the standard enthalpy change of combustion of hydrogen as -285.8 kJ mol^{-1}. A value for the enthalpy change of formation of water, calculated from bond energies, is -283.1 kJ mol^{-1}. Suggest why these values are slightly different.

Bond	$E(X-Y)$ (kJ mol^{-1})
H–H	+436
C–C	+347
C=C	+612
C–H	+413
O=O	+498
O–H	+464
C–O	+358
C=O	+805

● **Table 13.1** Some common bond enthalpies.

Measuring energy transfers and enthalpy changes

Simple laboratory experiments can give us estimates of the energy transferred during some reactions. Enthalpy changes may then be calculated.

Enthalpy changes of combustion

Measurements of $\Delta H_c^{\ominus}$ are important as they help to compare the energy available from the oxidation of different flammable liquids, which may be used as fuels.

The type of apparatus used for a simple laboratory method is shown in *figure 13.9*. A fuel, such as an alkane or an alcohol, burns at the wick. Measurements are made of:

- the mass of cold water in the metal calorimeter (m g),
- the temperature rise of the water (ΔT K),
- the loss in mass of the fuel (y g).

It is known that 4.2 J of energy are needed to raise the temperature of 1 g of water by 1 K. (This is called the **specific heat capacity of water** and equals 4.2 J g^{-1} K^{-1}.)

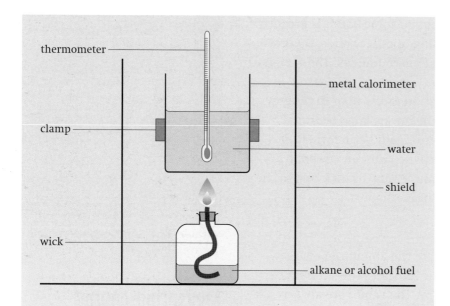

• **Figure 13.9** Apparatus used for approximate measurements of energy transferred by burning known masses of flammable liquids.

The specific heat capacity of a liquid is given the general symbol c. The energy required to raise m g of water by ΔT K is given by the general relationship:

energy transfer (as heating effect) = $mc\Delta T$ joules

Therefore, in the experiment, $m \times 4.2 \times \Delta T$ joules of energy are transferred during the burning of y grams of the fuel. Therefore, if one mole of the fuel has a mass of M grams, $m \times 4.2 \times \Delta T \times M/y$ joules of energy are transferred when one mole of the fuel burns. The answer will give an approximate value of the enthalpy change of combustion of the fuel in joules per mole ($J\,mol^{-1}$). Divide this answer by 1000 to find the value for $\Delta H_c^\ominus$ in kilojoules per mole ($kJ\,mol^{-1}$).

We shall now look at an example. In an experiment using the simple apparatus above to find the enthalpy change of combustion of propanol (C_3H_7OH), the following measurements were made:

mass of water in the calorimeter (m)	= 100 g
temperature rise of the water (ΔT)	= 21.5 K
loss in mass of propanol fuel (y)	= 0.28 g

We are given: A_r (H) = 1, A_r (C) = 12, A_r (O) = 16; and specific heat capacity of water c = 4.2 $J\,g^{-1}\,K^{-1}$

The energy transferred as heat from the burning propanol is

$mc\Delta T = 100 \times 4.2 \times 21.5\,J$

$\qquad = 9030\,J$

This is the energy transferred (heat produced) through burning 0.28 g of propanol. The mass of one mole of propanol is 60 g. Therefore energy transferred through burning one mole of propanol is

$\Delta H_c^\ominus = 9030 \times 60/0.28\,J\,mol^{-1}$

$\qquad = 193\,500\,J\,mol^{-1}$

$\qquad = 1935\,kJ\,mol^{-1}$

From this experiment, the value for $\Delta H_c^\ominus$ (C_3H_7OH) = $-1935\,kJ\,mol^{-1}$.

SAQ 13.5

The value for $\Delta H_c^\ominus$ (C_3H_7OH) in a book of data is given as $-2010\,kJ\,mol^{-1}$. Suggest why the value calculated from the experimental results above is so much lower.

An improved apparatus: the flame calorimeter

The simple apparatus shown in *figure 13.9* is not efficient because energy from burning of the fuel is lost in heating the apparatus and surroundings. A more effective apparatus is shown in *figure 13.10*.

In using this apparatus we need to know its **heat capacity**. This is the energy needed to raise the temperature of the whole apparatus by 1K. The heat capacity may be given by the manufacturer or calculated from measurements made using a fuel with known standard enthalpy change of combustion.

When the flame calorimeter is used, the energy transferred is found from:

energy transferred
$\qquad$ = heat capacity of apparatus $\times \Delta T$

The 'unknown' $\Delta H_c^\ominus$ is calculated as shown in the previous example.

Measuring enthalpy changes of other reactions

The experiments outlined above involved burning fuels. You may also undertake experiments in which the enthalpy changes are from reactions between chemicals in solutions. Here is an example.

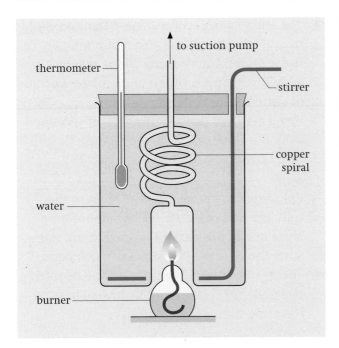

● **Figure 13.10** Flame calorimeter for measuring energy transfers during combustion of flammable liquids.

We shall look at the enthalpy change of neutralisation in the reaction between an acid and an alkali:

e.g. hydrochloric acid plus sodium hydroxide solution:

$$HCl(aq) + NaOH(aq)$$
$$\longrightarrow Na^+(aq) + Cl^-(aq) + H_2O(l)$$

The reaction that produces the enthalpy change here is shown more simply as:

$$H^+(aq) + OH^-(aq) \longrightarrow H_2O(l)$$

$Na^+(aq)$ and $Cl^-(aq)$ are **spectator ions** and take no part in the reaction producing the enthalpy change.

In such an experiment you would:

■ use a heat-insulated vessel, such as a vacuum flask or a thick polystyrene cup (*figure 13.11*), and stir the reactants;

■ use known amounts of all reactants and known volumes of liquids – if one reactant is a solid, make sure you have an excess of solvent or other liquid reactant, so that all the solid dissolves or reacts;

■ measure the temperature change by a thermometer reading to at least 0.2 °C accuracy;

■ calculate the energy transfers using the relationship

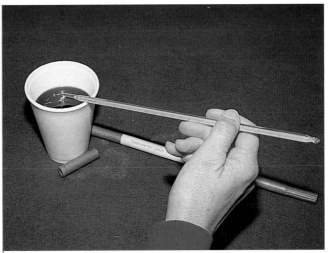

● **Figure 13.11** A simple apparatus used in school laboratories to measure enthalpy changes for reactions in aqueous solutions.

energy transferred (joules)
  $= mc\Delta T$
  = mass of liquid (g) × sp. heat cap. of aq. soln. ($J\,g^{-1}\,K^{-1}$) × temp. rise (K)

We shall now work through some typical results from an experiment. When 50 cm³ of HCl(aq) are added to 50 cm³ of NaOH(aq), both of concentration 1 mol dm⁻³, in an insulated beaker, the temperature rises by 6.2 K. The acid and alkali are completely neutralised.

We may calculate the molar enthalpy change of neutralisation (for the reaction between hydrochloric acid and sodium hydroxide) as follows:

50 cm³ HCl(aq) + 50 cm³ NaOH(aq)
                = 100 cm³ solution
mass of this solution (m) = 100 g
change in temperature (ΔT) = 6.2 K

We assume that the specific heat capacity (c) of the solution is the same as that for water ($4.2\,J\,g^{-1}\,K^{-1}$). Therefore the energy transferred (heat produced) by the reaction is

$mc\Delta T = 100 \times 4.2 \times 6.2$
    $= 2604\,J$

50 cm³ of HCl(aq) or NaOH(aq) of concentration 1 mol dm⁻³ contain 50/1000 mol = 5 × 10⁻² mol of HCl or NaOH. So, the molar enthalpy change of

neutralisation, for the reaction between 1 mol HCl and 1 mol NaOH to give 1 mol NaCl, is given by:

$$\Delta H_r^{\ominus} = -2604/5 \times 10^{-2}\,\text{J mol}^{-1}$$
$$= -52\,080\,\text{J mol}^{-1}$$
$$= -52.08\,\text{kJ mol}^{-1}.$$

The data book value for the molar enthalpy change of neutralisation is $\Delta H_r^{\ominus} = -57.1\,\text{kJ mol}^{-1}$. In the above experiment, heat is lost to the surroundings. The result obtained is thus less exothermic than the data book value.

SAQ 13.6

Suggest why the molar enthalpy changes of neutralisation for the reactions of acids such as hydrochloric, sulphuric, or nitric with alkalis such as aqueous sodium hydroxide or potassium hydroxide are all very similar in value, at about $-57.2\,\text{kJ mol}^{-1}$.

The enthalpy change of solution of sodium hydroxide

In this experiment, the temperature is measured over time and a graph is plotted. Extrapolation of the curve obtained as the mixture cools allows correction to be made to the estimated temperature rise. The corrected figure makes allowance for cooling losses to the surroundings.

Method

1 Weigh a polystyrene cup of the kind shown in *figure 13.11*.
2 Weigh 100 g of distilled water into the polystyrene cup. (How could you work out roughly how much to add in advance?)
3 Measure the temperature of the water in the cup. Keep a check on it until the temperature is steady. Record this temperature.
4 Add a few pellets of solid sodium hydroxide straight from a previously sealed container. (Solid sodium hydroxide absorbs water from the air, so it gets heavier if you leave it standing. **Take care** – it is also very **corrosive**. Wash it off immediately with water if you get it on your skin, and report to your teacher.)
5 Stir the mixture immediately, and start a stop-watch. Keep stirring with the thermometer, and record the temperature every 30 seconds.

6 The temperature will reach a maximum, and then it will start to fall. When it has fallen for five minutes, you can stop taking readings.
7 Weigh the cup + solution to calculate the mass of sodium hydroxide you dissolved.
8 Plot a graph of temperature against time, and work out the maximum temperature the mixture might have reached (see graph in *figure 13.12*).
9 Calculate the amount of heat input to the solution, and calculate the amount of heat given out by the sodium hydroxide and water.
10 Scale the result to tell you how much heat energy would have been released on dissolving one mole (40 g) of sodium hydroxide to make the same strength of solution.

A typical set of results

The example below will help you to understand the procedure and calculations:

Mass of polystyrene cup	=	8.00 g
Mass of polystyrene cup + distilled water	=	108.15 g
Mass of distilled water used	=	100.15 g
Mass of cup + water + sodium hydroxide	=	114.35 g
Mass of sodium hydroxide that dissolved	=	6.20 g
Initial temperature of water in the cup	=	15.0 °C

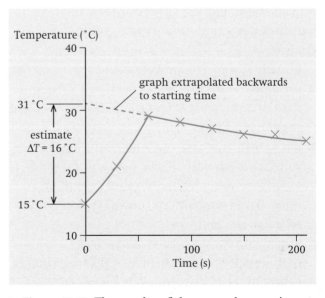

● **Figure 13.12** The results of the example experiment.

Table showing temperature at fixed times after mixing:

Time (s)	0	30	60	90	120	150	180	210
Temperature (°C)	15.0	21.0	29.0	28.0	27.0	26.0	26.0	25.0

Calculation

Estimated temperature rise caused by 6.20 g NaOH is $\Delta T = 15.0\,°C = 16\,K$

Energy transferred = $m \times c \times \Delta T$

where m = mass of water, c = specific heat capacity of water $(4.18\,J\,g^{-1}\,K^{-1})$, and ΔT = maximum temperature rise. So

$$\text{Energy transferred} = 100.15\,g \times 4.18\,J\,g^{-1}\,K^{-1} \times 15.0\,K$$
$$= 6.70\,kJ$$

6.20 g NaOH releases 6.28 kJ energy on dissolving it in water.

Enthalpy changes by different routes: Hess's law

When we write a reaction equation, we usually show only the beginning and end, that is, the reactants and products. But there may be many different ways that the reaction actually occurs in between. The reaction may have different routes.

For example, consider a reaction system, with initial reactants A + B and final products C + D, in which two different routes (1 and 2) between A + B and C + D are possible (*figure 13.13*). What can be said about the enthalpy changes for the two different routes? Are they different too?

The answer to this question was first summarised in 1840 by Germain Hess and is now called **Hess's law**. A concise form is: The total enthalpy change for a chemical reaction is *independent* of the route by which the reaction takes place, provided the initial and final conditions are the same.

In the case of our example above, Hess's law tells us that the enthalpy change for route 1 would equal the total of the enthalpy changes for route 2; that is

$$\Delta H_1 = \Delta H_2 + \Delta H_3 + \Delta H_4$$

The overall enthalpy change is affected only by the initial reactants and the final products, not by what happens in between.

Hess's law seems fairly obvious in the light of the more universal first law of thermodynamics (law of conservation of energy – see page 148). If different routes between the same reactants and products were able to transfer different amounts of energy, energy would be created or destroyed. We could

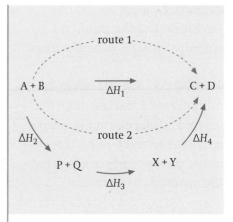

● **Figure 13.13** Two different routes between reactants and products. Hess's law tells us that $\Delta H_1 = \Delta H_2 + \Delta H_3 + \Delta H_4$.

make 'perpetual motion' machines (*figure 13.14*) and gain free energy for ever! Unfortunately, as in most aspects of life, you cannot get something for nothing.

Using Hess's law: enthalpy cycles

Chemists often use an **enthalpy cycle** to calculate the enthalpy change for a reaction which cannot easily be measured directly. We shall look at three examples. The first example makes use of bond enthalpies; the second,

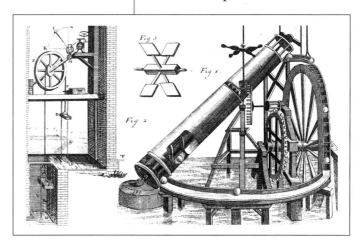

● **Figure 13.14** An attempt to design a mechanical perpetual motion machine. The heavy spheres cause the wheel to rotate. This operates the 'screw', which lifts the spheres back to the top of the wheel. Why does it not work?

enthalpy changes of formation and the third, enthalpy changes of combustion.

Calculating $\Delta H_f^\ominus$ from bond enthalpy data

An important reaction which is covered in more detail in chapter 15 is the reaction for the Haber process (see page 184) for the synthesis of ammonia

$$N_2(g) + 3H_2(g) \rightarrow 2NH_3(g)$$

Bond enthalpy data is shown in *table 13.2*.

When calculating $\Delta H_r^\ominus$ from bond enthalpy data, you will find it helpful to draw the enthalpy cycle showing the bonds present in the reactants and products. Remember that bond enthalpy is the enthalpy change for the formation of atoms from one mole of the bonds in the gaseous state.

The enthalpy cycle for the Haber process is shown in *figure 13.15*. Look at the equation for route 1. The following bonds are broken:

- one N≡N triple bond;
- three H–H single bonds;

and the following bonds are formed:

- three N–H single bonds per molecule of ammonia – a total of six as two ammonia molecules are produced from one nitrogen and three hydrogen molecules.

Route 2 shows the input of

Bond	Bond enthalpy (kJ mol^{-1})
N≡N	945
H–H	436
N–H	391

- **Table 13.2** Bond enthalpies important for the Haber process.

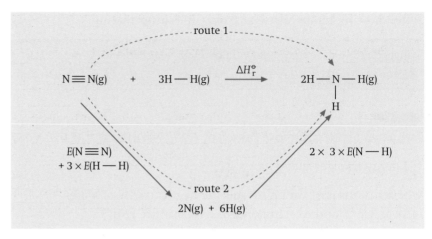

- **Figure 13.15** The enthalpy cycle for the production of ammonia by the Haber process.

enthalpy to break the bonds in the reactants, $E(N≡N) + 3 \times E(H–H)$ and the release of enthalpy when ammonia forms, $2 \times 3 \times E(N–H)$.

As, by Hess's Law, the enthalpy change for route 1 = total enthalpy change for route 2:

$$\Delta H_r^\ominus = \text{enthalpy change for bonds broken} -$$
$$\text{enthalpy change for bonds formed}$$
$$= E(N≡N) + 3 \times E(H–H) - 6 \times E(N–H)$$
$$= 945 + (3 \times 436) - (6 \times 391)$$
$$= 2253 - 2346$$
$$= -93 \text{ kJ mol}^{-1}$$

Remember that bond breaking is endothermic, bond formation is exothermic (hence the negative sign before $6 \times E(N–H)$).

Figure 13.16 will help you to visualise which bonds are being broken and which formed with the help of molecular models.

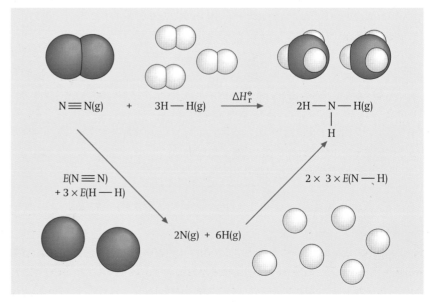

- **Figure 13.16** Bond breaking and bond formation in the enthalpy cycle for the Haber process.

	A	B	C	D	E	F
1	**Enthalpy of formation of ammonia from bond enthalpies**					
2						
3						
4	Bond	Bond enthalpy $(kJ\,mol^{-1})$	Number of bonds broken	Enthalpy input $(kJ\,mol^{-1})$	Number of bonds formed	Enthalpy output $(kJ\,mol^{-1})$
5						
6	N≡N	945	1	945		0
7	H–H	436	3	1308		0
8	N–H	391		0	6	−2346
9						
10		Total enthalpy input:		2253		
11		Total enthalpy output:				−2346
12						
13				Enthalpy of reaction $(kJ\,mol^{-1})$:		−93

● **Table 13.3** Bond enthalpy calculation for the Haber process.

Bond enthalpy calculations lend themselves to use of a spreadsheet on a computer. *Table 13.3* shows such a spreadsheet for the Haber process.

SAQ 13.7
A balanced chemical equation for the complete combustion of methane is:

$$CH_4(g) + 2O_2(g) \rightarrow CO_2(g) + 2H_2O(g)$$

a Re-write this equation to show the bonds present in each molecule.
b Using your equation, draw an enthalpy cycle showing bonds broken in the reactants, forming gaseous atoms, and bonds formed in the products from these gaseous atoms.
c Use the bond enthalpies given on page 151 to calculate the enthalpy change of combustion for methane (use a spreadsheet if possible).
d Compare the value for $\Delta H_c^\ominus$ with the experimentally determined value of -890 kJ mol^{-1}. Which value is more accurate?

Enthalpy change of reaction from enthalpy changes of formation
Enthalpy changes of formation of many compounds have been determined experimentally under carefully controlled conditions. Often these have been found indirectly from other experimental enthalpy changes such as enthalpy changes of combustion

(see page 158). Many data books provide detailed tables of enthalpy changes of formation. These enthalpy figures help chemists and chemical engineers to design a new chemical production plant. In such a plant, an exothermic process may release sufficient energy to cause a fire or explosion. Careful design of the plant allows the release of energy to be controlled and even re-used for heating or electricity generation.

Imagine that you are building a plant to make slaked lime from quicklime (see page 71). The equation for this exothermic reaction is:

$$CaO(s) + H_2O(l) \rightarrow Ca(OH)_2(s); \qquad \Delta H_r^\ominus = ?$$

The enthalpy changes of formation for each of the reactants and the product are

$$Ca(s) + \tfrac{1}{2}O_2(g) \rightarrow CaO(s);$$
$$\Delta H_f^\ominus [CaO(s)] = -635.1\,kJ\,mol^{-1}$$
$$H_2(g) + \tfrac{1}{2}O_2(g) \rightarrow H_2O(l);$$
$$\Delta H_f^\ominus [H_2O(l)] = -285.8\,kJ\,mol^{-1}$$
$$Ca(s) + H_2(g) + O_2(g) \rightarrow Ca(OH)_2(s);$$
$$\Delta H_f^\ominus [Ca(OH)_2(s)] = -986.1\,kJ\,mol^{-1}$$

We can now draw the enthalpy cycle (*figure 13.17*).
■ As both CaO(s) and H$_2$O(l) appear in the top left-hand corner of the cycle, we must add the enthalpy changes of formation of each compound.
■ Route 1 contains the $\Delta H_r^\ominus$ which we wish to determine.

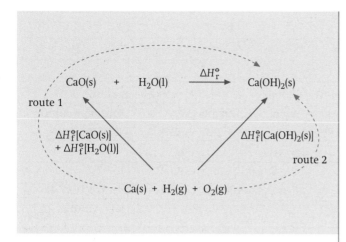

● **Figure 13.17** The enthalpy change for the reaction of quicklime with water.

The total enthalpy change for route 1 is:

$\Delta H_f^\ominus [\text{CaO(s)}] + \Delta H_f^\ominus [\text{H}_2\text{O(l)}] = (-635.1) + (-285.8)$
$+ \Delta H_r^\ominus \qquad\qquad\qquad + \Delta H_r^\ominus \text{ kJ mol}^{-1}$

and for route 2 is:

$\Delta H_f^\ominus [\text{Ca(OH)}_2\text{(s)}] = -986.1 \text{ kJ mol}^{-1}$

By Hess's Law, the enthalpy change for route 1 = enthalpy change for route 2.

Thus:

$(-635.1) + (-285.8) + \Delta H_r^\ominus = -986.1 \text{ kJ mol}^{-1}$

or $\Delta H_r^\ominus = (-986.1) - [(-635.1) + (-285.8)] \text{ kJ mol}^{-1}$
$= -65.2 \text{ kJ mol}^{-1}$

Notice the brackets inserted round each enthalpy change figure. These help ensure that you do not make a mistake over the signs!

SAQ 13.8

The balanced equation for the decomposition of magnesium carbonate is:

$\text{MgCO}_3\text{(s)} \rightarrow \text{MgO(s)} + \text{CO}_2\text{(g)}$

a Draw an enthalpy cycle showing the formation of each of the reactants and products from their elements in their standard states.

b Use the following enthalpy changes of formation to calculate the enthalpy change for the decomposition of magnesium carbonate.

	$\text{MgCO}_3\text{(s)}$	MgO(s)	$\text{CO}_2\text{(g)}$
$\Delta H_f^\ominus$ (kJ mol^{-1})	−1096	−602	−394

Enthalpy change of formation from enthalpy changes of combustion

Consider the formation of methane from carbon and hydrogen:

(a) $\text{C(s)} + 2\text{H}_2\text{(g)} \longrightarrow \text{CH}_4\text{(g)}; \qquad \Delta H_f^\ominus = ?$

This could be a very useful reaction for making methane gas starting with a plentiful supply of carbon such as coal or wood charcoal. Scientists are trying to find ways of making it occur directly and need to know the value of the enthalpy change of formation of methane. The best way is to use different routes, from reactants to product, with reactions that are known to occur.

Carbon, hydrogen and methane all burn in oxygen and the enthalpy changes of combustion of each can be measured.

(b) $\text{C(s)} + \text{O}_2\text{(g)} \longrightarrow \text{CO}_2\text{(g)};$
$\qquad\qquad\qquad \Delta H_c^\ominus = -393.5 \text{ kJ mol}^{-1}$

(c) $\text{H}_2\text{(g)} + \frac{1}{2}\text{O}_2\text{(g)} \longrightarrow \text{H}_2\text{O(l)};$
$\qquad\qquad\qquad \Delta H_c^\ominus = -285.8 \text{ kJ mol}^{-1}$

(d) $\text{CH}_4\text{(g)} + 2\text{O}_2\text{(g)} \longrightarrow \text{CO}_2\text{(g)} + 2\text{H}_2\text{O(l)};$
$\qquad\qquad\qquad \Delta H_c^\ominus = -890.3 \text{ kJ mol}^{-1}$

One helpful way to calculate the enthalpy change for reaction (a) above starts with an enthalpy cycle (*figure 13.18*):

■ As in previous enthalpy cycles, the balanced equation for the enthalpy change we wish to calculate is written at the top of the cycle.

■ In this example the common products of combustion are written at the bottom of the cycle. We add oxygen to both sides of the top equation to balance the equations for the

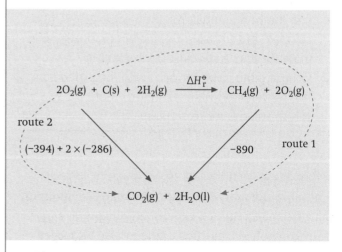

● **Figure 13.18** An enthalpy cycle used to calculate the enthalpy change of formation of methane.

downward pointing arrows. This does not alter the reaction in the top equation.

■ Note that, in route 2, one mole of carbon is oxidised by combustion together with two moles of hydrogen.

The enthalpy change for route 1
$= \Delta H_r^{\ominus} + (-890) \, kJ \, mol^{-1}$
The enthalpy change for route 2
$= (-394) + 2 \times (-286) \, kJ \, mol^{-1}$

Applying Hess's Law:

$$\Delta H_r^{\ominus} + (-890) = (-394) + 2 \times (-286)$$

Hence:

$$\Delta H_r^{\ominus} = (-394) + 2 \times (-286) - (-890) = -76 \, kJ \, mol^{-1}$$

SAQ 13.9

a Write the balanced chemical equation for the enthalpy change of formation of ethane, $C_2H_6(g)$.

b Using your equation, draw an enthalpy cycle, given the enthalpy change of combustion of ethane is -1560 kJ mol⁻¹.

c Using the enthalpy changes of combustion of carbon and hydrogen in the above example, calculate the enthalpy change of formation of ethane.

SUMMARY

♦ Chemical reactions are often accompanied by transfers of energy to or from the surroundings, mainly as heat. In exothermic reactions, energy is transferred away from the reacting chemicals; in endothermic reactions, energy is gained by the reacting chemicals.

♦ Changes in energy of reacting chemicals at constant pressure are known as enthalpy changes (ΔH). Exothermic enthalpy changes are shown as negative values (−) and endothermic enthalpy changes are shown as positive values (+).

♦ Standard enthalpy changes are compared under standard conditions of pressure, temperature, concentration and physical states.

♦ Standard enthalpy changes of formation $\Delta H_f^{\ominus}$ and of combustion $\Delta H_c^{\ominus}$ are defined in terms of one mole of compound formed or of one mole of element or compound reacting completely with oxygen; their units are kJ mol⁻¹.

♦ Bond breaking is an endothermic process; bond making is an exothermic process.

♦ Bond energy is a measure of the energy required to break a bond. The values quoted are usually average bond enthalpies, as the strength of a bond between two particular atoms is different in different molecules.

♦ Enthalpy changes may be calculated from measurements involving temperature change in a liquid, using the relationship:
enthalpy change = mass of liquid
× specific heat capacity
of liquid
× temperature change.
$$\Delta H = mc\Delta T$$

♦ Hess's law states that 'the total enthalpy change for a chemical reaction is independent of the route by which the reaction takes place provided the inital and final conditions as the same'.

♦ The principle of Hess's law may be used to calculate enthalpy changes for reactions that do not occur directly or cannot be found by experiment. For example:
● the enthalpy change of reaction for the formation of ammonia may be calculated from the average bond enthalpies of the reactants ($N_2 + H_2$) and of the N–H bonds in ammonia, NH_3;
● the enthalpy change of reaction for the slaking of quicklime from the enthalpy changes of formation of the reactants, $CaO(s)$ and $H_2O(l)$, and product, $Ca(OH)_2(s)$;
● the enthalpy change of formation of methane from the enthalpy changes of combustion of carbon, hydrogen and methane.

Questions

1 Considerable scientific research is taking place to develop hydrogen as a fuel for the future. Scientists are especially interested in developing hydrogen as a motor fuel because it burns more cleanly and more efficiently than petrol.

  a Suggest what is meant by the statement **hydrogen burns more cleanly than petrol**.

  b Fuel scientists use a term called the 'energy density' to compare fuels. Energy density is the energy produced from the combustion of **one gram** of a fuel. It can be calculated from the standard enthalpy change of combustion of a fuel.

   (i) Define the term standard enthalpy change of combustion.

   (ii) Calculate the energy density of hydrogen and of petrol. You may assume that petrol consists of the hydrocarbon C_8H_{18}.
   [$\Delta H_c^{\ominus}$ (H_2): $-287\,kJ\,mol^{-1}$;
   $\Delta H_c^{\ominus}$ (C_8H_{18}): $-5473\,kJ\,mol^{-1}$,
   A_r: H, 1.00; C, 12.00.]

  c Suggest two reasons why petrol is the preferred fuel for motor vehicles even though hydrogen has a greater energy density.

2 In an investigation to find the enthalpy change of combustion of ethanol, C_2H_5OH, a chemist found that 1.60 g of ethanol could heat 150 g of water from 22.0 °C to 71.0 °C.

  a Explain what is meant by the enthalpy change of combustion of ethanol.

  b Use the chemist's results to calculate a value for the enthalpy change of combustion of ethanol.

  c Explain, with reasons, how you would expect this result to compare with the theoretical value of the standard enthalpy change of combustion of ethanol.

3 Methane production as 'biogas' is growing rapidly as an alternative energy supply, particularly in some countries. Methane can be used as a fuel because of its exothermic reaction with oxygen.
$CH_4(g) + 2O_2(g) \rightarrow CO_2(g) + 2H_2O(l)$;
$\Delta H_c^{\ominus}$ ($CH_4(g)$) = $-890.3\,kJ\,mol^{-1}$

  a Explain what is meant by $\Delta H_c^{\ominus}$ ($CH_4(g)$) = $-890.3\,kJ\,mol^{-1}$

  b The enthalpy change of formation of methane, $\Delta H_f^{\ominus}$ ($CH_4(g)$), cannot be measured directly.

   (i) Using the data below, calculate the enthalpy change of formation of methane.

Compound	$\Delta H_c^{\ominus}$ (kJ mol^{-1})
$CH_4(g)$	−890.3
C(s)	−393.5
$H_2(g)$	−285.9

   $C(s) + 2H_2(g) \quad \rightarrow \quad CH_4(g)$

   (ii) Suggest why the enthalpy change of formation of methane cannot be measured directly.

  c A typical biogas plant in China, using the dung from five cows, can produce 3000 dm^3 of biogas in a day. The biogas produced contains 60% of methane by volume.

   (i) Using the data in the table in part b(i), calculate the maximum heat energy that can be produced each day from the methane in this biogas. [Assume that 1 mole of methane occupies 24 dm^3 under these conditions.]

   (ii) Suggest a practical difficulty of using biogas as a fuel on a large scale.

CHAPTER 14

Reaction rates

By the end of this chapter you should be able to:

1 describe qualitatively, in terms of *collision theory*, the effect of concentration changes on the rate of a reaction;

2 explain why an increase in the pressure of a gas, increasing its concentration, may increase the rate of a reaction involving gases;

3 explain qualitatively, using the Boltzmann distribution and enthalpy profile diagrams, what is meant by the term *activation energy*;

4 describe qualitatively, using the Boltzmann distribution and enthalpy profile diagrams, the effect of temperature changes on the rate of a reaction;

5 explain what is meant by a *catalyst*;

6 explain that, in the presence of a catalyst, a reaction proceeds via a different route, i.e. one of lower activation energy, giving rise to an increased reaction rate;

7 interpret catalytic behaviour in terms of the Boltzmann distribution and enthalpy profile diagrams;

8 state what is meant by *homogeneous catalysis* and *heterogeneous catalysis*;

9 outline, as an example of homogeneous catalysis, how gaseous chlorine free radicals, formed by the action of ultraviolet radiation on CFCs, catalyse the breakdown of the gaseous ozone layer into oxygen;

10 describe catalysts as having great economic importance, for example in fertiliser production;

11 for carbon monoxide, oxides of nitrogen and unburnt hydrocarbons, describe their presence in and/or formation from the internal combustion engine and state their environmental consequences;

12 outline, as an example of heterogeneous catalysis, how a catalytic converter removes carbon monoxide and nitrogen monoxide emissions from internal combustion engines.

Speed, rates and reactions

In a race, the fastest car, horse or runner is the winner. The winner needs to cover the given distance in the shortest possible time. We measure the speed of the winner by measuring the distance travelled in one hour. For example, in the 1999 Japanese Grand Prix, Mika Häkkinen completed the 310.8 kilometre race in 1 hour, 31 minutes and 18.79 seconds. Häkkinen's average speed was $204.2 \, \text{km h}^{-1}$, the distance travelled divided by the time taken.

The speed of the winner of a car race is much higher than that of the winning horse or runner in their respective races. Different chemical reactions also proceed at very different speeds. Some reactions can be very fast whilst others may be very slow (*figure 14.1*). Reactions also proceed at different speeds when conditions are changed. For example, glucose will burn rapidly in air, but when used as an energy source in our bodies, it is oxidised much more slowly. In both cases the products are the same (carbon dioxide and water).

For chemical reactions we use the term **rate** instead of speed to describe how fast a reaction proceeds. The rate of a reaction is found by measuring the amount in moles of a reactant which is used up in a given time. The study of rates of reactions is referred to as **chemical kinetics**.

In the 1999 Japanese Grand Prix, Häkkinen's speed on timed sections of the course varied from $100\,km\,h^{-1}$ to $300\,km\,h^{-1}$. His speed built up at the start of the race, was higher in clear straight sections, and lower on bends or corners. The rate of a chemical reaction also varies throughout a reaction but in a very different way. Unlike Häkkinen's speed, a reaction rate starts high and then decreases throughout the reaction. When all the reactants have been used up, the rate has dropped to zero. Häkkinen, however, was still driving very fast as he passed the chequered flag!

Rates of reaction – why bother?

There are many reasons why chemists study reaction rates, for example to:

- improve the rate of production of a chemical;
- help understand the processes going on in our bodies or in the environment;
- gain an insight into the mechanism of a reaction.

During the manufacture of a chemical such as a fertiliser or a medicine, the reaction rate is one of the factors which determine the overall rate of production. In the next chapter, you will see how an understanding of how fast a reaction proceeds helps chemists and chemical engineers to choose the conditions used in the manufacture of a particular chemical.

The consequences of improving a reaction rate may have far-reaching consequences on chemical manufacture. For example, before the Second World War, it took about a week to make nitroglycerine, a high explosive, in commercial quantities. During the war, research by an ICI chemist increased the rate by about seven times – very useful at the time.

The rate of formation of ozone in the stratosphere is dependent on the intensity of ultraviolet (UV) radiation reaching the Earth from the Sun. In chapters 9, 10 and 12, you learnt how ozone depletion has been caused by chlorine free radicals. The ozone layer normally helps to filter out UV radiation from sunlight, but its destruction leads to high levels of UV radiation reaching the Earth's surface where it causes problems such as skin cancer. The chlorine free radicals are formed by the action of UV radiation on chlorofluorocarbons (see page 141). A knowledge of the rates of these various reactions has enabled chemists to contribute much to an understanding of this environmental problem, highlighting the urgent need to control the use of chlorofluorocarbons.

Also in chapters 9, 10 and 12 you met several reaction mechanisms. Many of these mechanisms have been discovered by a study of reaction rates.

● **Figure 14.1   a** A variety of rapid combustion reactions take place following the ignition of fireworks.   **b** Fortunately, rusting is a very slow reaction.

It is the slowest step in a mechanism which determines the overall rate of reaction. The slowest step in a reaction mechanism is called the **rate determining step**. In the formation of ozone in the stratosphere, the slowest step involves the photodissociation (breakdown by light) of oxygen molecules by high-energy ultraviolet radiation into oxygen atoms. Environmental chemists have studied the rates of many of the reactions which take place in the atmosphere. Such research has contributed much to our understanding of these reactions and of the effects of pollutant gases. It is this work which has both demonstrated the need for the control of man-made pollutants and led to the development of more environmentally friendly products.

Factors that affect the rate of a reaction

Factors that may affect the rate of a chemical reaction are:

1 **Concentration of reactants**, for example increasing the concentration of hydrochloric acid in the reaction of magnesium with the acid (see page 70), will cause the reaction rate to increase. This will be seen in the more vigorous evolution of hydrogen gas. For reactions involving gases, an increase in pressure will increase the reaction rate, as pressure is proportional to concentration. The Haber process is operated under high pressure in order to increase the rate of reaction (see page 183).

2 **Temperature**. A catalytic converter only functions properly when it is hot as the rate of the reactions on the surface of the catalyst are negligible when the converter is cold. Nearly all reactions show an increase in rate as the temperature is increased. In general, an increase of 10 kelvin causes the rate of many reactions to approximately double.

3 If the **surface area** of a solid or liquid reactant is increased, the reaction rate will be increased. For example, powdered magnesium produces hydrogen more rapidly than magnesium ribbon when treated with hydrochloric acid.

4 Some reactions require visible or ultraviolet radiation for reaction to occur. An increase in the **intensity of the radiation** will increase the reaction rate, for example in the free radical substitution of methane by chlorine (see page 113).

5 **Catalysts** are well known for their ability to speed up reactions (see page 171), for example nickel in the hydrogenation of vegetable oils to make margarine (see page 119).

Methods of following rates of reaction

We can measure reaction rates in a variety of ways to study the factors which affect chemical reaction rates. Each of these factors is a variable which we could investigate. However, as there are several variables which affect the rate of a reaction, experiments need to be designed with care if the measurements made are to be of value. For example, if we wish to study how an increase in temperature affects the rate of a reaction, we must keep other variables, such as the concentrations of reactants, the same for each experiment we carry out over the range of temperatures chosen. A fair test is required.

We must also be certain of the stoichiometry (see page 27) of the reaction. In other words, we need to know the mole ratios of reactants and products as shown by the balanced chemical equation. We must be sure that there are no side reactions taking place, as these will affect our measurements.

Armed with the above information, we can now decide which variable to investigate and which others will need to be controlled. If the reaction is taking place in a solution, concentrations of reactants can be controlled by ensuring that a large excess of each is present with the exception of the reactant under investigation.

Lastly we must decide how we can monitor the progress of the reaction. This might involve following the change in concentration of a reactant or of a product. There are two types of method accessible to us:

■ A destructive method based on chemical analysis (for example, a titration). As this takes time, the reaction mixture must be quenched to slow down or stop the reaction. Quenching by cooling in ice might be sufficient. Alternatively, a reagent might be removed by a rapid reaction – an acid catalyst could be neutralised using a base.

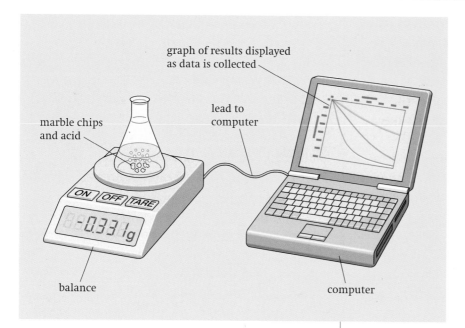

● **Figure 14.2** The apparatus used to measure the mass loss during the reaction of marble chips with hydrochloric acid.

■ Non-destructive methods using a variety of physical techniques (measuring, for example, a decrease in mass of a reaction mixture, the volume of a gas evolved, change in colour intensity, change in pH or change in electrical conductivity). As these changes do not involve interfering with the progress of the reaction, there is no need to quench the reaction mixture.

An outline follows of some of these methods for monitoring reaction rates.

Monitoring reaction rate using mass loss

When a gas is evolved during a reaction, monitoring mass loss may provide a suitable method of measuring the reaction rate. There needs to be sufficient loss in mass to be followed with reasonable accuracy on the balance available. For example, 2.00 g of small marble chips will give a satisfactory loss in mass when treated with

150 cm^3 of 2 mol dm^{-3} hydrochloric acid. *Figure 14.2* illustrates the equipment in use. Ideally, the mass loss can be monitored using a computer.

SAQ 14.1

The equation for the reaction of marble (calcium carbonate, CaCO$_3$) with hydrochloric acid is:

$$CaCO_3(s) + 2HCl(aq) \rightarrow CaCl_2(aq) + CO_2(g) + H_2O(l)$$

a Calculate the amounts, in moles, of calcium carbonate (marble chips) and hydrochloric acid used in this experiment.

b Which reagent is present in excess?

c By how much is it present in excess?

d Explain why a reagent is present in excess.

Figure 14.3 shows some results obtained with 1.0, 2.0 and 4.0 mol dm^{-3} solutions of hydrochloric acid at room temperature.

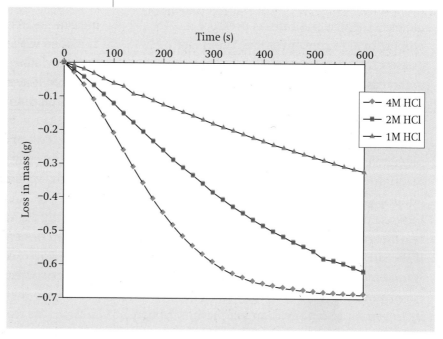

● **Figure 14.3** Graphs showing results obtained for the loss in mass when marble chips react with hydrochloric acid. The rate of reaction can be found by measuring the mass lost in a given time. The steeper the curve the faster the rate of reaction. When no more gas is evolved, the reaction rate is zero and the line on the graph becomes horizontal.

a Determine the mass lost after 300 seconds from the graph shown in *figure 14.3* for the 1.0 and 2.0 moldm^{-3} solutions of hydrochloric acid.

b These two masses are a measure of the relative reaction rates over 300 seconds. How has the reaction rate changed on doubling the acid concentration from 1.0 to 2.0 moldm^{-3}?

c Suggest a mathematical relationship between the reaction rate and the acid concentration.

● **Figure 14.5** Ribena drinks of different concentrations.

Monitoring reaction rate using volume of gas evolved

The reaction of calcium carbonate with hydrochloric acid may also be monitored by collecting the carbon dioxide evolved. The gas may be collected in a gas syringe or in an inverted, water-filled burette (*figure 14.4*). The volume of carbon dioxide produced over a period of time is proportional to the reaction rate.

Monitoring reaction rate using colour intensity

Figure 14.5 shows three glasses of Ribena diluted with water. Can you tell in which glass the concentration is greatest? Could you rank them in order of concentration? Could you tell how much Ribena is in each glass?

The answer to the first two questions should be 'yes'. The answer to the third cannot be found without getting an idea of what the colour actually means in terms of concentration.

● **Figure 14.6** 'Standard' Ribena solutions with an unknown alongside. Try to estimate the concentration of the unknown.

It would be possible to hazard a good guess. You could prepare calibration solutions like these:

a 2.0 cm^3 Ribena in 10 cm^3 solution
b 1.6 cm^3 Ribena in 10 cm^3 solution
c 1.2 cm^3 Ribena in 10 cm^3 solution
d 0.8 cm^3 Ribena in 10 cm^3 solution
e 0.4 cm^3 Ribena in 10 cm^3 solution

You could put them in specimen tubes like the ones shown in *figure 14.6*. They must all be filled to the same level.

You could take a sample of Ribena from one of the glasses and put it into an identical tube, to exactly the same depth. It may be better to look down from above to distinguish the colours. This increases the amount of liquid that the light passes through, so that faint colours show up better. It also helps to standardise how far away from the samples your eyes are.

This method could be used to estimate the concentration of copper ions in the experiment shown in

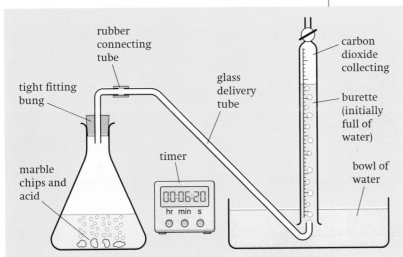

● **Figure 14.4** Cross section of the apparatus used to monitor reaction rate by measuring volume of gas evolved.

figure 14.8. You could have a range of coloured solutions, each representing a concentration from (say) 1 to 0.1 mol dm⁻³. There might be better methods of course, and scientists spend much of their time inventing improved methods and equipment. For example, a simple **colorimeter** for measuring the concentration of chlorine is shown in figure 14.7. The colorimeter measures the amount of light of a specific colour that passes through a sample.

A spectrophotometer is often used to measure colour concentration. The word 'spectrophotometer' means 'light-measurer making use of part of the spectrum'. In practice the spectrophotometer measures how much light of a particular wavelength can pass through a sample, liquid or gas.

The beaker in figure 14.8a contains 1 dm³ of 1.00 mol dm⁻³ aqueous copper sulphate, so it contains one mole of copper ions (63.5 g of them). Iron wool reacts with the copper ions in solution, displacing them and changing the colour of the solution as a result.

$$Cu^{2+}(aq) + Fe(s) \longrightarrow Fe^{2+}(aq) + Cu(s)$$

Solutions appear coloured because they absorb radiation in the visible region of the spectrum. Aqueous copper sulphate, $CuSO_4(aq)$, absorbs radiation in the yellow, orange and red regions. Blue light passes through the solution, so the solution appears blue.

A **colorimeter** measures the absorbance of radiation over a selected narrow range of wavelengths. The wavelength range is selected by choosing a filter which transmits light over the

● **Figure 14.8** Copper ions replacing atoms of iron. After several minutes the blue colour of the solution (**a**) has become paler and a red-brown deposit has formed on the iron wool (**b**).

range absorbed by the compound under study. Hence a yellow, orange or red filter would be appropriate for measurements of absorption by aqueous copper sulphate.

Monitoring reaction rates of gases using pressure changes

Measurements of pressure change at a given temperature can be used to calculate concentration change as a reaction proceeds. For example, this method can be used to monitor the production of carbon dioxide from limestone in a sealed container (figure 14.9).

Monitoring reaction rates of solutions using chemical analysis

If there is a change in acidity or basicity as a reaction proceeds, suitable titrations can be made to

● **Figure 14.7** A colorimeter is used to analyse the concentration of chlorine in drinking water.

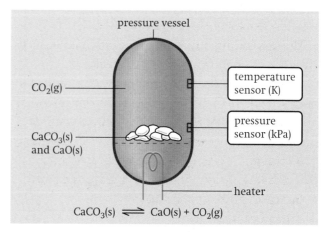

● **Figure 14.9** A notional system to investigate the effect of heat on the decomposition of limestone.

follow the rate. The rate of formation of sulphurous acid, H_2SO_3 (a component of acid rain formed by the reaction of sulphur dioxide with water), could be followed by measuring the increase in concentration of hydrogen ions produced. This is monitored by titrating samples of the increasingly acidic solution against a basic solution of known concentration, for example $0.001\,mol\,dm^{-3}$ aqueous sodium hydroxide. The more sodium hydroxide that is needed to neutralise the sample, the more sulphurous acid is present.

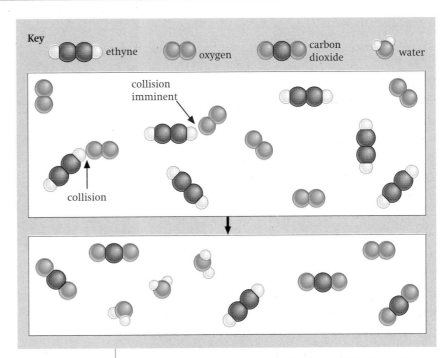

● **Figure 14.10** Molecules of ethyne, $C_2H_2(g)$, and oxygen, $O_2(g)$, can collide. If the collision is big enough, chemical bonds are broken. They are re-formed when the fragments combine to make new molecules: carbon dioxide, $CO_2(g)$, and steam, $H_2O(g)$.

The collision theory of reactivity

Collisions occur between billiard balls in a game of snooker. There are a few stories from the second half of the nineteenth century of explosions occurring when two billiard balls collided with exceptional force. One story describes how such an explosion set off a gunfight in a Colorado saloon.

Why should billiard balls explode? At the time billiard balls were made from celluloid (a mixture of nitrocellulose and camphor). Sometimes the balls were varnished with a nitrocellulose paint. If two such billiard balls collided with sufficient energy they might conceivably explode. As modern billiard balls are no longer made of celluloid, this is not something we are likely to experience, however many hours we spend watching snooker on television!

The 'exploding billiard balls' story enables us to visualise the collision theory of reactivity. Collision theory helps to provide explanations for the following experimental observations, made by measuring rates of reaction. The measurements show that the rate of reaction can be increased by:

■ increasing the concentration of a reactant;
■ increasing the pressure of a gaseous reactant;
■ increasing the temperature;
■ using a catalyst.

An example of a reaction, well known to welders, is the combustion of ethyne in oxygen when using

an oxyacetylene torch. (Acetylene is a more traditional name for ethyne. This gas is an example of an alkyne. Alkynes contain a C≡C triple bond.) This gaseous reaction involving two reactants is shown in *figures 14.10* and *14.11*. The reactant molecules are moving around and occasionally, random collisions will occur.

SAQ 14.3

Write the balanced equation for the reaction in *figure 14.10*.

It is not hard to imagine that, like the exploding billiard balls, collision of an ethyne and an oxygen molecule can result in a reaction. However, again like our nineteenth century billiard balls, only a few of these collisions result in a reaction. Not all the collisions are effective. A collision is not necessarily followed by a reaction. Effective collisions occur when the kinetic energy of the colliding molecules provides sufficient energy for reaction. We shall explore this aspect later (see page 170). However, a reaction certainly *cannot* occur if the molecules don't collide.

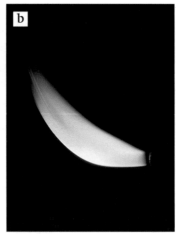

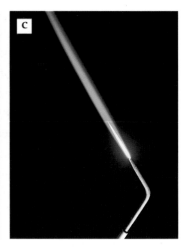

● **Figure 14.11**
a Ethyne, mixed with oxygen, is used in an oxyacetylene torch. Here the gas is not ignited, and you can see it bubbling through water.
b The ethyne is now ignited, but is not completely combusting because the yellow flame indicates the presence of carbon: the temperature of the flame is relatively low.
c The ethyne is now being completely converted into carbon dioxide and water: the temperature of the flame is much higher.

This simple notion is the basis of the **collision theory of reactivity**. When there are more balls on a billiard table, more collisions are likely to occur. If we increase the pressure of a gas, the molecules are closer together and more collisions will occur. Increasing the number of collisions will increase the number of effective collisions and so the reaction proceeds at a faster rate (*figure 14.12*).

The theory also generally applies to reactions in solutions. The reactants in solution behave rather like those in a gas – in each case the reactants are separated from each other. An increase in pressure increases the number of gas molecules in a given volume, which means the concentration is increased. When we increase the concentration of reagents in solution, the rate of reaction also increases.

In studying the influence of concentration on rate, we have to be careful to keep temperature constant, because a change in temperature will alter the reaction rate. The qualitative influence is for an increase in temperature to increase reaction rate, and using the simple collision theory model it is not hard to see why. There will be a wide distribution of energies (and therefore speeds) of molecules, but increasing the temperature will certainly increase the average speed of the molecules. Indeed, an increase in temperature is the same thing as an increase in the random kinetic energies, and hence the speeds, of the molecules. The increased speeds of molecules will lead to more molecules gaining sufficient energy to react on collision.

● **Figure 14.12** The larger number of molecules in **a** than in **b** leads to more collisions between molecules and a faster reaction rate.

We can summarise all this as follows:

■ Molecules will react only if they collide with each other.

■ Reactions will occur only if there is enough energy in the collison.

■ Increased concentration of molecules increases the likelihood of collision, which increases reaction rate.

■ Increased temperature increases the proportion of molecules with sufficient energy to react which increases reaction rate.

The Boltzmann distribution

In any mixture of moving molecules, the energy of each molecule varies enormously. Like bumper cars at a fairground, some are belting along at high speeds while others are virtually at a stand-still. The situation changes moment by moment: a car (or particle) travelling at a fairly gentle pace can get a shunt from behind and speed off with much greater energy than before; the fast car (or particle) that caused the collision will slow down during the collision.

The Boltzmann distribution represents the numbers of cars (or particles) with particular energies. It does not work too well for bumper cars, but it does with samples of gas, where there are billions and billions of molecules in constant random motion. A few are almost motionless. A minority have momentary speeds far in excess of the average. The majority have speeds around an average value. This is illustrated by the graph shown in *figure 14.13*.

This average value will increase if the temperature of the entire collection of molecules is increased. Some molecules will still be almost immobile, but at any one time there is a greater number at a higher speed than before. The new distribution is shown in *figure 14.14*. The effect of this shift in the distribution is to increase the proportion of molecules with sufficient energy to react. This energy value is called the **activation energy**. The collision energy of the exploding billiard balls mentioned earlier must have exceeded the activation energy for reaction.

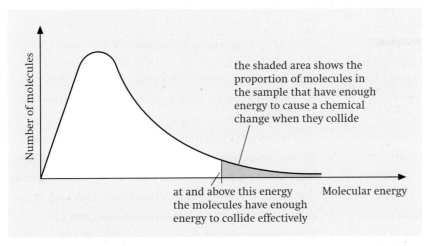

● **Figure 14.13** The Boltzmann distribution for molecular energies in a sample of gas. Since the mass of each molecule is the same, the difference in energies is due to a difference in speed. Note the asymmetric shape of the curve.

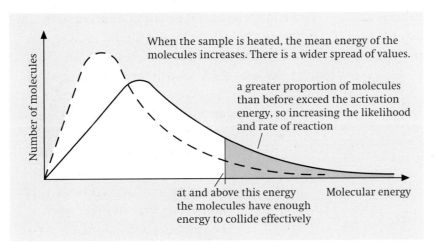

● **Figure 14.14** Note how the Boltzmann distribution flattens and shifts to the right at the higher temperature. The areas under both curves are the same – they represent the total number of molecules in the sample, and this should not change before a reaction occurs.

Activation energy

Just as two cars with effective bumpers may collide at low speed with no real damage being done (apart from frayed tempers), so low-energy collisions will not result in reaction. The molecules will bounce apart unchanged (*figure 14.15*). On the other hand, a high speed collision between one

- **Figure 14.15** These collisions, frequent as they are, are not effective. They do not, we hope, result in permanent damage – chemical change.

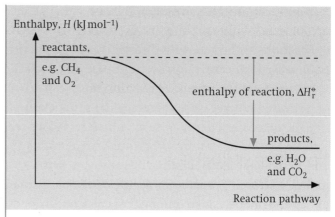

- **Figure 14.16** A 'down-hill-all-the-way' reaction. Fortunately, it does not happen for methane and oxygen at normal temperatures and pressures. For an explanation of enthalpy, see page 148.

car and another will result in permanent damage, and the configuration of each vehicle will be drastically altered (and the same may go for the drivers). In the same sort of way, molecules have to collide with a certain minimum energy E_a for there to be a chance of reaction. E_a is referred to as the **activation energy** for the reaction. Like other energy changes, activation energy has units of kJ mol⁻¹.

But why should we have to surmount this energy barrier E_a to bring about reaction? After all, as we saw in chapter 13, if a reaction is exothermic the sum of the bond energies in the product molecules is less than the sum of the bond energies in the reactant molecules. Why doesn't a reaction, such as the combustion of methane in oxygen, flow spontaneously downhill to give carbon dioxide and water (a less energetic, more stable, state) as illustrated in *figure 14.16*? Before we consider the answer to this question, it must be pointed out that such a situation would be inconvenient, if not catastrophic. Methane (or other hydrocarbons) would ignite spontaneously on contact with air! The equation for the complete combustion of methane is:

$$CH_4(g) + 2O_2(g) \longrightarrow CO_2(g) + 2H_2O(l)$$

We have to ignite the methane; that is, we must give it sufficient

energy for the reaction to get started. There is no reaction between the two gases (methane and oxygen) before ignition, and without this boost they sit together quite contentedly for an indefinite length of time. This is because, as the methane and oxygen molecules approach one another, the outer electrons of one molecule repel the outer electrons of the other. It's only if this repulsion can be overcome by a substantial input of energy that bonds can be broken and the attractive forces (between the electrons of one molecule and the positive nuclear charge of the other) can take over. The redistribution of electrons that occurs results in the bond-breaking and bond-making processes – it sets off a molecular reaction. Once the reaction has started, enough heat energy is produced to keep the reaction going (it is **self-sustained**). *Figure 14.17* shows the situation diagrammatically.

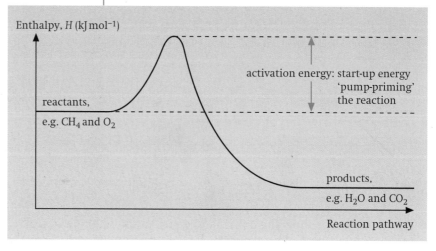

- **Figure 14.17** A reaction pathway diagram, showing the activation energy. This is an exothermic reaction.

Overall the reaction pathway (or coordinate) lies downhill, but initially the path lies uphill.

SAQ 14.4

In the case of the reaction between methane and oxygen, where could the activation energy come from?

Catalysis

A catalyst is something added to a reaction that increases its rate, but does not itself change in concentration: the same amount remains after the reaction as before. However, it is not true to say that the catalyst is unchanged.

Catalysts work by providing a different reaction pathway (route or mechanism) for the reaction. A reactant (in some case more than one reactant) will combine weakly with the catalyst to form an activated complex. This activated complex will undergo further reaction to form the products, releasing the catalyst for re-use. The catalyst takes part in the reaction but is restored at the end of the reaction.

The reaction rate increases because the catalysed reaction pathway has a lower activation energy than that of the uncatalysed reaction. This is shown in *figure 14.20*. The Boltzmann distribution in *figure 14.21* shows how the lower activation energy for the catalysed reaction increases the number of molecules that will react on collision.

There are two forms of catalysis:

- **homogeneous catalysis**, the catalyst and reactants are present in the same phase (solid, liquid or gas), often in aqueous solution;
- **heterogeneous catalysis**, the catalyst is present in a different phase to the reactants, for example gaseous reactants with a solid catalyst.

Why should endothermic reactions go at all?

If we have a reaction that is exothermic, it is obvious why the reaction should proceed to give the more stable products, so long as it is provided with a boost to enable it to surmount its particular activation barrier. But why ever should we be able to get an endothermic reaction to go?

Not only do we have the activation barrier to get over, but even when we do this, the energy of the product molecules is greater than the energy of the reactant molecules (*figure 14.18*). We have an apparent decrease in stability – the reaction has 'gone uphill'. We can only say that this is a very legitimate question to which the answer is that there is another factor that influences the relative stability of a system. It is called **entropy**. Entropy is a measure of the disorder or randomness of a system. The greater the degree of disorder, the greater the stability; and thus the total free energy of a system is the sum of the enthalpy and the entropy.

At this stage we can say no more, but if you proceed beyond this level with your studies of physics and chemistry, you will hear a lot more about entropy. It is a fascinating and essential idea in understanding the chemical changes in our environment.

SAQ 14.5

Examples of ordered instability and disordered stability are shown in *figure 14.19*. Which has the lower entropy? Which has the higher entropy and with it the greater stability?

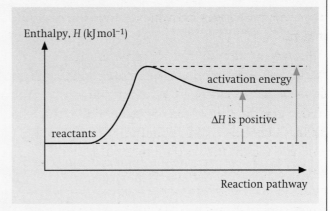

● **Figure 14.18** An enthalpy pathway diagram for an endothermic reaction. ΔH is the enthalpy change of the reaction.

● **Figure 14.19** Entropy at work.

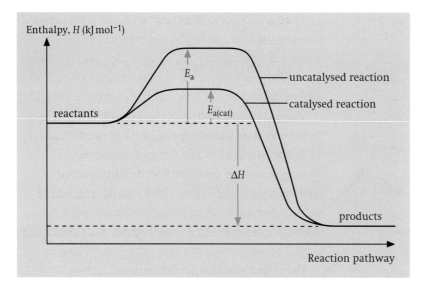

● **Figure 14.20** The catalysed reaction follows a different route (pathway) with a lower activation energy, $E_{a(cat)}$.

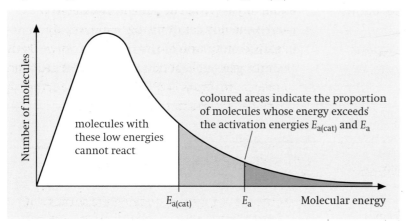

● **Figure 14.21** The route with the lower activation energy does not alter the Boltzmann distribution; however, it does increase the number of molecules with energies above the activation energy.

A good example of a reaction that involves homogeneous catalysis is the esterification of ethanol (see page 129). The products of this reaction are ethyl ethanoate and water:

$$H_3C - \overset{\displaystyle O}{\underset{\displaystyle O-H}{C}} \quad + \quad \overset{\displaystyle H}{\underset{\displaystyle O-CH_2-CH_3}{}} \longrightarrow H_3C - \overset{\displaystyle O}{\underset{\displaystyle O-CH_2-CH_3}{C}} \quad + \quad H_2O$$

ethanoic acid   ethanol   ethyl ethanoate   water

This reaction is catalysed by an acid. For example, concentrated sulphuric acid is usually added to a mixture of ethanol and ethanoic acid. The catalyst and the two reactants are all in the same liquid phase. The rate of formation of the products is increased by the presence of the acid. Although hydrogen ions from the catalyst take part in the reaction mechanism, the concentration of acid at the end of the reaction is the same as it was when the reagents were mixed.

A second example of homogeneous catalysis is the loss of ozone from the stratosphere as a result of the use of CFCs (see page 140). In this gas phase reaction, chlorine free radicals catalyse the decomposition of ozone into oxygen. When CFCs, such as CCl_2F_2, reach the stratosphere, ultraviolet light breaks carbon–chlorine bonds, generating chlorine free radicals, $Cl\cdot$.

Overall, this reaction is:

$$2O_3(g) \rightarrow 3O_2(g)$$

The two steps in the mechanism which involve the chlorine free radical are as follows:

$$Cl\cdot + O_3 \rightarrow ClO\cdot + O_2$$
$$ClO\cdot + O \rightarrow Cl\cdot + O_2$$

The chlorine free radicals regenerated in the second step are available for further reaction with ozone molecules. The reaction rate is fast and a few chlorine free radicals rapidly destroy many ozone molecules. It has been estimated that, during its lifetime, one chlorine free radical could destroy up to 100 000 ozone molecules.

The oxygen free radicals, O in the second equation, are formed continuously in the stratosphere. Ultraviolet light produces oxygen free radicals from oxygen molecules, O_2, or ozone molecules, O_3.

The role of the intermediate $ClO\cdot$ free radical was conclusively proved in 1987. A high-altitude plane carrying an American-led international team of scientists was flown into the ozone hole from the tip of South America. Concentrations of ozone and the $ClO\cdot$ free radical were measured as the plane flew south. The dramatic measurements they recorded are shown in *figure 14.22*. The concentration of ozone fell as the concentration of $ClO\cdot$ free radicals soared. The measurements the scientists obtained provided convincing

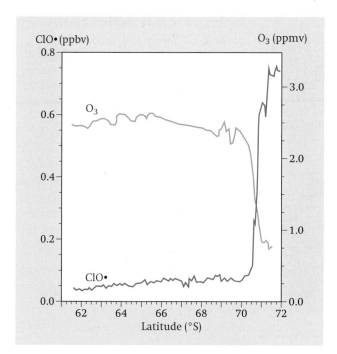

ClO• (ppbv)   O₃ (ppmv)

• **Figure 14.22** Chlorine oxide and ozone concentrations over Antarctica at 18 km altitude, 21 September, 1987, as measured on aircraft. ppbv = parts per billion by volume; ppmv = parts per million by volume.

evidence for the role of chlorine free radicals in the loss of ozone from the stratosphere.

Many economically important industrial processes involve the use of heterogeneous catalysts. For example:

1 the cracking, isomerisation and re-forming reactions which provide us with appropriate blends of petrol for our cars (see page 102);

2 hydrogenation of vegetable oils to produce margarine using a nickel catalyst (see page 119). An unsaturated fat is converted to a saturated fat by the addition of a hydrogen molecule to each of the carbon–carbon double bonds in the fat:

$$-CH=CH- + H_2 \xrightarrow{\text{nickel}} -CH_2-CH_2-$$

The nickel catalyst must be finely divided to provide a large surface area for reaction.

3 the production of ammonia by the Haber process. Before the German chemist Fritz Haber developed this process, much nitrogen was converted to ammonia using an expensive electrical discharge process. The Haber process uses a gas-phase reaction between nitrogen and hydrogen:

$$N_2(g) + 3H_2(g) \rightarrow 2NH_3(g)$$

The major part of the ammonia produced is used to manufacture fertilisers for increasing the yield of food crops. It is often said that, without such fertilisers, a far greater proportion of the world's human population would have suffered starvation during the twentieth century. Fritz Haber's discovery gained him the 1918 Nobel prize for Chemistry.

The Haber process reaction is catalysed by contact with a finely divided iron catalyst. Without a catalyst, the activation energy needed to break the very strong N≡N triple bond is extremely high. In the presence of the iron catalyst, molecules of nitrogen are weakly adsorbed on to iron atoms. This process weakens the nitrogen triple bond sufficiently for reaction to take place (*figure 14.23*). We will look further at the Haber process in the next chapter.

SAQ 14.6

Why is the iron catalyst finely divided?

Chemists are engaged in studying the surfaces of catalysts to find out just how they work, with the aim of developing new catalysts or improving existing ones. Improving the rates of large scale chemical processes leads to savings in energy and other costs such as that of the chemical plant. In recent years progress has been more rapid due to new techniques such as scanning probe microscopy (SPM). This technique enables the positions of gaseous molecules or atoms to be seen on a metal surface and provides support for models of heterogeneous catalysts such as that in *figure 14.23*. SPM provides powerful evidence to support reaction pathways such as adsorption of reactants, breaking of covalent bonds in reactant molecules and the presence of atoms on catalyst surfaces (*figure 14.24*).

Catalytic converters

Another area where chemists have contributed to an improvement in air quality is the development of catalytic converters. It is now a legal requirement for the exhausts of all new cars sold in the

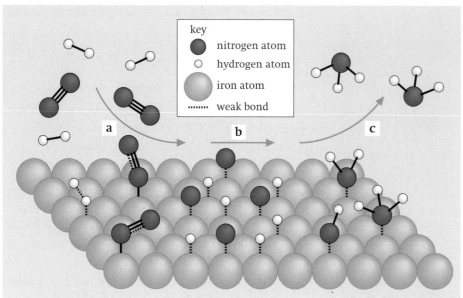

● **Figure 14.23** A possible model for the reaction pathway for the formation of ammonia from nitrogen and hydrogen by the Haber process. Heterogeneous catalysts bond to reactants which are **adsorbed** onto the catalyst atoms. Covalent bonds in the reactants are weakened and broken. New bonds form to give the product molecules which are **desorbed** from the catalyst.

a Adsorption of nitrogen and hydrogen molecules onto iron catalyst surface. Each molecule bonds weakly to iron atoms, causing bonds in the molecules to weaken.

b Nitrogen and hydrogen molecules dissociate into atoms as covalent bonds break on the surface of the catalyst. Nitrogen and hydrogen atoms bond to iron atoms.

c Nitrogen and hydrogen atoms combine in steps to form ammonia molecules. Desorption of ammonia molecules readily occurs as weak bonds to iron break.

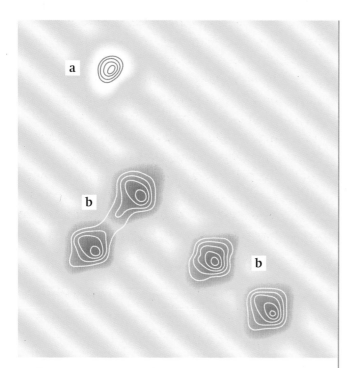

● **Figure 14.24** A scanning probe microscope (SPM) picture of oxygen on a copper surface. The diagonal rows coloured orange are copper atoms. **a** is an oxygen molecule, O_2, adsorbed on the surface. **b** are four O^- ions. The distance between these is about 0.80 nm, which is large enough to show they are not bonded together.

UK to be fitted with a catalytic converter. *Figure 14.25* shows a modern catalytic converter.

These pollutant gases are present in the gaseous mixture produced following the combustion of petrol in the engine of the car (see *table 14.1*). Carbon monoxide is formed by the incomplete combustion of fuel. This will occur when there is insufficient air mixed with the fuel. An equation for the incomplete combustion of octane is:

$$C_8H_{18} + 8\tfrac{1}{2}O_2 \rightarrow 8CO + 9H_2O$$

● **Figure 14.25** A three–way catalytic converter is designed to remove carbon monoxide, oxides of nitrogen and unburnt hydrocarbons from an engine's exhaust gases.

Name of gas	Formula	Origin	Effect
Carbon monoxide	CO	Incomplete combustion of hydrocarbons in petrol	Poisonous gas that combines with oxygen-carrying haemoglobin in the blood, and prevents oxygen from being carried
Nitrogen dioxide	NO_2	Atmospheric nitrogen and oxygen combine under the high-temperature conditions of the engine to form nitrogen monoxide. This is oxidised in the atmosphere to form nitrogen dioxide	Nitrogen dioxide is involved in the formation of photochemical smog and low level ozone
Hydrocarbons	C_xH_y	Some hydrocarbons in petrol may not be combusted at all	Some hydrocarbons (for example benzene) are toxic and may cause cancer

● **Table 14.1** Pollutants in vehicle exhaust fumes.

Nitrogen(II) oxide (monoxide) forms at the very high temperatures inside the engine (around 1000 °C). This high temperature provides sufficient energy for nitrogen and oxygen molecules to combine to form nitrogen(II) oxide:

$$N_2(g) + O_2(g) \rightarrow 2NO(g)$$

SAQ 14.7

What is the source of nitrogen in the engine?

Nitrogen(II) oxide is oxidised when it mixes with air:

$$2NO(g) + O_2(g) \rightarrow 2NO_2(g)$$

The product, nitrogen(IV) oxide, $NO_2(g)$, is a brown gas; nitrogen(II) oxide, NO(g), is colourless.

The catalytic converter helps to promote the following reactions:

■ The oxidation of carbon monoxide to carbon dioxide:

$$2CO(g) + O_2(g) \rightarrow 2CO_2(g)$$

■ The reduction of nitrogen monoxide back to nitrogen:

$$2NO(g) + 2CO(g) \rightarrow N_2(g) + 2CO_2(g)$$

■ The oxidation of hydrocarbons to water and oxygen. For example:

$$C_6H_6(g) + 7\tfrac{1}{2}O_2(g) \rightarrow 6CO_2(g) + 3H_2O(l)$$

The catalyst can be expensive, as it is made of an alloy of platinum, rhodium and palladium. Research to reduce costs has led to oxides of transition metals like chromium being used instead. As with other examples of heterogeneous catalysis, the above reactions will involve adsorption of the reactants on the surface of the catalyst, followed by chemical reaction and then desorption of the products as gaseous molecules. Catalytic converters must be hot to start working (typically 150–240 °C). They are not effective on short journeys.

If carbon monoxide, nitrogen(II) oxide and unburnt hydrocarbons are not removed from the car exhaust, they can lead to the formation of photochemical smog. Such smog has become a major source of irritation to humans, and to animals and plants. For photochemical smog to occur, bright sunlight and the still air conditions present in a temperature inversion are also required. Under these conditions, low-level ozone is formed from nitrogen(IV) oxide. Energy from the bright sunlight breaks down the nitrogen(IV) oxide into nitrogen(II) oxide and oxygen atoms:

$$NO_2(g) \rightarrow NO(g) + O(g)$$

Oxygen atoms combine with oxygen molecules to form ozone:

$$O(g) + O_2(g) \rightarrow O_3(g)$$

Temperature inversion

Close to the Earth's surface, air temperature normally decreases with height above ground level. In a temperature inversion, a layer of cool air becomes trapped under less dense warmer air. In this still air, pollutants from car exhausts build up.

High level ozone in the stratosphere is beneficial as it protects us from the harmful effects of high energy ultraviolet radiation. However, close to ground level, ozone is harmful to humans and affects the growth of plants. In still conditions, the gaseous cocktail of ozone and other pollutant gases from car exhausts produces a variety of compounds such as aldehydes and peroxyacetyl nitrate (PAN) by many different reactions. Ozone and PAN are particularly irritating to the eyes, nose and throat.

The steadily increasing reliance of the world's population on cars is the key factor in the formation of photochemical smog. In addition, whilst the work of chemists and other scientists has enabled catalytic converters to be developed, there are still many older vehicles in use without them. We can expect to see scenes such as the one shown in *figure 14.26*, for some time into the 21st century unless we take action to curb the use of private cars.

● **Figure 14.26** Photochemical smog caused by light reacting with pollutant molecules.

SUMMARY

◆ The rate of a chemical reaction is measured by the amount (in moles) of a reactant used up in a given time. Chemical kinetics is the study of rates of chemical reactions.

◆ Chemists study rates of reaction to:
  ● improve the rate of production of a chemical;
  ● help understand the processes going on in our bodies or in the environment;
  ● gain an insight into the mechanism of a reaction.

◆ The factors that affect the rate of a chemical reaction are:
  ● concentration (or pressure of gases);
  ● temperature;
  ● surface area or intensity of radiation;
  ● catalysts.
  The progress of a chemical reaction may involve sampling, followed by quenching to slow or stop the reaction prior to chemical

analysis by, for example, titration. Alternatively a physical method, such as following mass loss, volume of produced, absorbance of light by coloured solution, pH or conductivity may be used.

◆ The increase in rate of a chemical reaction when there is an increase in concentration (or pressure) of a reactant may be explained using collision theory. At higher concentration (or pressure), more collisions occur between reactant molecules. The proportion of these collisions which are effective also increases. Effective collisions are those where the molecules have sufficient energy for reaction to occur.

◆ The activation energy of a reaction is the minimum energy required for reaction to occur. Enthalpy profile diagrams show how the activation energy provides a barrier to reaction.

◆ The Boltzmann distribution represents the numbers of molecules in a sample with particular energies. The change in the Boltzmann distribution as temperature is increased shows how more molecules have kinetic energy which is above the activation energy. This, in turn, leads to an increase in reaction rate.

◆ A catalyst increases the rate of a reaction by providing an alternative reaction pathway with a lower activation energy. More molecules have sufficient energy to react, so the rate of reaction is increased.

◆ In homogeneous catalysis, both reactants and catalyst are in the same phase. Examples include: the acid catalysed formation of an ester from an alcohol and a carboxylic acid; the destruction of ozone by chlorine free radicals in the stratosphere.

◆ In heterogeneous catalysis, the reactants are in the liquid or gas phase with the catalyst in the solid phase. Examples include: the cracking, isomerisation and reforming reactions for modern petrol; the hydrogenation of vegetable oil to make margarine; the production of ammonia by the Haber process; catalytic converters for removing pollutants from car exhaust gases.

◆ The pollutants in car exhaust gases are carbon monoxide, nitrogen(II) oxide and unburnt hydrocarbons. If these gases are not removed by catalytic converters, they lead to the formation of low level ozone and photochemical smog. Both low level ozone and photochemical smog can be harmful to humans, animals and plants.

Questions

1 Catalysts are widely used in industry to alter the rate of a chemical reaction. Describe how catalysts carry out this function. Your answer should contain reference to activation energy, homogeneous catalysis and heterogeneous catalysis. Include diagrams and appropriate examples.

2 The atmospheric pollutant NO_2 is present in car exhaust gases. State two environmental consequences of nitrogen oxides and outline their catalytic removal from car exhaust gases.

3 In the stratosphere, ozone, $O_3(g)$, is formed by the action of ultraviolet radiation on oxygen, $O_2(g)$. At the same time it is being lost by reactions such as the one shown in equation 1.

Equation 1: $O_3(g) + O(g) \rightarrow 2O_2(g)$; $\Delta H^\ominus = -390 \, kJ \, mol^{-1}$

a Use collision theory to explain why, when the concentration of oxygen atoms, $O(g)$, is increased, the rate of the reaction shown shown in equation 1 is also increased.

b The reaction shown in equation 1 is catalysed by gaseous chlorine free radicals. The chlorine free radicals are formed by the action of ultraviolet radiation on CFCs.

(i) Write equations which show the two steps involved when chlorine acts as a catalyst for this reaction.

(ii) Catalysts act by providing a different reaction route with a lower activation enthalpy. What is meant by the term **activation energy**?

(iii) Draw a labelled enthalpy profile to illustrate the effect of a catalyst on the activation energy for the reaction shown in equation 1.

4 In the Haber process, ammonia is produced from nitrogen and hydrogen as shown in the equation below.

$N_2(g) + 3H_2(g) \rightarrow 2NH_3(g)$

a Describe, using the Boltzmann distribution, the effect of an increase in temperature on the rate of this reaction.

b The rate of formation of ammonia in the Haber process is increased by using an iron catalyst. This is an example of heterogeneous catalysis.

(i) Explain what is meant by the term heterogeneous catalysis.

(ii) Describe a model to show how a heterogeneous catalyst, such as iron in the Haber process, catalyses a reaction. Explain any scientific terms that you use. In your answer, you should refer to:
 ● the adsorption of reactants on to the surface of the catalyst;
 ● chemical reaction on the catalyst surface;
 ● desorption of the product from the catalyst.

CHAPTER 15

Equilibria

By the end of this chapter you should be able to:

1 explain the features of a *dynamic equilibrium*;

2 state *Le Chatelier's principle* and apply it to deduce qualitatively (from appropriate information) the effect of a change in temperature, concentration or pressure on a homogeneous system in equilibrium;

3 describe and explain the conditions used in the *Haber process* for the formation of ammonia, as an example of the importance of a compromise between chemical equilibrium and reaction rate in the chemical industry;

4 outline the importance of ammonia and nitrogen compounds derived from ammonia, for example fertilisers, polyamides and explosives;

5 describe an *acid* as a species that can donate a proton;

6 describe ammonia as a *base* in terms of its reaction with an acid to form ammonium salts;

7 describe the reactions of an acid, typified by hydrochloric acid with metals, carbonates, bases and *alkalis*, and interpret them using ionic equations to emphasise the role of $H^+(aq)$;

8 explain qualitatively, in terms of dissociation, the differences between *strong* and *weak* acids.

Reversible reactions

You will be familiar with a number of reversible physical processes. For example, if you decrease the temperature of water below $0\,°C$, ice forms. Allow the ice to warm to room temperature and it soon melts. The process can be represented as follows:

$$H_2O(s) \rightleftharpoons H_2O(l)$$

The $\rightleftharpoons$ sign in this equation is used to indicate that the process is reversible.

Another reversible physical process is the dissolving of carbon dioxide in water. You will have met aqueous carbon dioxide in the form of fizzy drinks such as cola. Carbon dioxide is dissolved in the drink under pressure. When the drink is poured, the carbon dioxide escapes as bubbles of gas producing a pleasant sensation

when the cola is consumed. An equation for this reversible change is:

$$CO_2(aq) \rightleftharpoons CO_2(g)$$

The solubility of carbon dioxide in water is enhanced by chemical reaction with water, producing hydrogen ions, $H^+(aq)$, and hydrogen carbonate ions, $HCO_3^-(aq)$:

$$H_2O(l) + CO_2(aq) \rightleftharpoons H^+(aq) + HCO_3^-(aq)$$

This reaction is also easily reversed. Boiling the water will decompose the hydrogencarbonate ions and drive off carbon dioxide.

Many other chemical reactions are reversible. An environmentally important reversible reaction is the formation of ozone, $O_3(g)$, from oxygen. Ultraviolet light is needed to form ozone; chlorine atoms (from CFCs) have the overall effect of reversing the reaction, causing damage to the ozone layer:

$$3O_2(g) \underset{CFCs}{\overset{UV\ light}{\rightleftharpoons}} 2O_3(g)$$

In this chapter we shall explore the nature of reversible reactions in more detail.

Equilibrium – a state of balanced change

The notion of a system being in equilibrium is a familiar one. You can stir salt into water until no more will dissolve. At this point the solution is described as a saturated solution and is in equilibrium with the undissolved solid. Although the concentration of the saturated solution stays the same, the ions and molecules are in a constant state of motion. We describe this as a **dynamic equilibrium**. Ions in the crystal lattice of the undissolved solid continue to go into solution. However, they are immediately replaced elsewhere in the lattice by the same numbers and kinds of ion. The dynamic nature of the equilibrium is only observable at the ionic or molecular level. The situation is one of continued but balanced change (*figure 15.1a*).

A similar situation exists when you close the tap on a cylinder of butane gas, in a camping gas stove for example. Evaporation and condensation go on until the liquid and gas phases are in equilibrium with one another. Again the equilibrium is dynamic. At equilibrium some of the molecules of liquid butane are evaporating, but only at the same rate as molecules of gaseous butane are condensing (*figure 15.1b*).

In general, in a dynamic equilibrium, the rate of reaction in the *forwards* direction equals the rate of reaction in the *reverse* direction.

Equilibrium and chemical change

If you heat calcium carbonate it decomposes, forming calcium oxide and carbon dioxide:

$$CaCO_3(s) \longrightarrow CaO(s) + CO_2(g)$$

On the other hand, if you leave calcium oxide in an atmosphere of carbon dioxide, the reverse reaction occurs, and calcium carbonate forms:

$$CaO(s) + CO_2(g) \longrightarrow CaCO_3(s)$$

If these substances are put in a sealed container at a high temperature (say 700 K) and left to get on with it, an equilibrium is set up. Both of the above reactions occur until a balance is reached. At this point the rate of formation of calcium carbonate equals its rate of decomposition.

All chemical reactions can reach equilibrium, a situation where the reactants are in equilibrium with the products. Again, these are dynamic equilibria: reagents are constantly being converted to products, and vice versa. At equilibrium the rate of the forward process is the same as that of the backward one. The idea that *all* chemical reactions can reach equilibrium seems to conflict with experience, e.g. the burning of magnesium in air. In many cases the degree of conversion of reactants to products is so large that, at the conclusion of the reaction, no reactants can be detected by normal analytical means. At other times two reagents, e.g. the nitrogen and oxygen in the air, do not seem to react at all. Such reactions are often considered to be irreversible one-way reactions under those conditions.

Suppose, for example, we mix an equal number of molecules of hydrogen with either chlorine or bromine. The green colour of the chlorine or the orange colour of the

Example: NaCl(s) $\rightleftharpoons$ NaCl(aq)   Example: C_4H_{10}(l) $\rightleftharpoons$ C_4H_{10}(g)

a

b

- Cl^- ion
- Na^+ ion
- water molecule
- butane molecule

- **Figure 15.1** Two physical equilibria. In both situations there is a constant interchange of particles, which maintains a steady balance. In **a** ions leave a crystal structure, while others join it. In **b** molecules escape from the crush in a liquid to relative isolation in a gas, while others leave the gas to join the liquid.

bromine disappears, and we are left with hydrogen chloride or hydrogen bromide. The reverse reaction is so minimal that both reactions go to apparent completion as indicated by these equations:

$$H_2(g) + Cl_2(g) \longrightarrow 2HCl(g)$$
$$H_2(g) + Br_2(g) \longrightarrow 2HBr(g)$$

When we mix hydrogen gas and iodine vapour, however, we find that the violet colour of the iodine persists. There is an equilibrium set up between the three components in which all three are present in significant amounts, as shown in the equation below and in *figure 15.2*:

$$H_2(g) + I_2(g) \rightleftharpoons 2HI(g)$$

The equation tells us that when a molecule of hydrogen reacts with a molecule of iodine, two molecules of hydrogen iodide are formed. It also enables us to examine the reaction in reverse. If two molecules of hydrogen iodide dissociate (i.e. split apart), then a molecule each of hydrogen and iodine are formed.

When you cook on a camping gas stove, butane gas is released and burned. The liquid butane will evaporate to maintain the gas supply. However, equilibrium will not be restored in the cylinder unless the gas is turned off at the tap. We must have a **closed system** to achieve a dynamic equilibrium.

SAQ 15.1

A beaker contains saturated aqueous sodium chloride in contact with undissolved solid sodium chloride. Is this a closed system? Explain your answer.

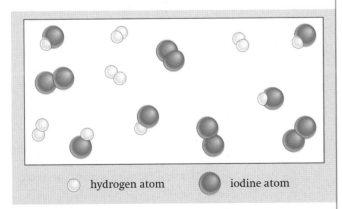

| ○ hydrogen atom | ● iodine atom |

● **Figure 15.2** A snapshot of the dynamic equilibrium between hydrogen gas, iodine gas and hydrogen iodide gas.

When we view a system at equilibrium, we are not aware that constant change is taking place. From our viewpoint the system looks static because all the dynamic change is occurring at the molecular or ionic level. The properties that we can see or measure remain constant. We call these macroscopic properties. In a camping gas cylinder with the tap closed, the volume of liquid and the pressure do not change once dynamic equilibrium is achieved. The concentration of salt in a saturated solution is also constant at equilibrium. The temperature of both systems must also be constant. Another feature of a dynamic equilibrium is this **constancy of macroscopic properties**.

In summary the characteristic features of an equilibrium are:
- It is dynamic at the molecular or ionic level.
- Both forward and reverse processes occur at equal rates.
- A closed system is required.
- Macroscopic properties remain constant.

Changing conditions: Le Chatelier's principle

Now that we have established the characteristic features of an equilibrium, we can ask the question "What happens to the equilibrium if we change the conditions in some way?" We could, for example, alter the temperature or change the concentration of a reactant.

Suppose we add more water to the equilibrium mixture of solid sodium chloride and saturated aqueous sodium chloride we saw in *figure 15.1*. The mixture will no longer be in equilibrium. However, more of the solid will dissolve and, providing there is sufficient solid, the solution will again become saturated. The system readjusts to restore equilibrium.

Raising the temperature of our sealed container of calcium carbonate in equilibrium with calcium oxide and carbon dioxide provides the energy that allows more calcium carbonate to decompose. Again, the system adjusts to restore equilibrium. Intially, more calcium oxide and carbon dioxide is formed. Equilibrium is restored when the rate of formation of the calcium oxide and carbon dioxide is the same as the rate of the reverse reaction to form calcium carbonate.

Observations of this type led the French chemist Henri Louis Le Chatelier in 1884 to put forward an important principle. The essence of **Le Chatelier's principle** is that:

> when any of the conditions affecting the position of a dynamic equilibrium are changed, then the position of that equilibrium will shift to minimise that change.

Next we will consider how we can qualitatively predict the effect of changing temperature, pressure or concentration on the equilibrium position using Le Chatelier's principle.

The effect of temperature on the position of equilibrium

We know that calcium carbonate decomposes to calcium oxide and carbon dioxide at a high temperature. At room temperature, no change is seen. The white cliffs of Dover are still calcium carbonate, as they were when first seen by Julius Caesar!

When calcium carbonate is heated in a closed system (see page 71), an equilibrium mixture containing both reactant and products results. The reaction is endothermic and, on raising the temperature, the equilibrium shifts towards the formation of calcium oxide and carbon dioxide. In the closed system, the higher the temperature, the greater is the proportion of products at equilibrium.

The dissociation of hydrogen iodide is an example of a homogeneous endothermic reaction:

$$2HI(g) \rightleftharpoons H_2(g) + I_2(g)$$

The effect of different temperatures on the equilibrium concentration of hydrogen can be seen in *table 15.1* and *figure 15.3*. As the temperature rises, the equilibrium concentration of hydrogen rises. The position of equilibrium in this gas phase reaction shifts towards the formation of hydrogen and iodine at higher temperature.

Temperature (K)	Equilibrium concentration of hydrogen iodide (mol dm^{-3})	Equilibrium concentration of hydrogen (or iodine) (mol dm^{-3})
298	0.934	0.033
500	0.864	0.068
700	0.786	0.107
764	0.773	0.114
1100	0.714	0.143

● **Table 15.1** The dissociation of hydrogen iodide, HI(g), at various temperatures.

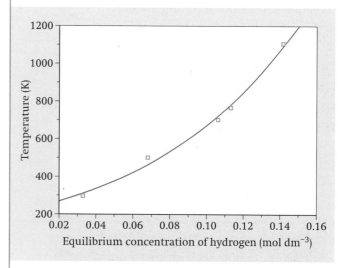

● **Figure 15.3** In an endothermic reaction such as the dissociation of hydrogen iodide, as the temperature is increased the equilibrium concentration of the products increases. The graph shows the increase in concentration of hydrogen with increasing temperature.

When we raise the temperature of an endothermic reaction, there is an increase in the enthalpy in the system. According to Le Chatelier's principle, the equilibrium position should shift towards the products in order to compensate for the additional enthalpy input.

Suppose we consider an increase in temperature for an exothermic reaction. The reverse reaction will be endothermic, so Le Chatelier's principle tells us that the equilibrium will shift towards the reactants to compensate for the extra enthalpy input.

Table 15.2 summarises the effects of temperature changes on the equilbrium position for exothermic and endothermic reactions.

Example	Endothermic reaction, $2HI(g) \rightleftharpoons H_2(g) + I_2(g)$	Exothermic reaction, $2SO_2(g) + O_2(g) \rightleftharpoons 2SO_3(g)$
Temperature increase	equilibrium position shifts towards products: more hydrogen and iodine form	equilibrium position shifts towards reactants: more sulphur dioxide and oxygen form
Temperature decrease	equilibrium position shifts towards reactant: more hydrogen iodide forms	equilibrium position shifts towards product: more sulphur trioxide forms

● **Table 15.2** The effect of temperature change on the equilibrium positions of reactions involving gases.

The effect of changes in concentration on the equilibrium position

We will consider the formation of an ester, such as ethyl ethanoate. When ethanol is warmed with ethanoic acid in the presence of a few drops of concentrated sulphuric acid, ethyl ethanoate is formed (see pages 129 and 172)

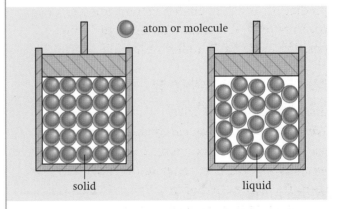

ethanoic acid   ethanol   ethyl ethanoate   water

The sulphuric acid catalyses this reaction. An equilibrium is soon established in the reaction mixture with significant concentrations of both products and reactants present. Suppose we increase the concentration of ethanol in the mixture. The position of equilibrium is disturbed. Applying Le Chatelier's Principle, more ethyl ethanoate and water will form and the concentration of ethanol and ethanoic acid will fall until a new position of equilibrium is established. The position of equilibrium moves towards the products.

SAQ 15.2

Consider the equilibrium involved in the formation of ethyl ethanoate.

a Use Le Chatelier's principle to predict how the position of equilibrium would change on adding more water to the mixture.

b Ethyl ethanoate is a useful solvent. It is used, for example, in nail varnish remover. Suggest how a chemical company might optimise the conversion of ethanol and ethanoic acid to ethyl ethanoate.

The effect of pressure on equilibria

Pressure has virtually no effect on the chemistry of solids and liquids. As shown in *figure 15.4*, pressure does not affect the concentration of solids and liquids – the molecules concerned are already in contact and it is difficult to push them closer together.

Pressure does have significant effects on the chemistry of reacting gases. As *figure 15.5* shows, the concentrations of gases increase with an increase in pressure, and decrease with a decrease in pressure. Since chemical equilibria are influenced by concentration changes, pressure

atom or molecule

solid   liquid

● **Figure 15.4** Pressure has little, if any, effect on the concentrations of solids and liquids.

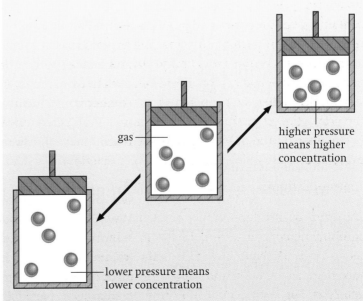

gas

higher pressure means higher concentration

lower pressure means lower concentration

● **Figure 15.5** Pressure has a considerable effect on the concentrations of gases.

changes also have an effect on equilibria where one or more of the reagents is a gas.

Again we can apply Le Chatelier's principle to predict how pressure change will affect an equilibrium. Imagine a reaction in the gaseous phase where two molecules, A and B, combine to form a single molecule, C:

$$A(g) + B(g) \rightleftharpoons C(g)$$

The situation is illustrated in *figure 15.6*.

It helps to remember that the pressure of a gas depends on the number of molecules in a given volume of the gas. The greater the number of molecules, the greater the number of collisions per second, and hence the greater the pressure of the gas. In the reaction above, when the pressure is increased *the equilibrium shifts to minimise this increase*, that is, to reduce the pressure overall. Therefore, there must be fewer molecules present than before. This can only happen if A and B molecules react to make more molecules of C.

This reasoning is summarised in *table 15.3*, which summarises the effects of increasing and decreasing the pressure on reactions in which **a** there are fewer molecules on the right of the equilibrium, and **b** there are more molecules on the right of the equilibrium.

SAQ 15.3
Predict the effect on the equilibrium position of increasing the pressure on the following reactions
a $2HI(g) \rightleftharpoons H_2(g) + I_2(g)$
b $N_2(g) + 3H_2(g) \rightleftharpoons 2NH_3(g)$

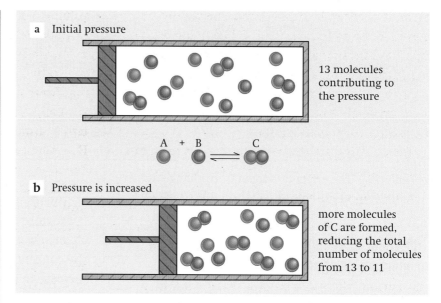

a Initial pressure

13 molecules contributing to the pressure

$A + B \rightleftharpoons C$

b Pressure is increased

more molecules of C are formed, reducing the total number of molecules from 13 to 11

● **Figure 15.6** An increase in pressure in this case causes the equilibrium to shift to the right, to produce more molecules of C than before, but fewer molecules in the reaction vessel overall.

Example	Fewer molecules on right $2SO_2(g) + O_2(g) \rightleftharpoons 2SO_3(g)$	More molecules on right $N_2O_4(g) \rightleftharpoons 2NO_2(g)$
Pressure increase	equilibrium position shifts towards products: more SO_3 forms	equilibrium position shifts towards reactants: more N_2O_4 forms
Pressure decrease	equilibrium position shifts towards reactants: more SO_2 and O_2 form	equilibrium position shifts towards products: more NO_2 forms

● **Table 15.3** The effect of pressure change on the equilibrium position of reactions involving gases.

The effect of catalysts on equilibria

As you know, a catalyst reduces the activation energy of a reaction, and hence speeds it up. A catalyst affects the rate of reaction, but does not feature in the overall equation for the reaction. More catalyst could mean a faster reaction, one in which an equilibrium was established more quickly, *but does not change the equilibrium concentration of reactants or products.*

An equilibrium of importance: the Haber process

We will now gather together these ideas using a reaction that is important from the theoretical, the practical and the industrial points of view. It is the Haber process for the 'fixation' of atmospheric nitrogen. We need large amounts of nitrogen compounds, particularly for fertilisers. Air is 80% nitrogen, so atmospheric nitrogen is the most plentiful and readily available source. At the same time, it cannot be used directly in the gaseous form; it needs to be 'fixed' into a chemically combined form to make a useful compound. One possible conversion might be to ammonia. Unlike nitrogen, ammonia is a reactive gas readily soluble in water, is readily convertible to ammonium salts, and can be converted to nitric acid by the Ostwald process of oxidation.

The equation for the reaction to form ammonia is as follows:

$$N_2(g) + 3H_2(g) \rightleftharpoons 2NH_3(g); \qquad \Delta H = -93 \, kJ \, mol^{-1}$$

ΔH refers to the enthalpy change of reaction (see chapter 13). The unreactive nature of nitrogen is, of course, a problem. Although the reaction is exothermic, the triple bond within nitrogen molecules lends them great strength, so the reaction has a high activation energy. How may the equilibrium be influenced to give a good yield of ammonia? This problem was solved in the early 1900s by the German chemist Fritz Haber, and the process that he developed is essentially that which is still in use today.

The obvious thing to do would seem to be to increase the temperature. However, by using Le Chatelier's principle, since the reaction is exothermic, increasing the temperature will drive the equilibrium to the left (table 15.2). This effect is quite dramatic (table 15.4); at 373 K and 25 atm the percentage of ammonia resulting from an initial mixture of 1 volume of nitrogen and 3 volumes of hydrogen is 91.7%: at 973 K this percentage drops to 0.9%.

Pressure is another variable. We can reason that an increase of pressure will drive the equilibrium to the right. From Avogadro's hypothesis, we know that equal volumes of all gases under the same conditions of temperature and pressure contain the same number of molecules. One mole of any gas therefore occupies the same volume, at standard temperature, 298 K, and pressure, 1 atm $\doteq$ 101 kPa. From this we can deduce the proportions by volume of the gases as follows:

$$N_2(g) + 3H_2(g) \rightleftharpoons 2NH_3(g);$$
1 volume   3 volumes   2 volumes $\qquad \Delta H = -93 \, kJ \, mol^{-1}$

According to Le Chatelier's principle, an increase in pressure should drive the equilibrium to the right, since this will result in a decrease in volume. This is found in practice, and table 15.4 gives the relevant figures.

Imagine you were asked to design a chemical production plant for the manufacture of ammonia. From our discussion we might consider using the highest possible pressure with a suitably low temperature, for example about 500 atm and 300 K. However, such a choice would create difficulties. The high activation enthalpy means that the rate of reaction is effectively zero at 300 K. Very high pressures increase the rate of reaction but dramatically increase the cost of the plant. The cost of labour for running the plant also increases as the type of pumps required for maintaining high pressure require more maintenance.

The problem of the very low rate of reaction can be partially overcome by the choice of a suitable catalyst (see page 171) such as porous iron (figure 15.7). Small amounts of the oxides of potassium, magnesium, aluminium and silicon improve the efficiency of the catalyst. The catalyst enables the reaction to proceed by a different route with a lower activation energy (see page 169). The rate can also be increased by raising the temperature and accepting a reduced equilibrium percentage of ammonia in the mixture. Modern plants operate at much lower pressures than older plants despite the reduction in the equilibrium percentage of ammonia. Such compromises reduce the overall production costs sufficiently to justify replacing an old plant.

There are two more ways in which the efficiency of an ammonia plant may be improved:

■ Ammonia is removed as it is formed so that the reaction mixture is not left to reach equilibrium. This means that the reaction rate stays reasonably high. If the reaction is allowed to

Temperature (K)	Percentage of ammonia at equilibrium			
	25 atm	50 atm	100 atm	200 atm
373	91.7	94.5	96.7	98.4
573	27.4	39.6	53.1	66.7
773	2.9	5.6	10.5	18.3
973	0.9	1.2	3.4	8.7

● **Table 15.4** Percentage of ammonia in the equilibrium mixture at various temperatures and pressures.

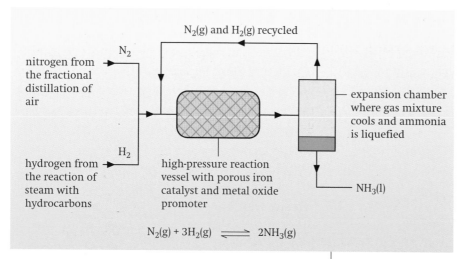

N₂(g) and H₂(g) recycled

nitrogen from the fractional distillation of air

hydrogen from the reaction of steam with hydrocarbons

high-pressure reaction vessel with porous iron catalyst and metal oxide promoter

expansion chamber where gas mixture cools and ammonia is liquefied

$NH_3(l)$

$$N_2(g) + 3H_2(g) \rightleftharpoons 2NH_3(g)$$

● **Figure 15.7** The production of ammonia by the Haber process.

approach equilibrium, the reaction rate decreases as concentrations of the reactants decrease.

■ The plant operates continuously and, after passing through the reaction vessel, the reaction mixture is passed into an expansion chamber where rapid expansion cools the mixture and allows ammonia to liquefy (*figure 15.7*). The liquefied ammonia is run off to pressurised storage vessels and the unreacted nitrogen and hydrogen is recirculated over the catalyst in the reaction vessel.

Modern Haber process plants (*figure 15.8*):
■ are highly efficient in conversion of nitrogen and hydrogen to ammonia;

■ have a low energy consumption (around 35 MJ per kg of nitrogen converted to ammonia);
■ are smaller, so they are less expensive to build;
■ have less environmental impact;
■ may be sited where they are needed, reducing transport costs.

The conditions used in modern plant are:
■ a pressure between 25 and 150 atm;
■ a temperature between 670 and 770 K;
■ a finely divided or porous iron catalyst with metal oxide promoters.

80% of ammonia production goes into making fertilisers such as ammonium sulphate. It has been claimed that without the invention of the Haber process, a much higher proportion of the World's population would have died of starvation. The increasing human population requires ever more intensive agricultural production techniques. In order to grow crops repeatedly in the same soil, artificial fertilisers are added to maintain fertility.

Much smaller proportions of ammonia production are used for making nitric acid (which in turn is used to make explosives) and polymers such as nylon. These proportions are shown in *figure 15.9*.

● **Figure 15.8** This modern ammonia plant is based on the chemical reaction devised by Fritz Haber in the early 1900s.

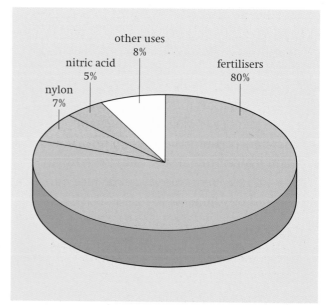

other uses
8%

nitric acid
5%

nylon
7%

fertilisers
80%

● **Figure 15.9** The uses of ammonia.

Acids and their reactions

You will have learnt to recognise an **acid** by its behaviour. For example, an acid:

■ turns blue litmus red;

■ has a pH of less than 7;

■ produces carbon dioxide when added to a carbonate, such as magnesium carbonate;

■ is neutralised by an **alkali** (such as sodium hydroxide) or a **base** (such as magnesium oxide).

Hydrochloric acid is a typical acid. It is formed by dissolving hydrogen chloride gas in water. Hydrogen chloride is a polar covalent molecule which ionises completely in water, producing $H^+(aq)$ and $Cl^-(aq)$ ions:

$$HCl(g) \xrightarrow{\text{water}} H^+(aq) + Cl^-(aq)$$

We call the aqueous solution of $H^+(aq)$ and $Cl^-(aq)$, hydrochloric acid. $H^+(aq)$ is a hydrated proton (a hydrogen *atom* consists of a proton and an electron; a hydrogen *ion* is simply a proton). We sometimes represent the $H^+(aq)$ ion as the **oxonium ion** $H_3O^+(aq)$. We can rewrite the equation for the reaction of hydrogen chloride gas with water as follows:

$$HCl(g) + H_2O(l) \rightarrow H_3O^+(aq) + Cl^-(aq)$$

Equations like this, which show the presence of ions, are called ionic equations (see also page 25). Chemists find ionic equations useful when discussing reactions of acids. Ionic equations are also useful when discussing other reactions involving ions, such as redox reactions (see page 68).

Chemists often define an acid as having the ability to transfer a proton to another molecule or ion. In *figure 15.10*, hydrogen chloride has donated a proton to a water molecule. Hence we can define hydrogen chloride as an acid. Some of the reactions of a typical acid are summarised in *table 15.5*.

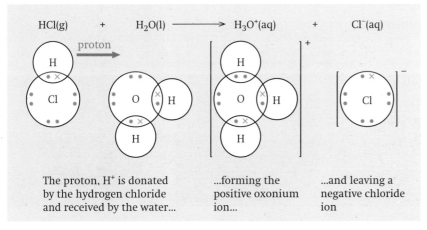

HCl(g)　　+　　H$_2$O(l) $\longrightarrow$ H$_3$O$^+$(aq) 　+　 Cl$^-$(aq)

proton

The proton, H$^+$ is donated by the hydrogen chloride and received by the water...

...forming the positive oxonium ion...

...and leaving a negative chloride ion

● **Figure 15.10** An acid is a proton donor. Hydrogen chloride is the acid in this reaction.

Salt formation by acids

The reaction of hydrogen chloride with ammonia

Hydrogen chloride gas will also react with ammonia gas. You may have seen the experiment shown in *figure 15.11*.

The pieces of cotton wool soaked in concentrated hydrochloric acid and in concentrated ammonia readily give off fumes of the two gases. These fumes diffuse along the glass tube. At the point where they meet, a reaction occurs producing ammonium chloride as a white solid. This appears about a third of the way along the tube from the concentrated hydrochloric acid end. This is because NH_3 molecules are lighter and smaller than HCl molecules, so they diffuse faster. An equation for this reaction is

$$HCl(g) + NH_3(g) \rightarrow NH_4Cl(s)$$

Ammonium chloride is a salt containing ammonium ions, NH_4^+, and chloride ions, Cl^-. We could rewrite the equation as:

$$HCl(g) + NH_3(g)$$
$$\rightarrow NH_4^+(s) + Cl^-(s)$$

Again, by our definition, hydrogen chloride has behaved as an acid, in this reaction donating a proton to an ammonia molecule. By neutralising the acid, the ammonia molecule is behaving as a base.

Type of reactant	Example	Equation
metal	zinc	$Zn(s) + 2H^+(aq) \rightarrow Zn^{2+}(aq) + H_2(g)$
base	copper(II) oxide	$2H^+(aq) + CuO(s) \rightarrow Cu^{2+}(aq) + H_2O(l)$
carbonate	sodium carbonate	$2H^+(aq) + Na_2CO_3(s) \rightarrow 2Na^+(aq) + CO_2(g) + H_2O(l)$
alkali	aqueous potassium hydroxide	$H^+(aq) + OH^-(aq) \rightarrow H_2O(l)$

● **Table 15.5** Some reactions of a typical acid. With hydrochloric acid, the chloride salt of the metal is formed.

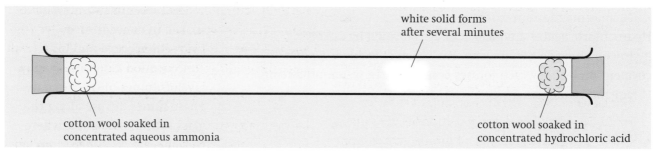

white solid forms after several minutes

cotton wool soaked in concentrated aqueous ammonia

cotton wool soaked in concentrated hydrochloric acid

● **Figure 15.11** An experiment to show that hydrogen chloride gas (an acid) and ammonia gas (a base) react to form solid ammonium chloride.

The production of a fertiliser salt

The reaction of ammonia with dilute sulphuric acid is a particularly important reaction as the product is the fertiliser ammonium sulphate, $(NH_4)_2SO_4$. The full equation for the reaction of ammonia with dilute sulphuric acid is:

$$2NH_3(aq) + H_2SO_4(aq) \longrightarrow (NH_4)_2SO_4(aq)$$

The sulphuric acid has donated protons to ammonia molecules to form $NH_4^+(aq)$. As with hydrochloric acid, ammonia is behaving as a base by neutralising the acid. The ionic equation is:

$$2NH_3(aq) + 2H^+(aq) + SO_4^{2-}(aq)$$
$$\longrightarrow 2NH_4^+(aq) + SO_4^{2-}(aq)$$

The sulphate ions are unchanged during the reaction and the equation may be simplified to:

$$NH_3(aq) + H^+(aq) \longrightarrow NH_4^+(aq)$$

We describe ions which are unchanged in a reaction as **spectator ions**. They are present to balance the charges of oppositely charged ions in the reaction mixture.

The formation of salts with metals, metal oxides and metal carbonates

The reactions of hydrochloric acid with magnesium, magnesium oxide or magnesium carbonate are described on page 70. In each case a

salt (magnesium chloride, $MgCl_2$) is formed. Such behaviour is typical of all acids. For example, black copper(II) oxide dissolves in dilute sulphuric acid on warming to give a blue solution of copper sulphate (*figure 15.12a*). With hydrochloric acid, copper(II) oxide forms a green solution of copper(II) chloride (*figure 15.12b*). Metal oxides which dissolve in an acid are termed bases as the oxide ions accept protons.

The ionic equation for the reaction of copper(II) oxide with hydrochloric acid is:

$$2H^+(aq) + 2Cl^-(aq) + CuO(s)$$
$$\longrightarrow Cu^{2+}(aq) + 2Cl^-(aq) + H_2O(l)$$

● **Figure 15.12** Small beakers of black copper(II) oxide dissolving in **a** sulphuric acid and **b** hydrochloric acid.

$2Cl^-(aq)$ appears on both sides of the equation. It is unchanged, so we can simplify the equation to:

$$2H^+(aq) + CuO(s) \longrightarrow Cu^{2+}(aq) + H_2O(l)$$

In this reaction two protons from hydrochloric acid have been donated to an oxide ion, O^{2-}, in copper(II) oxide to form a water molecule. Like the sulphate ions in the production of ammonium sulphate fertiliser, the chloride ions are also spectator ions.

SAQ 15.4

a Write balanced ionic equations for the reaction of hydrochloric acid with (i) calcium (ii) strontium oxide, SrO(s) and (iii) barium carbonate, $BaCO_3(s)$.

b Name and give the formula of the salt formed for each reaction in part a.

Strong and weak acids

Hydrochloric acid is described as a strong acid. Molecules of strong acids, such as hydrogen chloride, are fully dissociated to ions in aqueous solution. Nitric and sulphuric acids are also strong acids.

Many organic acids are described as weak acids. This term signifies that their molecules are only partially ionised in aqueous solution. An equilibrium exists between the undissociated molecules and the ions. For example, ethanoic acid is a weak acid; the equilibrium equation can be written as:

$$CH_3COOH(aq) \rightleftharpoons CH_3COO^-(aq) + H^+(aq)$$

In water, approximately one in a thousand molecules of ethanoic acid are dissociated into ions.

SUMMARY

- A reversible reaction is a reaction that may proceed in either direction (forward or reverse), depending on the applied conditions.

- Dynamic equilibrium occurs when the rate for the forward reaction is equal to the rate of the reverse reaction, so that products are formed at the same rate as they are decomposed. The equilibrium is dynamic because it is maintained despite continual changes occurring between molecules.

- A closed system is needed for equilibrium to be established in a chemical reaction. Equilibria are characterised by the constancy of macroscopic properties such as concentration.

- Le Chatelier's principle states that the equilibrium will shift so as to minimise the effect of a change in concentration, pressure or temperature.

- A catalyst may accelerate the rate at which the reaction achieves equilibrium.

- The conditions used in the Haber process for the production of ammonia are a compromise between ideal reaction conditions and the expense involved in producing those conditions. The key requirement is to produce the most yield for the least cost.

- Large quantities of ammonia are used for producing fertilisers such as ammonium sulphate.

- Acids are proton donors. Acids form salts and hydrogen with many metals. Acids are neutralised by: basic metal oxides to form salts and water; metal carbonates to form salts, water and carbon dioxide; alkalis to form salts and water. Ammonia behaves as a base as it is neutralised by sulphuric acid to form the salt ammonium sulphate.

- Strong acids, such as hydrochloric acid, are fully dissociated into ions. Weak acids, such as ethanoic acid, are only partially dissociated into ions. An equilibrium exists between the weak acid molecules and ions.

Questions

1 The dissociation of hydrogen iodide can be represented by the equation below:

$$2HI(g) \rightleftharpoons H_2(g) + I_2(g); \Delta H^\ominus = -53 \, kJ \, mol^{-1}$$

a Using this reaction as an example, explain what is meant by
   (i) a reversible reaction;
   (ii) a dynamic equilibrium.
b Explain, giving a reason, the effect on the equilibrium above of:
   (i) increasing the temperature whilst keeping the pressure constant;
   (ii) increasing the pressure whilst keeping the temperature constant.
c State the effect on the equilibrium above of adding a catalyst whilst keeping pressure and temperature constant.

2 Ammonia is made by the Haber process from nitrogen and hydrogen. The conditions used are a compromise to obtain a reasonable yield at a satisfactory rate. Typically, a temperature between 650 and 720 K is chosen with an iron catalyst containing promoters such as potassium hydroxide. In the most up-to-date Haber process plant, the pressure used is 110 atmospheres. These conditions typically produce about 15% conversion to ammonia.

The equation and enthalpy change for the reaction are as follows.

$$N_2(g) + 3H_2(g) \rightleftharpoons 2NH_3(g);$$
$$\Delta H^\ominus = -92 \, kJ \, mol^{-1}$$

a (i) State Le Chatelier's principle.
   (ii) Use Le Chatelier's principle and the equation for the Haber process reaction to explain why a pressure of 110 atm is used rather than a lower pressure.
   (iii) When a temperature lower than 650 K is used, a higher percentage conversion is achieved. Use Le Chatelier's principle and the enthalpy change for the Haber process to explain this effect.
   (iv) Explain why a temperature in the range 650–720 K is used even though a lower temperature produces a higher percentage conversion of ammonia.
b Large quantities of ammonia are converted into ammonium sulphate by reaction of ammonia with sulphuric acid.
   (i) Write a balanced equation for this reaction.
   (ii) Suggest a use for the large quantities of ammonium sulphate produced in this way.

3 An acid, such as hydrochloric acid, will dissolve metals, carbonates, bases and alkalis to form salts.
a (i) Describe what is meant by an acid, using hydrochloric acid as an example.
   (ii) Hydrochloric acid is a strong acid; many organic acids are weak acids. Explain the difference between a strong acid and a weak acid.
b Write balanced equations for the following reactions:
   (i) The reaction of magnesium with hydrochloric acid to form magnesium chloride and hydrogen;
   (ii) The reaction of magnesium carbonate with hydrochloric acid to form magnesium chloride, carbon dioxide and water.
c One of the two reactions in **b** is a redox reaction. Use oxidation states to identify which reaction is the redox reaction. Identify which element is oxidised and which is reduced. Give your reasons.

Appendix: Periodic Table of the elements

Group

Key:

a
X
Name
b

a = relative atomic mass
X = symbol
b = proton number

1.0
H
Hydrogen
1

s-Block

Period	I	II
1		
2	6.9 Li Lithium 3	9.0 Be Beryllium 4
3	23.0 Na Sodium 11	24.3 Mg Magnesium 12
4	39.1 K Potassium 19	40.1 Ca Calcium 20
5	85.5 Rb Rubidium 37	87.6 Sr Strontium 38
6	133 Cs Caesium 55	137 Ba Barium 56
7	Fr Francium 87	Ra Radium 88

d-Block

45.0 Sc Scandium 21	47.9 Ti Titanium 22	50.9 V Vanadium 23	52.0 Cr Chromium 24	54.9 Mn Manganese 25	55.9 Fe Iron 26	58.9 Co Cobalt 27	58.7 Ni Nickel 28	63.5 Cu Copper 29	65.4 Zn Zinc 30
88.9 Y Yttrium 39	91.2 Zr Zirconium 40	92.9 Nb Niobium 41	95.9 Mo Molybdenum 42	Tc Technetium 43	101 Ru Ruthenium 44	103 Rh Rhodium 45	106 Pd Palladium 46	108 Ag Silver 47	112 Cd Cadmium 48
La to Lu 57	178 Hf Hafnium 72	181 Ta Tantalum 73	184 W Tungsten 74	186 Re Rhenium 75	190 Os Osmium 76	192 Ir Iridium 77	195 Pt Platinum 78	197 Au Gold 79	201 Hg Mercury 80
Ac to Lr	Rf Rutherfordium 104	Db Dubnium 105	Sg Seaborgium 106	Bh Bohrium 107	Hs Hassium 108	Mt Meitnerium 109	Unn Ununnillium 110	Uuu Unununium 111	Uub Ununbium 112

p-Block

III	IV	V	VI	VII	0
					4.0 He Helium 2
10.8 B Boron 5	12.0 C Carbon 6	14.0 N Nitrogen 7	16.0 O Oxygen 8	19.0 F Fluorine 9	20.2 Ne Neon 10
27.0 Al Aluminium 13	28.1 Si Silicon 14	31.0 P Phosphorus 15	32.1 S Sulphur 16	35.5 Cl Chlorine 17	39.9 Ar Argon 18
69.7 Ga Gallium 31	72.6 Ge Germanium 32	74.9 As Arsenic 33	79.0 Se Selenium 34	79.9 Br Bromine 35	83.8 Kr Krypton 36
115 In Indium 49	119 Sn Tin 50	122 Sb Antimony 51	128 Te Tellurium 52	127 I Iodine 53	131 Xe Xenon 54
204 Tl Thallium 81	207 Pb Lead 82	209 Bi Bismuth 83	Po Polonium 84	At Astatine 85	Rn Radon 86
	Uuq Ununquadium 114		Uuh Ununhexium 116		Uuo Ununoctium 118

f-Block

139 La Lanthanum 57	140 Ce Cerium 58	141 Pr Praseodymium 59	144 Nd Neodymium 60	Pm Promethium 61	150 Sm Samarium 62	152 Eu Europium 63	157 Gd Gadolinium 64	159 Tb Terbium 65	163 Dy Dysprosium 66	165 Ho Holmium 67	167 Er Erbium 68	169 Tm Thulium 69	173 Yb Ytterbium 70	175 Lu Lutetium 71
Ac Actinium 89	Th Thorium 90	Pa Protactinium 91	U Uranium 92	Np Neptunium 93	Pu Plutonium 94	Am Americium 95	Cm Curium 96	Bk Berkelium 97	Cf Californium 98	Es Einsteinium 99	Fm Fermium 100	Md Mendelevium 101	No Nobelium 102	Lr Lawrencium 103

Answers to self-assessment questions

Chapter 1

1.1 a U-235 has 92 protons, 92 electrons and 143 neutrons.
U-238 has 92 protons, 92 electrons and 146 neutrons.

b K^+-40 has 19 protons, 18 electrons and 21 neutrons.
Cl^--37 has 17 protons, 18 electrons and 20 neutrons.

1.2 All the isotopes have the same number and arrangement of electrons and this controls their chemical properties.

1.3 a Sodium has 11 electrons in all. There is one electron in its outer shell ($n = 3$) and this is the easiest to remove. The second ionisation energy shows the energy required to remove an electron from the next inner (filled) shell ($n = 2$).

The ninth electron to be removed is in shell $n = 2$ and the tenth is in shell $n = 1$, which is closest to the nucleus.

b The first electron is in the outer shell $n = 3$.

The relatively low increases from the second to the ninth ionisation energies show that eight electrons are in the same shell $n = 2$. The tenth and eleventh electrons are in the shell $n = 1$.

1.4 Group II. The first and second ionisation energies are fairly close in value. There is a large increase between the second and third ionisation energies, which shows that the second and third electrons are in a different shell. This indicates that there are two electrons in the outer shell.

1.5 See *figure*.

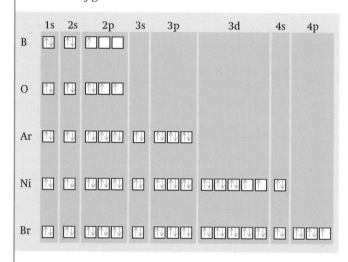

● **Answer for** SAQ 1.5

Chapter 2

2.1 Relative atomic mass of neon
$$= \frac{90.9 \times 20 + 0.3 \times 21 + 8.8 \times 22}{100} = 20.18$$

2.2 a $24.3 + 2 \times 35.5 = 95.3$

b $63.5 + 32.1 + 4 \times 16.0 = 159.6$

c $2 \times 23.0 + 12.0 + 3 \times 16.0$
$+ 10(2 \times 1.0 + 16.0) = 286.0$

2.3 a ^{90}Zr, ^{91}Zr, ^{92}Zr, ^{94}Zr, ^{96}Zr

b $A_r(Zr)$
$$= \frac{51.5 \times 90 + 11.2 \times 91 + 17.1 \times 92 + 17.4 \times 94 + 2.8 \times 96}{100}$$
$$= 91.3$$

2.4 a $\dfrac{35.5}{35.5} = 1\,\text{mol Cl atoms}$

b $\dfrac{71}{2 \times 35.5} = 1\,\text{mol Cl}_2\,\text{molecules}$

2.5 a 6×10^{23} Cl atoms

b $1\,\text{mol Cl}_2$ molecules $= 2\,\text{mol Cl atoms}$
$= 2 \times 6 \times 10^{23} = 1.2 \times 10^{24}$

2.6 **a** $CO_2 = 12.0 + 2 \times 16.0 = 44.0\,g$

∴ mass 0.1 mol $CO_2 = 0.1 \times 44.0$

$= 4.40\,g$

b $CaCO_3 = 40.1 + 12.0 + 3 \times 16.0$

$= 100.1\,g$

∴ mass 10 mol $CaCO_3 = 10 \times 100.1$

$= 1001\,g$

2.7 **a** From equation, mole ratio $H_2:Cl_2 = 1:1$

∴ mass ratio = 2.0 : 71.0 or 1 : 35.5

b $HCl = 1.0 + 35.5 = 36.5 = 1$ mol HCl

∴ as 1 mol H_2 produces 2 mol HCl,

0.5 mol H_2 produces 1 mol HCl.

∴ 2.0×0.5

$= 1.0\,g\ H_2$ produces $36.5\,g$ HCl.

2.8 1000 tonne Fe_2O_3 produce

$112 \times \dfrac{1000}{160}$ tonne = 700 tonne Fe

∴ 1 tonne Fe requires $\dfrac{1000}{700}$ tonne Fe_2O_3

$= 1.43$ tonne

∴ mass ore $= 1.43 \times \dfrac{100}{12} = 11.9$ tonne

2.9 **a** C_3H_7 **b** HO

2.10

	Cu	**O**
Amount (mol)	$\dfrac{0.635}{63.5} = 0.0100$	$\dfrac{0.080}{16.0} = 0.00500$
Ratio (mol)	2	1

∴ Empirical formula is Cu_2O.

2.11 **a** Mass C in 1.257 g CO_2

$= \dfrac{12.0}{44.0} \times 1.257 \quad = 0.343\,g$

Mass H in 0.514 g H_2O

$= \dfrac{2 \times 1.0}{18.0} \times 0.514 \quad = 0.057\,g$

(Check: 0.343 + 0.057 = 0.400 g = mass of hydrocarbon sample.)

	C	**H**
Amount (mol)	$\dfrac{0.343}{12.0} = 0.0286$	$\dfrac{0.057}{1.0} = 0.057$
Ratio (mol)	1	1.99

∴ Empirical formula is CH_2; $M_r(CH_2) = 14$.

b As $84 = 6 \times 14$, molecular formula is C_6H_{12}.

2.12 **a** $MgBr_2$ **d** Na_2SO_4

b HI   **e** KNO_3

c CaS   **f** NO_2

2.13 **a** Potassium carbonate

b Aluminium sulphide

c Lithium nitrate

d Calcium phosphate

e Silicon dioxide

2.14 **a** $2Al + Fe_2O_3 \rightarrow Al_2O_3 + 2Fe$

b $2C_8H_{18} + 25O_2 \rightarrow 16CO_2 + 18H_2O$

or $C_8H_{18} + \frac{25}{2}O_2 \rightarrow 8CO_2 + 9H_2O$

c $2Pb(NO_3)_2 \rightarrow 2PbO + 4NO_2 + O_2$

2.15 **a** $Cl_2(aq) + 2Br^-(aq) \rightarrow 2Cl^-(aq) + Br_2(aq)$

b $Fe^{3+}(aq) + 3OH^-(aq) \rightarrow Fe(OH)_3(s)$

2.16 **a** Amount nitric acid

$= \dfrac{25}{1000} \times 0.1 = 2.5 \times 10^{-3}$ mol

b Volume $= \dfrac{50}{1000} = 5 \times 10^{-2}\,dm^3$

∴ concentration $= \dfrac{0.125}{5 \times 10^{-2}}$

$= 2.5\,mol\,dm^{-3}$

2.17 **a** $CH_3COOH = 12.0 + 3 \times 1.0 + 12.0$

$+ 2 \times 16.0 + 1.0 = 60.0$

∴ concentration $= 0.50 \times 60 = 30.0\,g\,dm^{-3}$

b $NaOH = 23.0 + 16.0 + 1.0 = 40.0$

∴ concentration $= \dfrac{4.00}{40.0} = 0.100\,mol\,dm^{-3}$

(N.B. Three significant figures in these answers.)

2.18 **a** Amount KOH

$= \dfrac{20}{1000} \times 0.100 = 2 \times 10^{-3}$ mol

$KOH + HCl \rightarrow KCl + H_2O$

∴ amount KOH = amount HCl

$= 2 \times 10^{-3}$ mol

Volume HCl $= \dfrac{25.0}{1000} = 2.5 \times 10^{-2}\,dm^3$

∴ concentration HCl

$= \dfrac{2 \times 10^{-3}}{2.5 \times 10^{-2}} = 0.08\,mol\,dm^{-3}$

b $36.5 \times 0.08 = 2.92\,g\,dm^{-3}$

2.19 Amount HNO_3

$$= \frac{24}{1000} \times 0.050 = 1.20 \times 10^{-3}\,mol$$

∴ stoichiometric mole ratio nitric acid: iron hydroxide is

$1.20 \times 10^{-3} : 4.00 \times 10^{-4}$ i.e. 3:1

Iron hydroxide contains three hydroxide ions to exactly neutralise three HNO_3 molecules. So equation is

$3HNO_3(aq) + Fe(OH)_3(s)$
$\rightarrow Fe(NO_3)_3(aq) + 3H_2O(l)$

2.20 a Amount He $= \dfrac{2.4}{24} = 0.10\,mol$

b 0.5 mol propane = $0.5 \times 24 = 12\,dm^3$

1.5 mol butane = $1.5 \times 24 = 36\,dm^3$

∴ total volume = $48\,dm^3$

2.21   hydrocarbon $Y(g) + O_2(g) \rightarrow CO_2(g) + H_2O(l)$

gas volumes (cm^3)	20	60	40
gas volume ratio	1	3	2
gas mole ratio	1	3	2

As 2 mol of carbon dioxide are obtained from 1 mol of the hydrocarbon, each hydrocarbon molecule contains 2 carbon atoms.

2 mol of carbon dioxide requires 2 out of the original 3 mol of oxygen.

Hence 1 mole of oxygen molecules, $O_2(g)$, are left to combine with hydrogen atoms from the hydrocarbon to form water.

1 mole of $O_2(g)$ produce 2 mol of water. Hence there must be $2 \times 2 = 4$ hydrogen atoms present in the hydrocarbon.

a The formula of the hydrocarbon is C_2H_4. Strictly speaking, as this formula has been obtained from ratios, hydrocarbon Y could be any hydrocarbon with the empirical formula CH_2. The relative molecular mass of hydrocarbon Y is needed for a full identification. (In the worked example above SAQ 2.21, the formula of hydrocarbon X happens to be unique.)

b $C_2H_4(g) + 3O_2(g) \rightarrow 2CO_2(g) + 2H_2O(l)$

Chapter 3

3.1   At negative electrode: $Cu^{2+} + 2e^- \rightarrow Cu$
At positive electrode: $2Br^- \rightarrow Br_2 + 2e^-$

3.2   a–d See *figure*.

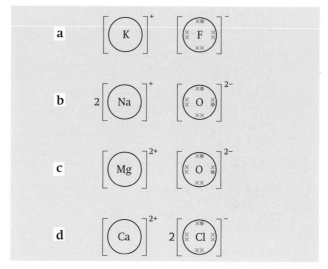

● **Answer for** SAQ 3.2a–d

3.3   a See *figure*.

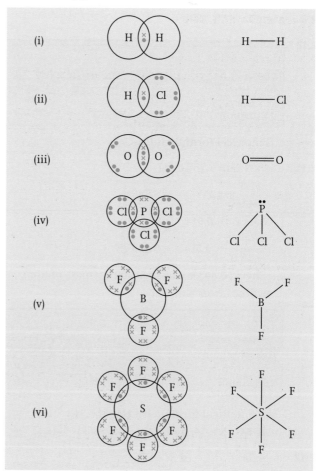

● **Answer for** SAQ 3.3a

b BF$_3$: Outer shell of boron contains six electrons.

SF$_6$: Outer shell of sulphur contains 12 electrons.

3.4 **a–c** See *figure*.

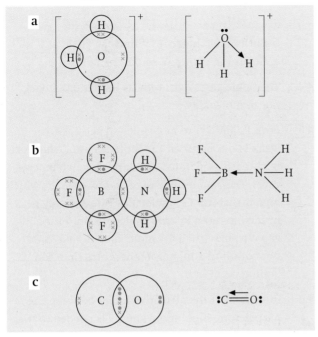

● **Answer for** SAQ 3.4a–c

3.5 **a–d** See *figure*.

Thus, **a** is non-polar; and **b**, **c** and **d** are polar.

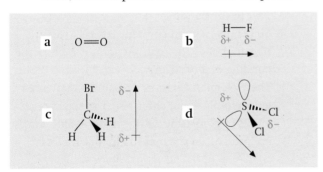

● **Answer for** SAQ 3.5a–d

3.6 **a**

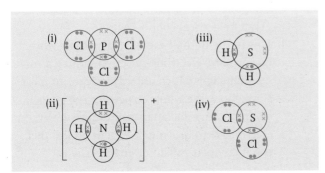

b (i) triangular pyramid

(ii) tetrahedral

(iii) non-linear

(iv) non-linear

3.7 **a** Copper provides better heat transfer as it has a thermal conductivity that is five times higher than that of iron (stainless steel has a lower thermal conductivity than iron).

b Copper has more than three times the density of aluminium. The electrical conductivity of copper is 1.5 times that of aluminium. Aluminium cables will be lighter than copper whilst still being good conductors of electricity. The lighter cables enable less massive (and less unsightly) pylons to be used. As the tensile strength of aluminium is low, aluminium cables are reinforced with a steel core to increase their strength.

c Copper has the highest electrical and thermal conductivities. Its high thermal conductivity helps to keep equipment such as transformers cool.

3.8 As water molecules are free to rotate, the positive charge on the rod repels the positive end of a water molecule whilst attracting the negative end. The overall effect is thus an attraction. The effect will be the same if the charge on the rod is negative rather than positive.

3.9 See *figure*.

● **Answer for** SAQ 3.9

Dotted lines show the dipole–dipole forces. (Note: Extrusion through spinnerets causes more molecules to line up closely, increasing the intermolecular forces (and hence the strength of the fibre) by the closer contact.)

3.10 Underlying increase is due to increasing instantaneous dipole–induced dipole forces as the number of electrons and protons present in the molecules rise. The value for water based on this underlying trend would be about 18 kJ mol^{-1}.

The much higher value observed for water is due to the presence of much stronger intermolecular forces.

3.11 The O–H···O distance in ice is 0.159 + 0.096 nm = 0.255 nm. The effect of this is to produce a structure that occupies more space than that required when ice melts and many hydrogen bonds break. For a given mass, ice occupies a greater volume than water, so its density is less.

3.12 Washing-up liquid lowers the surface tension of water. This reduces the hydrogen bonding at the surface to the point where it is no longer sufficient to keep the needle afloat.

3.13 **a** Underlying increase is due to increasing instantaneous dipole–induced dipole forces as the number of electrons and protons present in the molecules rise.
   b The much higher value observed for ammonia is due to the presence of hydrogen bonds, N–H···N.

3.14 **a**

   b See *figure*.

● Answer for SAQ 3.14b

Chapter 4

4.1 The properties predicted for eka-silicon are close to those now known for germanium.

4.2 **a** Elements may have several isotopes – atoms with the same number of protons but different numbers of neutrons and hence different masses. The mass of an isotope of an element is the same as its nucleon number. This equals the number of protons plus the number of neutrons. The relative atomic mass of the element is the 'weighted average' of the nucleon numbers of its isotopes.

   b Tellurium and iodine have several isotopes each. The weighted average A_r of tellurium is higher than the average for iodine. Thus, in a table based on relative atomic masses only, tellurium would have been placed higher than iodine.

4.3 **a** C $1s^2\,2s^2\,2p^2$ Si $1s^2\,2s^2\,2p^6\,3s^2\,3p^2$
   b Both outer shell configurations are $s^2\,p^2$
   c Ge also in Group IV so outer shell is $s^2\,p^2$.

4.4 The noble gases exist only as individual atoms, not in molecules.

4.5 Both P_4 and S_8 are molecular structures with weak bonds between the molecules and these are fairly easily separated at relatively low temperatures. Their molecular masses, however, are much higher than for Cl_2 molecules. More energy is needed to move P_4 or S_8 molecules into the vapour phase than Cl_2 molecules. S_8 and P_4 do not boil until a higher temperature than the boiling point of Cl_2.

4.6 In general, if the attractive forces between the particles are high, more energy is needed to overcome these forces and the melting point is high.
   a These elements all have a metallic structure. The metallic bonding is stronger moving from sodium to aluminium as there are more outer shell electrons available to be mobile and take part in the bonding.
   b Silicon has a giant covalent lattice structure like diamond. The melting point is high as the bonding is very strong.
   c These elements exist as non-polar small molecules (sulphur and chlorine) or as separate atoms (argon). Only weak van der Waals' forces are present, so the melting points are low.

4.7 **a** Group I to Group III elements are all metals with metallic structure and bonding. The number of shell $n = 3$ electrons which are available to join the conduction band increases from one to three per atom and this gives greater electrical conductivity.
   b This is due to their metallic structures, with one or more electrons per atom joining a conduction band, which allows electrons to move throughout the whole structure. The p-block elements are molecular in structure with electrons kept in strong covalent bonds; their conductivity is much lower than the conductivity of metals.

4.8 **a** Electronic configurations are:

Na $1s^2 2s^2 2p^6 3s^1$

Mg $1s^2 2s^2 2p^6 3s^2$

Al $1s^2 2s^2 2p^6 3s^2 3p^1$

Mg has a higher nuclear charge than Na. This makes it more difficult to remove a 3s electron and thus Mg has a higher first ionisation energy. Al has a lower first ionisaton energy than Mg as the electron being removed is in a 3p orbital, a little further from the nuclear charge (and of higher energy) than the 3s orbital.

b Si $1s^2 2s^2 2p^6 3s^2 3p^2$

P $1s^2 2s^2 2p^6 3s^2 3p^3$

S $1s^2 2s^2 2p^6 3s^2 3p^4$

The general increase in ionisation energy is mainly due to the effect of the increasing nuclear charge on the 3p electrons. The first ionisation energy of S is slightly lower than that of P for the same reason as the first ionisation energy of oxygen is lower than that of nitrogen (see text).

4.9 Francium is the most likely: it has only one electron in an s orbital, distant from the nucleus and well screened by several filled inner shells.

4.10 **a** Between the fifth and sixth successive ionisation energies.

b Group VII (the element is fluorine).

Chapter 5

5.1 **a** (i) the metallic radii increase from element to element down the Group;

(ii) the first ionisation energies decrease from element to element down the Group.

b (i) the radii increase as additional shells of electrons are added going down the Group from magnesium to barium.

(ii) the electron removed is further from the nucleus and shielded by the inner filled shells of electrons. The distance and shielding effects together are able to reduce the effect of the increasing nuclear charge from element to element down the Group. Hence the ionisation energy decreases from element to element down the group.

c As less energy is needed to remove an electron going down the Group from magnesium to barium, the electronegativity will also decrease from element to element down the Group.

5.2 C in CO_3^{2-} has an ox. state of +4.

Al in Al_2Cl_6 has an ox. state of +3.

5.3 Magnesium oxide.

0.33 g

5.4 **a** $2Sr(s) + O_2(g) \rightarrow 2SrO(s)$

b The metal burns with a red flame and a white solid is formed.

c Each strontium atom loses two electrons and changes oxidation state from 0 to +2. Strontium is oxidised.

Each oxygen atom gains two electrons and changes oxidation state from 0 to −2. Oxygen is reduced.

d Two electrons are lost from each metal atom in the reaction. Down the Group, the first two ionisation energies decrease from magnesium to barium. Consequently, the reactivity of the metals increase increase down the Group as less energy is required to remove the two electrons.

5.5 **a** Calcium carbonate dissolves rapidly in dilute hydrochloric acid with the evolution of carbon dioxide.

$CaCO_3(s) + 2HCl(g) \rightarrow CaCl_2(aq) + H_2O(l) + CO_2(g)$

b The calcium hydroxide contains hydroxide ions which will neutralise the acidity in the soil.

c $Mg(OH)_2(s) + 2HCl(g) \rightarrow MgCl_2(aq) + 2H_2O(l)$

Chapter 6

6.1 0, −1, +7, +4

6.2 See *figure*.

$$\left[Na \right]^+ \left[\begin{matrix} \times\times \\ \times\, Cl\, ^\times_\times \\ \times\times \end{matrix} \right]^-$$

$$H\, ^\times_\bullet Cl\, ^{\bullet\bullet}_{\bullet\bullet}$$

● **Answer for** SAQ 6.2

6.3 The halogens have covalent bonds and they are non-polar molecules. Polar molecules dissolve best in water, which is itself polar. Non-polar molecules dissolve best in non-polar solvents.

6.4 **a** The orange cyclohexane layer would turn purple:
$$Br_2(aq) + 2I^-(aq) \rightarrow 2Br^-(aq) + I_2(aq)$$
b No change.
c Given its position in Group VII, we would expect astatine to be darker in colour than iodine. The orange cyclohexane would turn this dark colour of astatine:
$$Br_2(aq) + 2At^-(aq) \rightarrow 2Br^-(aq) + At_2(aq)$$

Chapter 7

7.1 See *figure*.

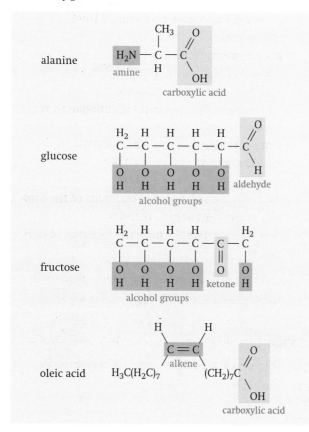

● **Answer for** SAQ 7.1

7.2 See *figure*.

a

b $(CH_3)_3CCl$

c

d C_4H_9Cl

e

● **Answer for** SAQ 7.2

7.3 **a** A heptane
B 3-methylhexane
C cyclopentane
D pentan-3-ol
E pentan-2-one
F 2-methylbutanoic acid
G 2,2-dimethylpropanal
b See *figure*.

(i)

$$CH_3CH_2C \overset{O}{\underset{H}{}}$$

(ii)

$$H_3C - \overset{H}{\underset{OH}{C}} - CH_3$$

(iii)

$$H_3C - \underset{H_2}{C} - C \overset{O}{\underset{C-CH_3}{}}$$
$$CH_3$$

(iv)

$$H_3C - \underset{H_2}{C} - \underset{H_2}{C} - NH_2$$

● **Answer for** SAQ 7.3b

7.4 See *figure*.

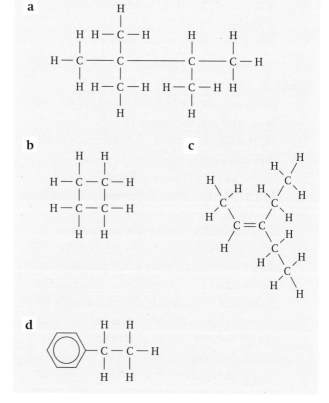

● **Answer for** SAQ 7.4

7.5

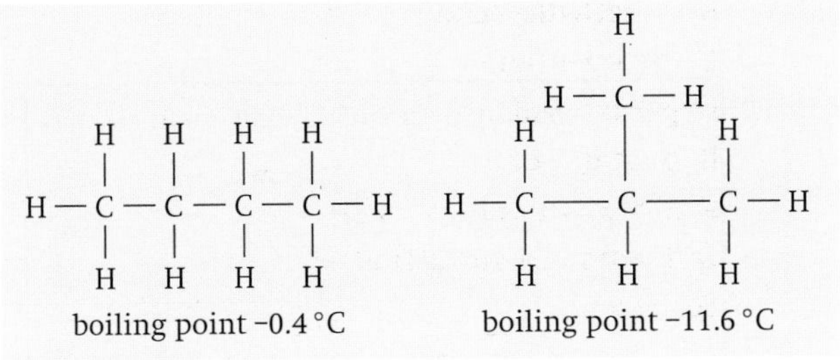

boiling point −0.4 °C   boiling point −11.6 °C

7.6   See *figure.*

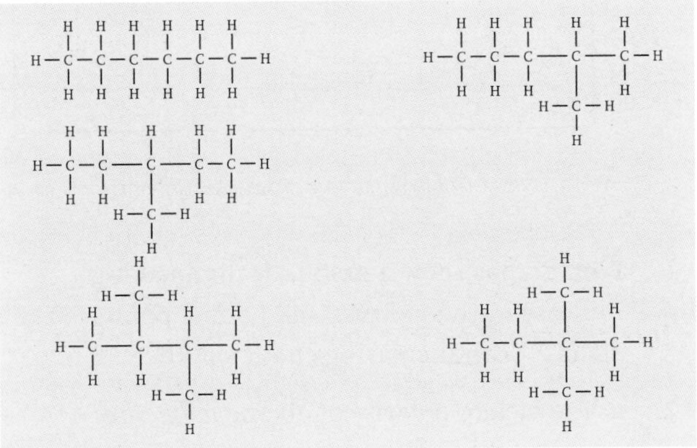

● **Answer for** SAQ 7.6

7.7   See *figure.*

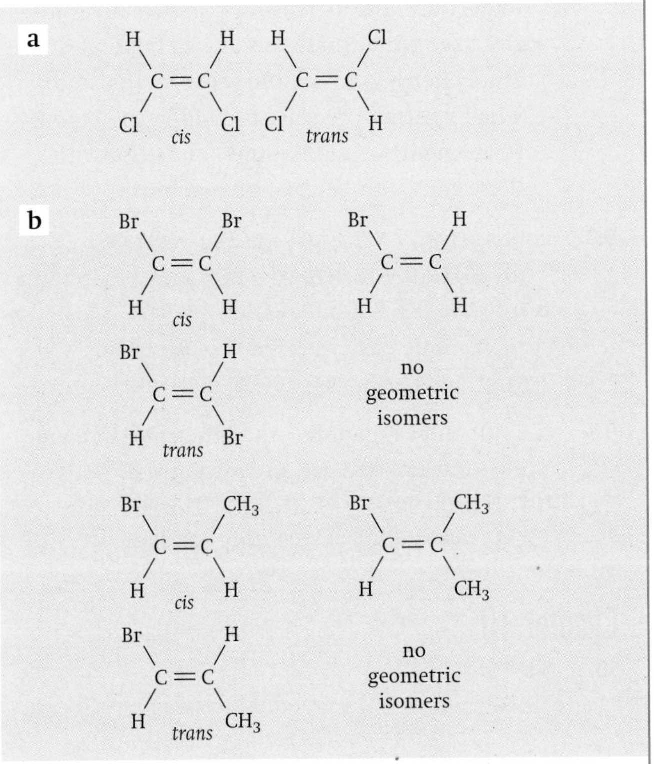

a

cis   trans

b

cis

trans   no geometric isomers

cis   no geometric isomers

trans

● **Answer for** SAQ 7.7

7.8   As 12 g of carbon are present in 1 mol (= 44 g) CO_2,

mass of carbon in 0.4800 g of CO_2 $= \dfrac{12}{44} \times 0.4800\,g$

$= 0.1309\,g$

$=$ mass of carbon in **W**

As 2 g of hydrogen are present in 1 mol (= 18 g) H_2O,

mass of hydrogen in 0.1636 g of H_2O $= \dfrac{2}{18} \times 0.1636\,g$

$= 0.0182\,g$

$=$ mass of hydrogen in **W**

As 14 g of nitrogen are present in 1mol (= 17 g) NH_3,

mass of nitrogen in 0.0618 g of NH_3 $= \dfrac{14}{17} \times 0.0618\,g$

$= 0.0509\,g$

$=$ mass of nitrogen in **W**

Hence

mass of C, H and N in 0.2000 g of **W** $= \dfrac{(0.1309 + 0.0182 + 0.0509)\,g}{}$

$= 0.2000\,g$

As this is the same as the total mass of the sample, **W** contains only C, H and N.

Now we calculate the numbers of moles of C, H and N:

	C	**H**	**N**
Mass (g)	0.1309	0.0182	0.0509
Amount (mol)	0.1309/12 $= 1.091 \times 10^{-2}$	0.0182/1 $= 1.82 \times 10^{-2}$	0.0509/14 $= 3.636 \times 10^{-3}$

Divide by the smallest amount to give whole numbers:

Atoms (mol)	3	5	1

Hence the empirical formula of **W** is C_3H_5N.

7.9   1 mol of butan-1-ol will produce 1 mol of 1-bromobutane. The quantity of butan-1-ol will determine the yield as the other reagents are in excess.

1 mol of butan-1-ol, C_4H_9OH, has a relative molecular mass of

$4 \times 12 + 9 \times 1 + 1 \times 16 + 1 = 74\,g$

1 mol of 1-bromobutane, C_4H_9Br, has a relative molecular mass of

$4 \times 12 + 9 \times 1 + 80 = 137\,g$

Hence

maximum yield of 1-bromobutane $= 10 \times \dfrac{137}{74} = 18.5\,g$

percentage yield $= \dfrac{12}{18.5} \times 100 = 65\%$

7.10 See *figure*.

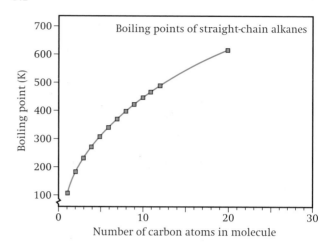

● **Answer for** SAQ 7.10

Free radicals have seven outer-shell electrons, electrophiles have six and nucleophiles have eight.

Chapter 8

8.1

Possible reactions include:

$CH_3CH_2CH_2CH_2CH_3 \longrightarrow CH_3CH_2CH_3 + H_2C = CH_2$

$\longrightarrow CH_3CH_2CH_2CH = CH_2 + H_2$

$\longrightarrow CH_3CH_2CH = CHCH_3 + H_2$

$\longrightarrow CH_3CH_3 + CH_3CH = CH_2$

$\longrightarrow CH_2 = CHCH = CHCH_3 + 2H_2$

$\longrightarrow H_3C - \overset{\displaystyle H}{\underset{\displaystyle CH_3}{C}} - C = CH_2 + H_2$

8.2 $C(s) + O_2(g) \rightarrow CO_2(g)$

$CH_4(g) + 2O_2(g) \rightarrow CO_2(g) + 2H_2O(l)$

$C_8H_{18}(l) + 12.5O_2(g) \rightarrow 8CO_2(g) + 9H_2O(l)$

$CH_3OH(g) + 1.5O_2(g) \rightarrow CO_2(g) + 2H_2O(l)$

$2H_2(g) + O_2(g) \rightarrow 2H_2O(l)$

8.3   A kilogram of hydrogen contains 500 moles of $H_2(g)$, whereas a kilogram of methane contains 62.5 moles of $CH_4(g)$.

8.4   **a** The volume of a liquid is much smaller than the volume of a gas of the same mass.

b A spherical shape gives the lowest surface area for the container of any given volume of liquid or gas. This saves material for making the container, and helps to keep the surface area of contents, affected by heating from the Sun, as small as possible.

8.5 $2NO_2(g) + H_2O(l) \rightarrow HNO_2(aq) + HNO_3(aq)$
          nitrous acid   nitric acid

$SO_2(g) + H_2O(l) \rightarrow H_2SO_3(aq)$
          sulphurous acid

$SO_3(g) + H_2O(l) \rightarrow H_2SO_4(aq)$
          sulphuric acid

Chapter 9

9.1

Both graphs show a gradually diminishing increase in the melting and boiling points of the alkanes with increasing chain length.

9.2   **a** The lack of polarity of alkane molecules means that only weak instantaneous dipole-induced dipole (van der Waals') force are present between molecules.

b As the number of electrons increases in the molecule (with increasing numbers of atoms), the strength of these forces also increases. More energy is needed to separate the atoms when melting the solid or boiling the liquid, so the melting and boiling points rise with increasing number of carbon atoms.

9.3   **a** (i) $C_8H_{18}(l) + 8.5O_2(g) \rightarrow 8CO(g) + 9H_2O(l)$
         (ii) $C_8H_{18}(l) + 12.5O_2(g) \rightarrow 8CO_2(g) + 9H_2O(l)$

b (i) 12.5 − 8.5 = 4 moles $O_2(g)$
     (ii) Volume of oxygen = 4 × 24.0 = 96 dm^3.
         Volume of air = 96 × 100/20 = 480 dm^3

9.4   **a** $Br_2(l)$ and $Cl_2(g)$ only – the others are in aqueous solution and are already ionised.

b $C_4H_{10}(g) + Br_2(l) \rightarrow C_4H_9Br(l) + HBr(g)$
     $C_4H_{10}(g) + Cl_2(g) \rightarrow C_4H_9Cl(l) + HCl(g)$

Chapter 10

10.1 See *figure*.

● **Answer for** SAQ 10.1

10.2 a D and E can also exist as *cis–trans* isomers.

b

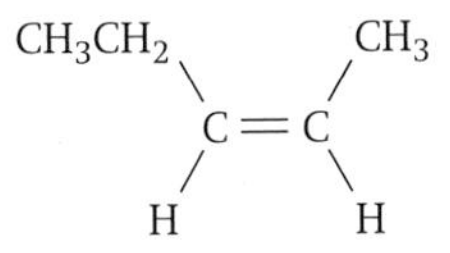

cis-pent-2-ene 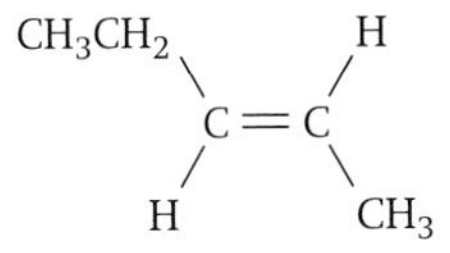   trans-pent-2-ene

10.3 See *figure*.

a The positive carbon atom has six electrons in its outer shell. It gains two more by accepting a lone-pair from the bromide ion.

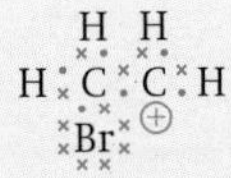

b

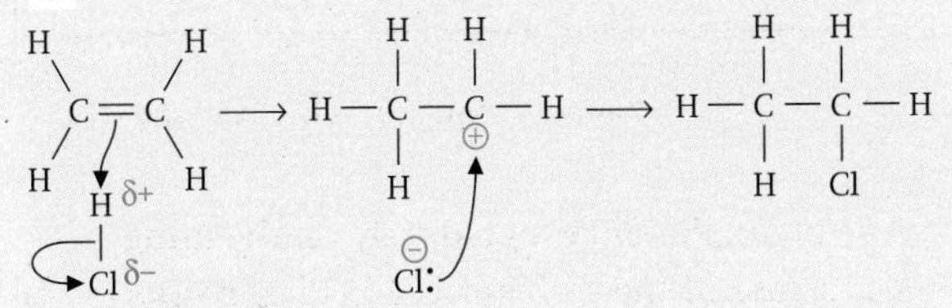

● **Answer for** SAQ 10.3

c CH_2ClCH_2Br

d Cl_2 Electrophile, polarisable like Br_2.

Na^+ No; does not usually form a covalent bond.

F^- No; negative charge, hence repelled by electron-rich centre.

H_2 No; not sufficiently polarisable.

SO_3 Electrophile, as sulphur will accept more electrons to form a new covalent bond.

ICl   Electrophile, as polar; iodine is positive (electrophilic) end of molecule.

10.4 See *figure*.

a

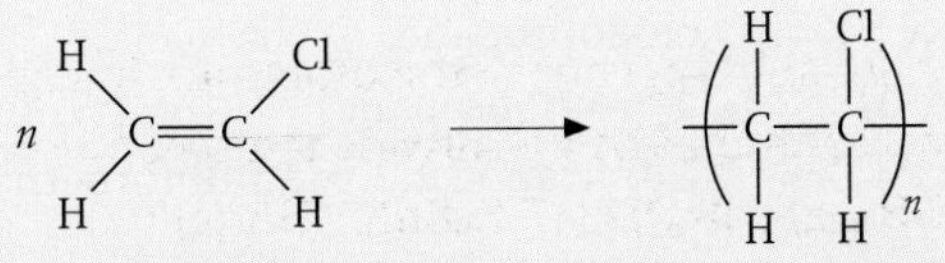

chloroethene   poly(chloroethene)

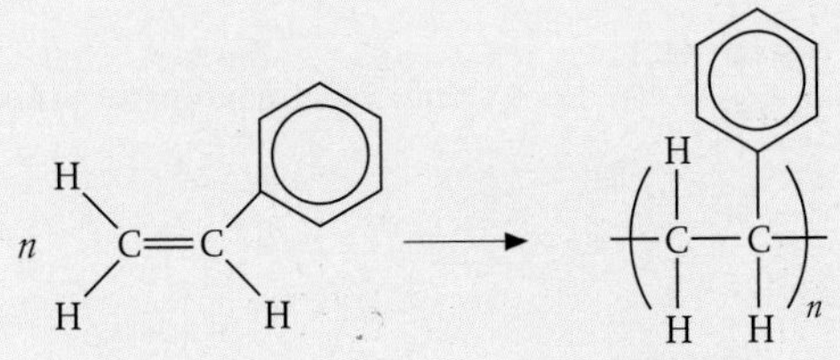

phenylethene   poly(phenylethene)

b

(i) poly(propene)   (ii) propene

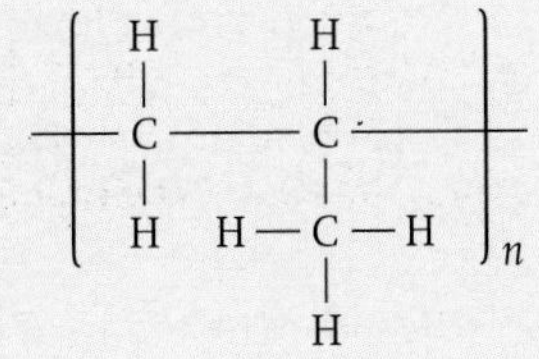

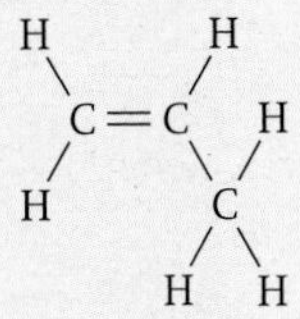

● **Answer for** SAQ 10.4

Chapter 11

11.1 Energy is absorbed when a bond is broken.

In order from strongest to weakest:

$E(O–H) > E(C–H) > E(C–O) > E(C–C)$

11.2 a C–O.

b The oxygen atom is very electronegative compared to hydrogen or carbon.

c An electrophile has a positively charged atom, which is attracted by an electron-rich centre. A nucleophile has a lone-pair of electrons, which is attracted to a positively charged centre.

11.3 See *figure*.

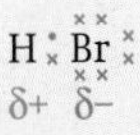

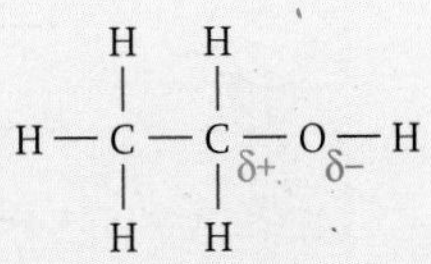

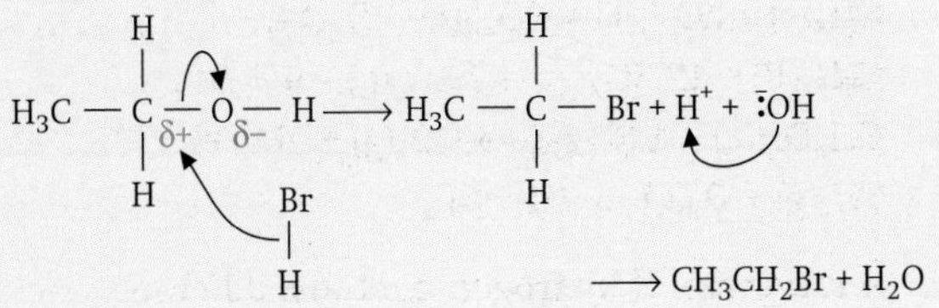

● **Answer for** SAQ 11.3

11.4 The hydrolysis of bromoethane requires aqueous ethanolic alkali and heat. The reverse reaction requires distillation with an excess of sodium bromide and concentrated sulphuric acid (no water is added). In the forward reaction, excess of water moves the reaction in the direction of hydrolysis. In the reverse reaction, absence of water and excess of hydrogen bromide (generated from the concentrated sulphuric acid and sodium bromide) moves the reaction towards the formation of bromoethane.

11.5

Alcohol	Molecular model	Structural formula	Classification
a pentan-1-ol	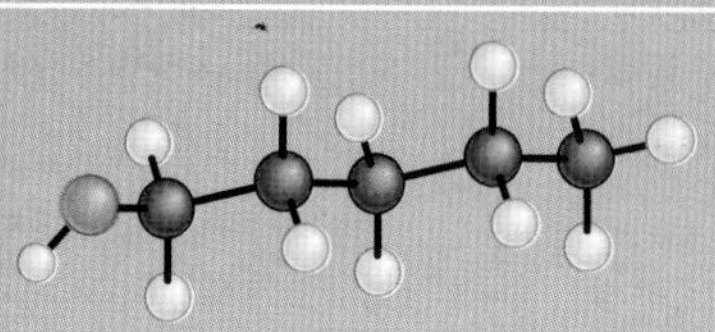	$CH_3CH_2CH_2CH_2CH_2OH$	primary
b pentan-2-ol	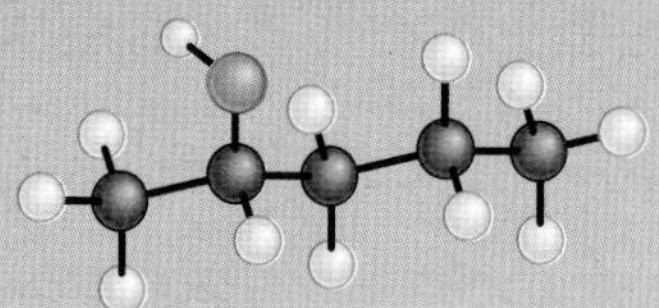	$\overset{\displaystyle OH}{\underset{\displaystyle \vert}{CH_3CH_2CH_2CHCH_3}}$	secondary
c 2-methylbutan-2-ol	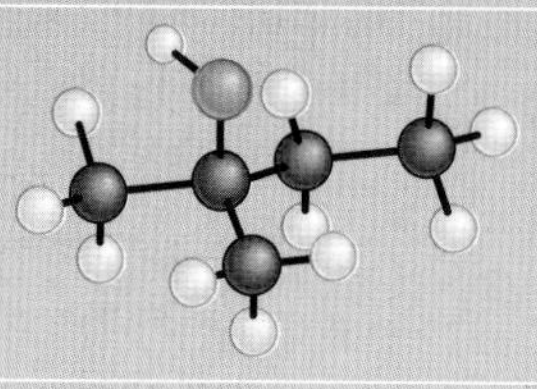	$CH_3\overset{CH_3}{\underset{OH}{C}}CH_2CCH_3$	tertiary
d 3-methylbutan-1-ol	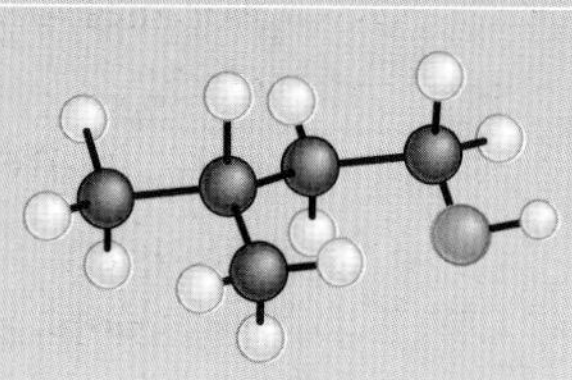	$CH_3\overset{CH_3}{\underset{\vert}{C}}HCH_2CH_2OH$	primary
e 3-methylbutan-2-ol	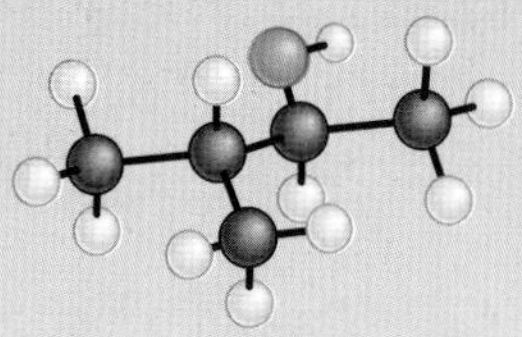	$CH_3\overset{CH_3}{\underset{OH}{C}}H-CHCH_3$	secondary
f 2-methylbutan-1-ol	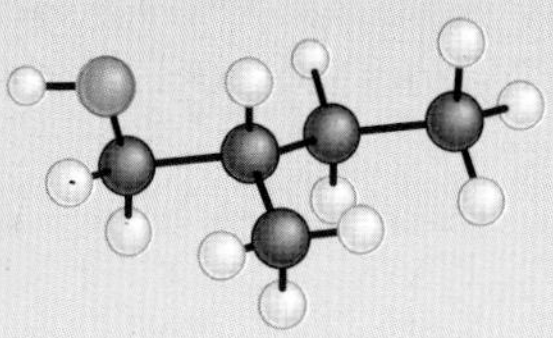	$CH_3CH_2\overset{CH_3}{\underset{\vert}{C}}HCH_2OH$	primary

11.6 **a**

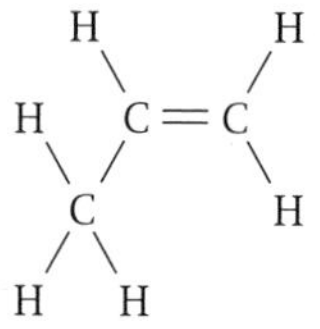

b $CH_3CH(OH)CH_3 \rightarrow CH_3CH=CH_2 + H_2O$

11.7 **a**

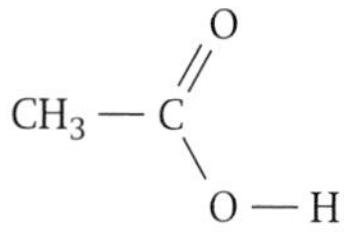

b C=O at 1710 cm^{-1}, strong and sharp.

11.8 In *figure 11.10* **a** is butanone as a strong, sharp absorption is present at 1710 cm^{-1}, characteristic of the C=O bond in butanone; **b** shows a strong, broad absorption at 3450 cm^{-1}, characteristic of the O–H bond in an alcohol.

Chapter 12

12.1 $CH_3CH_2CH_2I$: 1-iodopropane;
$CH_3CHBrCH_3$: 2-bromopropane;
$CBrF_2CBrF_2$: 1,2-dibromo-1,1,2,2-tetrafluoroethane.

12.2 Structural isomerism.

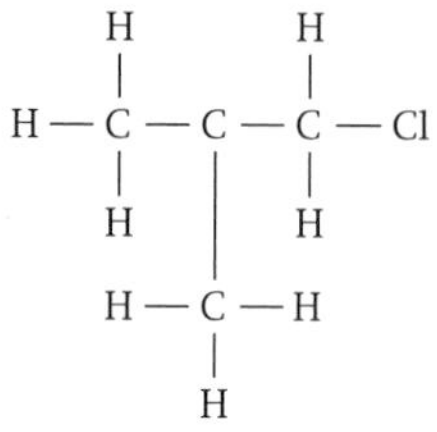

1 chloro-2-methylpropane (primary)

12.3 **a** 1-chloropropane is polar and has dipole–dipole intermolecular forces that are stronger then the instantaneous dipole-induced dipole forces in non-polar butane. More energy is needed to overcome the intermolecular forces in 1-chlorobutane, so its boiling point is higher.

b 1-chloropropane attracts water molecules by dipole–dipole forces that are weaker than the hydrogen bonds in water. An input of energy would be required for 1-chloropropane to mix with water and break some of these hydrogen bonds.

12.4

$$H_3C - \underset{\underset{CH_3}{|}}{\overset{\overset{CH_3}{|}}{C}} - Br + OH^- \longrightarrow H_3C - \underset{\underset{CH_3}{|}}{\overset{\overset{CH_3}{|}}{C}} - OH + Br^-$$

2-methylpropan-2-ol

12.5 Ammonia behaves as a nucleophile because the nitrogen atom possesses a lone-pair of electrons, which will form a covalent bond to carbon:

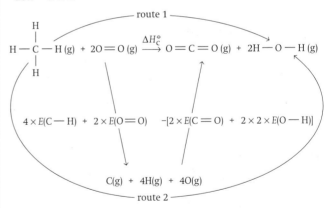

The hydrogen bromide will be neutralised by excess ammonia to form ammonium bromide:

$$HBr + NH_3 \rightarrow NH_4Br$$

Chapter 13

13.1 Exothermic: crystallisation; magnesium oxide formation.
Endothermic: evaporation; copper oxide from copper carbonate.

13.2 **a** (i) $2C(s) + 3H_2(g) \rightarrow C_2H_6(g)$;
$$\Delta H_f^\ominus = -84.7 \, \text{kJ mol}^{-1}$$
(ii) $2Al(s) + \frac{3}{2}O_2(g) \rightarrow Al_2O_3(s)$;
$$\Delta H_f^\ominus = -1669 \, \text{kJ mol}^{-1}$$

b

Enthalpy H axis (vertical), Reaction pathway (horizontal).
$2C(s) + 3H_2(g)$ at higher level.
$\Delta H_f^\ominus = -84.7 \, \text{kJ mol}^{-1}$ (downward arrow)
$C_2H_6(g)$ at lower level.

13.3 **a** *Figure 13.6a:* either $\Delta H_r^\ominus$ or $\Delta H_c^\ominus$
Figure 13.6b: $\Delta H_r^\ominus$

b (i) $C_8H_{18}(l) + 12\frac{1}{2}O_2(g) \rightarrow 8CO_2(g) + 9H_2O(l)$;
$$\Delta H_c^\ominus = -5512 \, \text{kJ mol}^{-1}$$
(ii) $C_2H_5OH(l) + 3O_2(g) \rightarrow 2CO_2(g) + 3H_2O(l)$;
$$\Delta H_c^\ominus = -1371 \, \text{kJ mol}^{-1}$$

c One mole of water is formed by burning one mole of hydrogen.

13.4 $\Delta H_c^\ominus(H_2)$ is calculated directly from experimental measurements. $\Delta H_f^\ominus(H_2O)$ is found from bond energies, which are average values calculated from measurements in a number of different experiments.

13.5 The value in the data book was calculated from much more accurate experimental data. Some of the energy transferred from the burning propanol would not change the temperature but would be 'lost' in heating the apparatus and surroundings.

13.6 The reaction that produces the enthalpy change is the same in each case of reaction between these acids and alkalis. Only $H^+(aq)$ and $OH^-(aq)$ are involved:
$$H^+(aq) + OH^-(aq) \rightarrow H_2O(l)$$

13.7 **a & b**

route 1

$$H - \underset{\underset{H}{|}}{\overset{\overset{H}{|}}{C}} - H \, (g) + 2O {=} O \, (g) \xrightarrow{\Delta H_c^\ominus} O {=} C {=} O \, (g) + 2H - O - H \, (g)$$

$4 \times E(C{-}H) + 2 \times E(O{=}O) \quad -[2 \times E(C{=}O) + 2 \times 2 \times E(O{-}H)]$

$C(g) + 4H(g) + 4O(g)$

route 2

c By Hess's law the enthalpy change for route 1 = enthalpy change for route 2.
Hence $\Delta H_c^\ominus = 4 \times E(C{-}H) + 2 \times E(O{=}O)$
$\quad - [2 \times E(C{=}O) + 2 \times 2 \times E(O{-}H)]$
$= 4 \times 413 + 2 \times 498 - (2 \times 805 + 2 \times 2 \times 464)$
$= -818 \, \text{kJ mol}^{-1}$

d Bond enthalpies used are based on average values and are based on breaking bonds in gaseous molecules. Water molecules are present in the gaseous state in the bond enthalpy calculation. $\Delta H_c^\ominus$ should refer to the liquid state for water, so the experimental value will be more accurate.

13.8 a

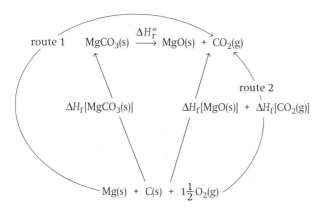

b The enthalpy change for route 1
= $\Delta H_f^{\ominus}[MgCO_3(s)] + \Delta H_r^{\ominus}$
The enthalpy change for route 2
= $\Delta H_f^{\ominus}[MgO(s)] + \Delta H_f^{\ominus}[CO_2(g)]$
Applying Hess's law
$\Delta H_f^{\ominus}[MgCO_3(s)] + \Delta H_r^{\ominus} = \Delta H_f^{\ominus}[MgO(s)] + \Delta H_f^{\ominus}[CO_2(g)]$
or
$(-1096) + \Delta H_r^{\ominus} = (-602) + (-394)$;

$\Delta H_r^{\ominus} = +100\,kJ\,mol^{-1}$

13.9 a & b

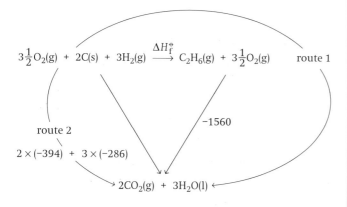

c Applying Hess's law
$\Delta H_f^{\ominus} + (-1560) = 2 \times (-394) + 3 \times (-286)$
$\Delta H_f^{\ominus} = 2 \times (-394) + 3 \times (-286) - (-1560)$
$= -86\,kJ\,mol^{-1}$

Chapter 14

14.1 a $CaCO_3 = 40 + 12 + (3 \times 16) = 100$

Amount of $CaCO_3 = \dfrac{2.00}{100} = 0.0200\,mol$

$150\,cm^3\,2\,mol\,dm^{-3}$ HCl contains $\dfrac{150}{1000} \times 2\,mol$ HCl

$= 0.300\,mol$ HCl

b From the equation, 2 mol HCl react with 1 mol $CaCO_3$. Therefore 0.0200 mol $CaCO_3$ require 0.0400 mol HCl. As 0.300 mol HCl is present, acid is in excess.

c The excess is 0.300 − 0.0400 = 0.260 mol.

d When the acid is in excess, the acid concentration is reasonably constant, so the concentration variable is controlled.

14.2 a 1.0 M HCl   −0.18 g
2.0 M HCl   −0.37 g

b Mass loss is approximately doubled, so rate is also doubled.

c Reaction rate is directly proportional to the concentration of HCl.

14.3 $2C_2H_2(g) + 5O_2(g) \rightarrow 4CO_2(g) + 2H_2O(g)$

14.4 A spark or match might provide the activation energy.

14.5 *Figure 14.19a* has lower entropy than *figure 14.19b*, so *figure 14.19b* represents the more stable state.

14.6 To provide a very large surface area for reaction.

14.7 Air.

Chapter 15

15.1 The system is not closed, water will evaporate.

15.2 a The position of equilibrium would move towards the reactants. A new position of equilibrium will be established with a lower concentration of the ester (and water).

b Use a large excess of ethanol or ethanoic acid. (Preferably whichever is cheaper!). Remove the ethyl ethanoate as it is formed (the ester may be distilled from the mixture).

15.3 a No change occurs as there are equal numbers of gaseous molecules on either side of the equation.

b There are fewer gaseous molecules on the right hand side of the equation. There is a reduction in volume moving from reactants to products so more $NH_3(g)$ is formed.

15.4 a (i) $Ca(s) + 2H^+(aq) \rightarrow Ca^{2+}(aq) + H_2(g)$
(ii) $2H^+(aq) + SrO(s) \rightarrow Sr^{2+}(aq) + H_2O(l)$
(iii) $2H^+(aq) + BaCO_3(s)$
$\rightarrow Ba^{2+}(aq) + CO_2(g) + H_2O(l)$

b (i) calcium chloride, $CaCl_2$;
(ii) strontium chloride, $SrCl_2$;
(iii) barium chloride. $BaCl_2$.

Glossary

acid a chemical species which can donate a proton, H^+. **Strong** acids dissociate fully into ions; **weak** acids only partially dissociate into ions.

activation energy the energy barrier which must be surmounted before reaction can occur.

addition polymer a polymer formed by a repeated addition reaction.

addition reaction the joining of two molecules to form a single product molecule.

adsorption weak bonds formed between, for example, gaseous molecules and atoms at the surface of a solid catalyst.

alkali a soluble base.

atomic number the number of protons in the nucleus of each atom of an element.

atomic orbital a representation of the region of space where there is a high probability of finding an electron in an electron subshell. Orbitals in different subshells have different shapes; s orbitals spherically surround the nucleus in the centre of the sphere, p orbitals have two spherical lobes either side of the nucleus.

atomic radius half the distance between the nuclei of two covalently bonded atoms.

Avogadro's constant, L the number of atoms or molecules in one mole of a substance ($L = 6.01 \times 10^{23}$).

base a base reacts with an acid to form a salt.

Boltzmann distribution the distribution of molecular energies.

bond enthalpy the amount of energy needed to break one mole of a bond in a gaseous molecule.

carbocation a carbon atom in an organic molecule which has lost an atom or a group of atoms from a carbon atom creating a single positive charge.

catalyst a catalyst increases the rate of a reaction but is not itself used up during the reaction.

***cis–trans* isomerism** occurs because a C=C cannot freely rotate. In some alkenes (with additional groups either side of the double bond) two isomers (*cis* or *trans*) are possible.

closed system a closed system can only transfer energy to or from its surroundings. Substances cannot be exchanged.

covalent bonding involves a pair of electrons between two atoms.

cracking the thermal decomposition of an alkane into a smaller alkane and an alkene.

dative covalent bond (co-ordinate bond) a covalent bond where both electrons come from one atom.

desorption weak bonds break between, for example, gaseous molecules and atoms at the surface of a solid catalyst.

displacement reaction a reaction in which one element produces another from an aqueous solution of its ions.

displayed formula shows all the covalent bonds and all the atoms present.

dynamic equilibrium an equilibrium is dynamic at the molecular level; both forward and reverse processes occur at the same rate; a closed system is required and macroscopic properties remain constant.

electron shielding the negative charge of filled inner shells of electrons repels electrons in the outer shells reducing the effect of the positive nuclear charge.

electronegativity describes the ability of an atom to attract the bonding electrons in a covalent bond.

electron-pair repulsion theory enables predictions of the shapes and bond angles in a molecule to be made from the numbers of bonding pairs and lone pairs of electrons present.

electrophile an atom (or group of atoms) which is attracted to an electron-rich centre or atom, where it accepts a pair of electrons to form a new covalent bond.

elimination when a small molecule is removed from a larger molecule.

empirical formula the simplest whole number ratio of the elements present in a compound.

endothermic term used to describe a reaction in which heat energy is absorbed from the surroundings (enthalpy change is positive).

enthalpy, H the term used by chemists for heat energy transferred during reactions.

enthalpy change of combustion the enthalpy change when one mole of an element or compound reacts completely with oxygen under standard conditions.

enthalpy change of formation the enthalpy change when one mole of a compound is formed from its elements under standard conditions; both compound and elements are in their standard states.

enthalpy change of reaction the enthalpy change when amounts of reactants, as shown in the reaction equation, react together under standard conditions to give products in their standard states.

enthalpy cycle a diagram displaying alternative routes between reactants and products which allows the determination of one enthalpy change from other known enthalpy changes using Hess's law.

enthalpy profile a diagram for a reaction to show the difference in enthalpy of the reactants compared with that of the products.

esterification the acid-catalysed formation of an ester from a carboxylic acid and an alcohol.

exothermic term used to describe a reaction in which heat energy is transferred to the surroundings (enthalpy change is negative).

feedstock a primary source of substance for the production of other chemicals.

free radical an atom or group of atoms with an unpaired electron.

functional group an atom or group of atoms which gives rise to an homologous series. Compounds in the same homologous series show similar chemical properties.

general formula a formula which may be written for each homologous series (C_nH_{2n+2} for alkanes).

Hess's law the total enthalpy change for a chemical reaction is independent of the route by which the reaction takes place, provided initial and final conditions are the same.

heterogeneous catalysis a catalyst that is present in a different phase to the reactants; frequently reactants are in a gaseous phase with a solid catalyst.

heterolytic fission when a bond breaks to form a positive ion and a negative ion.

homogeneous catalysis the catalyst and reactants are in the same phase, which is most frequently the aqueous phase.

homologous series a series of organic molecules with the same functional group.

homolytic fission when a bond breaks to form two free radicals.

hydrogen bond a weak intermolecular bond formed between molecules containing hydrogen bonded to the most electronegative elements (N, O, F).

initiation the first step in a free-radical substitution in which the free radicals are generated by heat or ultraviolet light.

intermolecular forces the weak forces of attraction between molecules based on instantaneous or permanent dipoles.

ion a positively or negatively charge atom or (covalently bonded) group of atoms.

ionic bonding the electrostatic attraction between oppositely charged ions.

ionisation energy the first ionisation energy is the energy needed to remove one electron from each atom in one mole of gaseous atoms of an element. Successive ionisation energies are the sequence of first, second, third, fourth, etc ionisation energies needed to remove the first, second, third, fourth, etc electrons from each atom in one mole of gaseous atoms of an element.

isomerisation the conversion of a straight-chain alkane to a branched-chain isomer.

isotopes are atoms of an element with the same number of protons but different numbers of neutrons.

isotopic abundance the abundance of each isotope present in a sample of an element.

Le Chatelier's principle when any of the conditions affecting the position of a dynamic equilibrium are changed, then the position of that equilibrium will shift to minimise that change.

mass number the total number of protons and neutrons in the nucleus of an atom.

molar mass the mass of one mole of a substance, calculated from its formula.

mole the unit of amount of substance (abbreviation: mol). One mole of a substance is the mass that has the same number of particles (atoms, molecules, ions or electrons) as there are atoms in exactly 12 g of carbon-12.

molecular formula shows the total number of atoms present in a molecule of the compound.

molecule a covalently bonded group of atoms.

monomer the small molecule used to build a polymer molecule.

nomenclature the international system of naming compounds such as organic compounds.

nucleophile a chemical that can donate a pair of electrons with the subsequent formation of a covalent bond.

oxidation the loss of electrons from an atom of an element.

oxidation state (number) a number (with a positive or negative sign) assigned to the atoms of each element in an ion or compound Oxidation states are determined using a set of rules devsied by chemsits.

π-bond a molecular orbital formed from overlap of atomic p orbitals in the formation of a double bond.

polymer the long molecular chain built up from monomer units.

principal quantum shell electron shells are numbered 1, 2, 3, 4, etc. Each quantum number corresponds to a principal quantum shell.

propagation the stage in a free-radical substitution which constitutes the two reaction steps of the chain reaction.

rate of reaction the amount in moles of a reactant which is used up in a given time.

redox reactions which involve reduction and oxidation processes.

reduction the gain of electrons by an atom of an element.

reforming the conversion of alkanes to cycloalkanes or arenes.

relative atomic mass, A_r, of an element is the mass of an atom of the element relative to the mass of an atom of carbon-12, which has a mass of exactly 12.

relative formula mass the mass of the formula of a compound relative to an atom of carbon-12.

relative isotopic mass the mass of an isotope of an atom of an element relative to an atom of carbon-12.

relative molecular mass the mass of a molecule of a compound relative to an atom of carbon-12.

saturated hydrocarbon contains only C–C single bonds.

skeletal formula shows the carbon skeleton only, hydrogen atoms are omitted, other atoms are shown as in a structural formula.

standard conditions (enthalpy changes) a temperature of 298 K and a pressure of 100 kPa.

stoichiometry the stoichiometry (or stoichiometric ratio) for a reaction shows the mole ratio of reactants and products in the balanced equation for the reaction.

structural formula shows how the atoms are joined together in a molecule.

structural isomerism structural isomers have the same molecular formula but different structural formulae.

substitution reaction an atom (or group of atoms) is substituted by a different atom (or group of atoms).

termination the step at the end of a free-radical substitution reaction which occurs when reactants are significantly depleted.

unsaturated hydrocarbon contains one or more C=C double bonds.

Van der Waals' forces the weak forces of attraction between molecules based on instantaneous or permanent dipoles.

volatility a measure of the ease with which a solid or liquid evaporates to a gas. Volatility increases as boiling point decreases.

Index